PETRA WILLE

STRONG
PRODUCT PEOPLE

A Complete Guide to Developing
Great Product Managers

Bibliographic information of the German National Library:

The German National Library lists this publication in the German National Bibliography; detailed bibliographic data is available on the internet at http://dnb.d-nb.de.

PART I: WHAT PRODUCT MANAGERS DO— DEFINE YOUR GOOD

PART II: MANAGE YOUR TEAM—FIND YOUR VOICE

PART III: FIND AND RECRUIT GOOD PRODUCT MANAGERS— ATTRACT THE BEST PEOPLE

PART IV: DEVELOP YOUR EXISTING PRODUCT TEAM— TRAIN FOR EXCELLENCE

PART V: CREATE THE RIGHT ENVIRONMENT— BUILD A GREAT CULTURE

FOREWORD

BY MARTY CAGAN

One of the strongest influences on my professional development was the legendary coach Bill Campbell, known as the "Coach of Silicon Valley." I was never personally coached by him, but I was fortunate enough to have met him, and to have worked directly for others who were personally coached by him, and so I grew up in my career learning his leadership principles.

Three lessons in particular made a lasting impression on how I think about my role as a leader in developing others:

First, "Leadership is about recognizing that there's a greatness in everyone, and your job is to create an environment where that greatness can emerge."

Second, "Coaching is no longer a specialty; you cannot be a good manager without being a good coach."

And finally, "Work the team, then the problem. When faced with a problem, the first step is to ensure the right team is in place and working on it."

I have found that if you take these three lessons to heart, and sincerely and genuinely try to be true to these ideals, your people can and will do amazing things.

But I hope you don't think any of this is easy. Many people mistakenly believe this type of leadership is about simply hiring smart people and getting out of their way. Unfortunately, it's not.

I have to explain to leaders all the time that strong product teams require stronger leadership, not less leadership.

- It takes much more effort to empower a product team, than it does to just give them a roadmap of features to build.

- It takes much more effort to provide weekly or when necessary even daily coaching, than it does to write up yearly performance evaluations.

- It takes much more effort to help a product manager create a strong written narrative, than it takes to review a few PowerPoint slides.

- It takes much more effort to provide critical but constructive feedback every single week, than it does to provide words of encouragement.

- It takes much more effort to personally make the case to senior leadership when your product manager has earned a promotion, than it does to simply send an email to HR.

If you're willing to put in this effort, then this book will help you do that.

I've known Petra for more than ten years now. When I first met her, she was a new product manager, with a solid technology background, a strong mind and work ethic, and a clear desire to learn the craft of product management.

I watched her develop as a product manager, then as a senior product manager, and then on to product leadership roles at multiple tech companies. But ultimately, I believed her highest and best use in technology would be to help develop others, and indeed she has.

So, with this book's help, I hope you go on to become a strong product leader, consistently developing strong product managers.

Marty Cagan
August 2020

FOREWORD

BY MARTIN ERIKSSON

Leadership. It's an odd word. It conjures up impossibly heroic images of military generals leading valiant charges from the front, or business leaders who set ambitious goals and drive their companies to achieve them through their own brilliance. The very word implies action, doing, getting out in front of your people, and showing how it's done by doing it best.

And yet the best leaders don't lead from in front. They spend more time worrying about whether their people are ready for action and have all the information, skills, and tools they need to be successful in that action.

As I look back on the leaders who have enabled every successful step forward through my 25-year career in product, and consider the many leaders I admire around me who I interviewed for my book or get to interact with on a daily basis through Mind the Product, it's clear that they all think like that.

And if it's all about our people, then it's all about building empowered, autonomous teams (and more and more evidence is piling up about the value of organizing ourselves this way), and it's clear that the old leadership model is broken. We can't empower a team and tell them what to do at the same time. So, we need a new model that focuses more on equipping our people with the tools they need to succeed on their own. And that means that developing our people becomes a leader's most important job.

The good news is that there are a lot of ways to learn how to adopt this new way of leading. From Marty Cagan's *Empowered,* through David Marquet's *Turn That Ship Around,* and our own *Product Leadership,* there are more and more books on the value of empowering our teams. And yet none of us *really* tackled the details of the hard work of *how* to develop our people's skills and prepare them for that empowerment. But in many ways, I'm glad we didn't, because who better to coach us through the art of coaching than Petra?

Petra has dedicated her life to helping others achieve greatness, and her insights and experience from doing just that permeates this entire book. In these pages you will find everything you need to know about how to develop your people and set them up for success. Something I wish more leaders had.

Martin Eriksson
London, September 2020

INTRODUCTION

STRONG

"In what ways can you tell you're developing as a product management personality?"
—From the 52 Questions Card Deck[1]

There are a lot of books on product management out there right now, and new ones keep popping up all the time. Why? Clearly, because heads of product, product managers, product teams, and stakeholders are hungry to learn more about how to create great products that deliver real value to users. The rewards can be tremendous—turning a startup that no one has heard of into a world-changing unicorn in just a matter of months.

Of course, as we all know, this is much easier said than done.

Creating great tech products takes much more than just having a great product idea. It takes competent, passionate, skilled product people—and a cross-functional product development team that shares the same characteristics—to deliver a successful product.

And becoming this kind of a product manager takes time, effort, and commitment. It's a long journey, and an especially hard one absent any guidance and feedback from someone who deeply cares about

---

1   Petra Wille (n.d.). 52 Questions. Retrieved from https://www.petra-wille.com/52questions

the personal and professional development of every product person on the team.

That's why I wrote *Strong*. My goal is to provide you, someone who actively manages product managers (PMs)—usually called head of product (HoP), product team lead, product manager lead, manager of product managers, or sometimes even director of product—with a comprehensive guide to helping your product managers leap over the obstacles that get in the way of creating great products.

I have, in fact, seen many of these obstacles up close and personal during the course of my own time as a product manager and head of product, and now working with product teams in companies all around the world as a freelance product discovery and people development coach. I have seen firsthand how organizations of all kinds are dealing with the obstacles they encounter—sometimes successfully (which is cause for celebration) and sometimes unsuccessfully (which is why I am called in to help). And in this book, I share what I've learned. I share how HoPs can become coaches of their product teams, and I write about the specific things HoPs can do to help PMs reach their full potential.

Before we dig deeper into this book, however, I would like to explain a few things.

How This Book Is Organized

You'll notice that I have devoted an entire chapter (Chapter 4: Define Your Good) to defining what it takes to be a "Good PM." It's important for you as head of product to understand that what makes a Good PM *good* varies from organization to organization. That is, PMs are only good in their context, their company, their current job, and their time. That's why it's so important for you to take the content of this book and translate it into your own unique environment. Not only that, but it's also important to revise this context-sensitive definition of *good* on a regular basis because times are changing. The best HoPs see change coming and start adapting their definition of good early enough to make sure their product team is ready for whatever the future might bring.

You'll also notice that I have organized the content of this book in a particular order:

PART I: What Product Managers Do—Define Your Good

PART II: Manage Your Team—Find Your Voice

PART III: Find and Recruit Good Product Managers—Attract the Best People

PART IV: Develop Your Existing Product Team—Train for Excellence

PART V: Create the Right Environment—Build a Great Culture

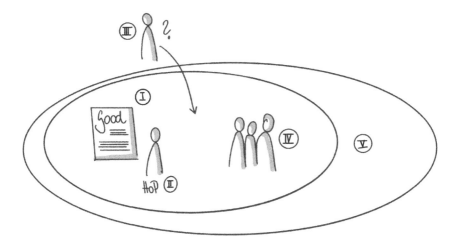

Figure 0-1: The Parts of the book in one illustration. I love drawing things because images open up a different level of understanding.

Here's how to use the content in each of these Parts:

Part I includes topics that are of direct interest to HoPs, and it provides you with the groundwork you need to work with your product managers in the most effective way.

Part II focuses on what it takes to be a great manager, and it is for heads of product who want to improve their people-development skills.

Part III is about recruiting and hiring great PMs, and it offers guidance on developing your product team.

Part IV takes a deep dive into the specific skills that every PM needs, and it touches on the most common product management coaching topics. Please note that this Part tries to accomplish two things: explain core concepts and also the plain basics—not because I think you have never heard about them, but because it will provide you with a concise summary you can quickly review before starting to coach one of your PMs on the topic. It's a shortcut that will hopefully save you a lot of time.

Finally, Part V focuses on broader organizational topics I know many HoPs need to work on to make sure their PMs can thrive, including how to influence the organization around the product team in the best possible way.

Your Personal Travel Guide

This is not a "read it front to back" kind of book. At least not for most readers.

If you are an HoP with some previous PM experience, then I recommend you use this book as your personal travel guide. If you want to find out more about a specific topic (destination), let's say, onboarding new PMs, then simply check the table of contents and flip to the appropriate chapter.

If you are an HoP who brings extensive PM experience and knowledge to the table, then skimming through the key concepts in this book might spark some new (and perhaps better) ideas for approaches that are different than the ones you are using now.

And if you've never worked as a product manager, and you don't have much experience in this field, then it might make sense for you to read the book in its entirety and later use it as a workbook.

It's also important to note that *Strong* does not contain every single topic that you need to know to be an ace HoP. For example, I don't provide advice on how to handle your CEO, or how you as HoP can nail stakeholder management, or how to best prepare for a board presentation. *Strong* focuses on the people part of an HoP's job—the things you need to do to help your PMs develop and succeed in their careers.

Please note that I have settled on the convention of randomly using the pronouns he/she, him/her, they/them throughout the book. As you know, great product managers come in every gender, so *Strong* reflects this fact. In addition, I don't use any examples from my own coaching. Those are, of course, confidential. So, although the examples you'll read are true to the kinds of experiences and situations you will encounter as an HoP, they are strictly hypothetical.

While I wrote this book with the assumption that you have the ability to influence your organization, I do understand that, particularly if your company is large and well-established, there may already be policies or procedures in place that prescribe how things are to be done. For example, the PM career ladder might already be spelled out by your company, or the progression/capabilities framework may already be in place. If this is the case in your organization, you may not be able to influence these things very much. That's okay—I am certain that there are other areas where you can exert influence over your company, and *Strong* will help you do that.

I truly hope that this book helps you create a *strong* product organization with *strong* product managers who create great tech products that deliver real value to your customers—even if you are leading and can influence only a part of the organization. With this book in hand, I know you can do just that.

One final thing: I personally drew the illustrations in *Strong.* They either illuminate something I want you to better understand, or they provide you with a simple visual you can draw yourself on a whiteboard when you have a conversation with your PMs—or sometimes *both*. Please feel free to use them in your own work.

As with every other product person I know, I *love* user feedback, so please don't hesitate to drop me a line with your thoughts at: strong@ petra-wille.com. While I can't promise to reply to each and every email message I receive, I do promise to read them all!

PART I

WHAT PRODUCT MANAGERS DO—DEFINE YOUR GOOD

As a head of product, you've been selected to lead a very important group of people in your organization: *product managers*. In this part, we'll take a close look at exactly what your key roles and responsibilities are as a head of product and what it takes to lead a product management team. In addition, we'll introduce a quick, top-level assessment you can use to gauge the capabilities of each product manager on your team, and we'll define and describe in detail the role of product managers and what it takes to be a "Good PM."

CHAPTER 1

YOUR ROLE IN THIS GAME

- What heads of product do
- Leading the product management team
- Creating the right environment

Congratulations! You've been chosen to lead a group of product managers. So, your job title is usually something like: Team Lead Product, Manager of Product Managers, VP Product, Director of Product—even CPO—or Head of Product (that's the most common term in my own experience, and what I use and call an "HoP" throughout the book). Whatever your title may be, your position is a critically important one because the work of product managers has a large—if not the main—impact on a company's success. Marc Andreesen was right when he said ten years ago that "software is eating the world." This is even more the case today.[2]

As HoP, you have some key roles and responsibilities to fulfill when it comes to building a first-class product organization. So, why not start the first chapter of this book with a really tough question: What are the key roles and responsibilities of a good HoP?

2 https://a16z.com/2011/08/20/why-software-is-eating-the-world/

I have asked many people that question—via a survey,[3] a Twitter poll, in my client interactions, and in numerous leadership forums—and I received many different responses, though perhaps it's no surprise that most were in the same general vein. One of my Twitter followers, Sally McBeth, suggested, for example, that HoPs should share a vision and strategy; create a space for PMs to do their best work through culture, advocacy, and codesign; and disseminate tools and methods to help improve standards. Product thought leader Martin Eriksson, on the other hand, suggested that HoPs should focus on direction, clarity, and freedom.

From these interactions with many product people all around the world, I have developed a consensus. At minimum, a competent head of product:

- Helps everyone understand the company's business and goals by translating them into its product strategy and then setting directions and goals for the product team.

- Builds the product management team. This includes such things as finding and hiring great product managers, developing and growing product manager capability and capacity, and monitoring product manager performance and performance of their products.

- Creates the right environment. This includes creating an environment that allows product managers to do their best work, and making sure decisions get made (but not making all the decisions).

Leading the Product Management Team

Joff Redfern is VP of Product for Atlassian. He has a vivid metaphor that neatly summarizes the roles and responsibilities of an HoP: building a

---

3   Download the "Next Bigger Challenge" assessment here: https://www.strong productpeople.com/downloads

better shipyard.[4] The people who run a shipyard don't actually build the ships themselves—they hire the best shipbuilders, they create a proper environment for building ships, and they provide their people with the support and tools they need to do great work. So, Joff suggests that your role as head of product is to build a better shipyard—the ships (the products) your teams build can only be as good as the shipyard that produces them. You are the one that is building the shipyard. Your role as HoP is to make sure the shipyard is in the best shape possible.

I particularly like this metaphor because as head of product you are not working directly on the products your organization builds—you instead *lead* the folks who build them. But because you are working on the shipyard itself, it usually takes longer to see the effects of your work as it filters through the organization and the people you lead. As a leader, your job is to get results through others. This requires an ability to influence people along with no small amount of patience. Former General Electric CEO Jack Welch explained that, "Before you are a leader, success is all about growing yourself. When you become a leader, success is all about growing others."[5]

Now let's dive a bit deeper into the role of the HoP. Let's use the widely known three-part model that is called the *3Ps of organizational success*. Good HoPs have the ability to influence each of these, leading to the outcomes they want:

- People

- Product

- Processes[6]

---

4   A Better Shipyard—Joff Redfern on the Product Experience (April 10, 2019). Retrieved from https://www.mindtheproduct.com/a-better-shipyard-joff-redfern-on-the-product-experience

5   https://www.inc.com/gene-hammett/3-lessons-from-jack-welch-on-leadership-that-you-dont-learn-in-business-school.html

6   Peter McLean (2013). The 3Ps of Organisational Success. Retrieved from https://petermclean.co/the-3ps-of-organisational-success/

As an HoP, you are usually able to impact all three of these Ps. In some cases, your impact may be direct—such as by hiring the right people—or indirect, by setting the right direction and goals.

Note: If you are leading a product organization in a startup, and you are still searching for product-market fit, you can supplement the second P—product—with purpose. You may not have figured out what your product is yet, but chances are you have a clear purpose that drives your people forward.

Are you devoting enough time to influencing all three Ps, or do you tend to favor one or two over another? Take a moment to think about how much time you devote to people, product, and processes—where do you put the lion's share of your time? Please review your schedule for the past four weeks. How much time did you spend on each of the three Ps? How much time is consumed by hiring, onboarding, and constantly developing your product people? How much time are you investing in setting and refining goals, setting directions, and making sure everybody understands them? And how much time are you investing in making sure everything runs as smooth as possible by creating the right processes?

I have created my own model (see Figure 1-1) that takes the three Ps and divides them into very specific buckets of HoP activities—showing at a glance the totality of what good heads of product do:

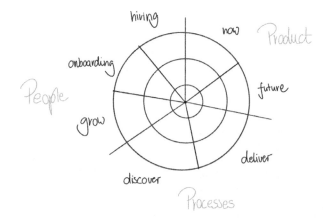

Figure 1-1: Circle graph of HoP activities (pieces of the pie represent average time distribution)

People includes:

- Hire: Reading applications, interviewing, employer-branding activities, etc.

- Onboard: Pre-first-day planning, admin—hardware, accounts, etc.—welcome day, stakeholder intros, initial 2-4 week 1:1s, etc.

- Grow: Reflecting on your team, empowering and inspiring them, reflecting on individual performance, coaching/1:1s, staying approachable, your own growth, etc.

Product includes:

- Now: Evangelizing, explaining why everyone is doing what they are currently doing, clarity, transparency, alignment, etc. within the product team and toward the rest of the organization.

- Future: Creating an overall product vision, strategy, principles, and goals that deliver user value while keeping the company alive, taking everyone along on this journey, keeping politics at a low level, etc.

Processes includes:

- Discover: Helping everyone understand the value of product discovery, making sure employees are getting in touch with real users, checking on hypotheses and experiment-driven product management, making sure decisions are based on data/gut feeling and user feedback, and ensuring there is an alignment process, that stakeholder management works, and PMs are telling their stories well, etc.

- Deliver: Making sure there's a plan but keeping it agile, ensuring maximum value is delivered with minimum effort, checking status with each PM, limiting distractions such as the next random "low-hanging-fruit" idea, removing obstacles like too many frontend devs, deescalating if things go wrong, making sure there are post-initial-launch iterations, making sure successes get celebrated, etc.

Now, color in the previous graphic, with the smallest ring just a little bit of your time for each of these activities, the middle ring a moderate amount, and the outside ring quite a lot. What do you see? Chances are, your time is not evenly divided between all the HoP activities. In fact, some may be missing altogether.

I personally really enjoy going through this three P exercise with heads of product. It's simple and straightforward, but it is powerfully accurate when you want to know if you're allocating enough time to each of your roles and responsibilities as an HoP.

Now, let's consider a common example and see what it tells us. The graph below is typical of what I see with many heads of product.

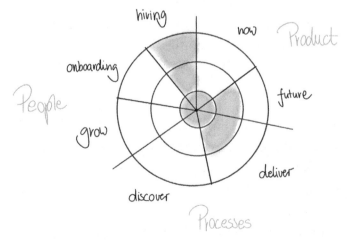

Figure 1-2: Example circle graph of actual HoP activities, post-self-assessment

You can see that this particular HoP has devoted at least a small amount of time to each of their seven key activities, however, in this case, *hiring* takes up a lot of the HoP's time—usually because they are sitting in so many interviews.

Many discussions are focused on how something should be done (OKRs, Agile methodology, experiments, user research, and so on)—that's *deliver*. And they are investing some time (never as much as they would like) setting directions and thinking about the overall product portfolio—that's *future*. This leaves them with precious little time—perhaps just an hour or two each week—to work with their product people on their personal development. 1:1s turn out to be mostly just status updates, which are routinely cancelled when other priorities come up. I see this a lot and putting people development on the back burner is an issue. Let me explain why.

Why Investing in Your People Pays Off

Let's assume that you want to start a soap bar empire with a team of three people because soap bars are the next big thing and you want to gain a first-mover advantage. You are the founder and head of product of this soap bar company (represented by the shaded person in Figure 1-3).

You invented these unique, hand-carved soap bars and you're obviously good at making them. You are, in fact, so good at making soap bars that, on your own, you can produce 15 a day. The other two people you hire to your team aren't as good as you are at making soap bars—they can each produce only five a day. Altogether, you and your team produce 25 bars a day.

However, you are convinced that you can increase production significantly by working closely with the two members of your team. So, you schedule an onboarding day, and you're so busy with onboarding that you can't produce your normal 25 soap bars that day—instead, you produce 12 soap bars.

Because you took the time to properly onboard the two members of your team, however, they figure out how to improve their production of soap bars and they are each now able to make 10 a day—5 more a day for each person. Now that you're spending more time supporting your team members, you'll also only be able to produce 10 bars for a total of 30 a day for your entire team.

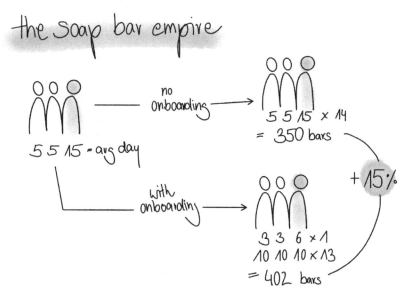

Figure 1-3: Soap bar empire—before and after onboarding

Before you took time to properly onboard your team, you could produce 350 soap bars in two weeks. After taking a day to properly onboard your team members, you are able to produce 402 soap bars in that two-week period, a 15 percent increase in production. This will further increase to 420 soap bars for subsequent two-week periods—all because you took time to onboard your people and then support them from that moment forward.

The point of this exercise is that, while taking time to properly onboard your employees will reduce your team's overall productivity for a short period of time, in the long run, your team will be more productive. Investing in your people definitely pays off.

It's your job to make sure your product people can be successful within their role. By devoting more time to this task, you'll improve the productivity of your people while you gain better outcomes for your organization.

And that is why this book is dedicated to exploring and improving the *people* part of product management.

Let's pause for a moment to reflect on what your answers are to these two questions:

■ What are the things I do to make my product people more successful in their role? For example, providing the training or support when they need to improve. . . . .
. . . .
. . . .

■ What are the things I would love to do more of in terms of people development? . . . .
. . . .
. . . .
. . . .

> **TIP:** This little framework could go into a meeting series in your calendar—it pops up once a quarter and you can invest 30 minutes to reflect on this.

Setting the Next Bigger Challenge

So, as head of product, how exactly can you help your PMs develop their full potential? There are two states for each of your PMs: *current*—how they exist today—and *potential* for what they can be tomorrow. I suggest that heads of product think about both as they consider how to help their PMs continue to improve. Here's how to help them get from as-is to their full potential:

- Set your expectations by analyzing what the company/ product/team currently needs. For example, you might want your PMs to focus more on discovery. Or you might want them to build a track record of removing technical debt while still delivering customer value. Let everyone know the expectations you have set. Then, let your PMs know when they do well against your expectations, and when they fall short. Help them calibrate their internal vs. external perspectives via peer feedback. More on this in Chapter 8: Monitoring Performance and Giving Feedback.

- Have a bigger vision for each of your PMs—one that is ideally aligned with their personal goals. Help them see the potential that you see within them and help them grow toward this potential by assigning them the right work packages and initiatives, and through constant coaching and holding them accountable for their personal growth. Be sure to follow up with your PMs to track progress.

It's important to have a bigger vision for each of your PMs. People always ask me, "Even beyond their current role?" and the answer is always yes. And people will then ask, "Even beyond their current position in our company?" and my answer to this question is yes as well. Because no matter if they stay or if they leave, you want to have a bigger vision for them to keep them motivated and to help them grow.

Of course, in addition to having a bigger vision for your PMs, you've also got to assign them to the right initiatives that help them grow. And, despite all you do, sometimes people need to leave their current organization at some point in time to grow even bigger. But, along the way, you'll get much more out of them if you help them.

To do all this with your PMs requires that you as HoP set aside time in your busy schedule to ...

- Observe. Make sure to actively observe how your PMs are doing—collect examples and personal anecdotes that make it easier to give personal feedback.

- Reflect and adapt your expectations. You need to pause and reflect every once in a while to see if what you *think* the company needs is still what the company really *does* need. You also need to assess if your PMs are still good at what you thought they are good at and if their personal motivations have changed.

- Plan. You need time to plan next steps for each product person on your team.

- Exchange and coaching (1:1s). You need time to share your observations and plans with your PMs. We'll address this in more detail in Chapter 7: The Power of Coaching.

Throughout all this, you want to be sure that your PMs are developing—that their skills and expertise are continuing to improve. This requires your attention. I have found that asking this leading question can help you in this effort:

Is This PM Ready for the Next Bigger Challenge?

I have developed a form you can fill out for each of your PMs (see Figure 1-4 on next page). Just use your gut feeling to answer the question. Here are a few examples for the next bigger challenge (and I'm sure you already have some things in mind that might be particularly relevant to your own company):

- A repositioning of your whole product with a lot of management attention

- Work with a completely new staffed product development team

- Taking care of the onboarding of new PM colleagues (while continuing to work on their product)

As you can see, if your answers for one of your PMs is "Yes," then you will assign them to the next bigger challenge that comes available so that they develop and acquire new skills on the job. If the answer is "Yes, but …" then you should still assign them to the next bigger challenge but help them to get a mentor. If the answer is "No," then ask yourself "Why not?" Make sure you are investing more time in observing this PM, reflecting on what he is already capable of and where he has some gaps. Discuss these gaps with your PMs and how they see themselves with them, and then figure out how you can support your PMs as they gain more skills and self-confidence. If the answer is "Maybe," then gather more info and keep observing until you've got a clear yes or no.

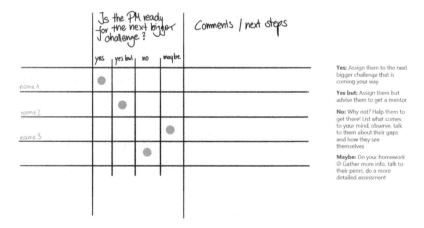

Figure 1-4: PM next bigger challenge assessment

So, what's next?

Going through this exercise will give you a good idea about the current state of your product team. If, however, you're finding it difficult to develop a list of skills that your PMs should have, and it's hard to identify their gaps, then continue through Part I of this book. If you work with the content, you'll develop a good job description and you'll better understand how to express your expectations in a more structured way.

If you have a crystal-clear definition of the perfect PM, and it's easy to identify the gaps in your people but you struggle to talk with them about their gaps, you'll find many helpful tips within Part II: Manage Your Team–Find Your Voice.

And if you have identified gaps in your people, and the things missing are tangible and product related (such as time management, for example) and you just need some more background info and tricks for how you can make the conversation work, then Part IV: Develop Your Existing Product Team–Train For Excellence is your friend.

Further Reading

This is the first Further Reading section in this book, which you will find at the end of most chapters. The purpose of this section is to provide you with more sources of product wisdom–written, video, and audio–you can explore to get some new ideas and views related to the topic of the chapter.

- The "Next bigger challenge" assessment is available for download here: https://www.strongproductpeople.com/further-readings#chapter-1_1

- 10 Top Tips from Product's Finest Leaders–Imogen Johnson: https://www.strongproductpeople.com/further-readings#chapter-1_2

- What Do Product Managers Want from Their Bosses? https://www.strongproductpeople.com/further-readings #chapter-1_3

CHAPTER 2

A QUICK TEAM ASSESSMENT

- The GWC assessment
- Using your insights to navigate this book

Before you assess whether or not each of your PMs has what it takes to be a successful PM, it can be very helpful to first do a quick, top-level assessment of your entire team. This is especially the case if you are a head of product who has never, ever thought about assessing your team in a structured way. Unfortunately, many HoPs have not reflected on whether they think their team is actually capable of doing the job that needs to be done.

I'm certain that, even if you have never formally assessed your team, you have a strong gut feeling about the individual PMs on your team. So, let's tap into that gut feeling for your first team assessment.

The GWC Assessment

The quick team assessment I recommend in this chapter is easy and it will help you to gain clarity on what you think about the members of your team. But you will need to set aside some uninterrupted time to reflect—perhaps 15–30 minutes, depending on how many people are on your team. All you'll need to conduct the assessment is a pen and a sheet of paper—it's that simple! Please note that this can be used for *any* role on your team, it's not specific only to PMs.

The method I use for doing a team assessment is called *GWC*, and it is described in Gino Wickman's book, *Traction*. According to Wickman, GWC stands for *get it, want it,* and *capacity to do it.*[7] These three parts of GWC can be turned into questions that you ask yourself as the manager/leader of PMs. Let's consider each in turn:

- Does your PM understand (as they say, **get**) what their role is as a PM? And do they get what's expected from them in this role in terms of outcome and output?

- If they get it, do they also **want** it? Is the work they do aligned with what they want to achieve in their career and personal life?

- And if they get what needs to be done, and they want to do it, do they have the **capacity** to do the job? Do they have what's required mentally, physically, and emotionally to do their jobs? Do they also have sufficient time and knowledge and are they provided with enough resources?

Are you ready to conduct your quick team assessment using GWC? I hope so because that's what we'll do now. Please grab that pen and piece of paper and draw a chart like the one in Figure 2-1 on page 29. Make sure there are enough spaces for each of your product managers.

---

7   Gino Wickman, *Traction: Get a Grip on Your Business,* BenBella Books (2012) p. 99

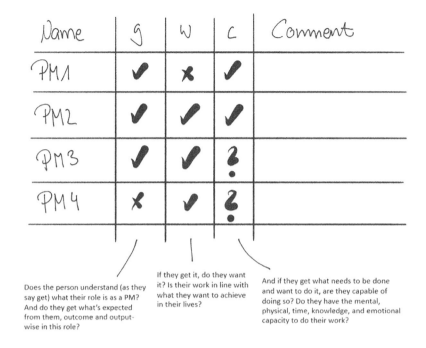

Does the person understand (as they say get) what their role is as a PM? And do they get what's expected from them, outcome and output-wise in this role?

If they get it, do they want it? Is their work in line with what they want to achieve in their lives?

And if they get what needs to be done and want to do it, are they capable of doing so? Do they have the mental, physical, time, knowledge, and emotional capacity to do their work?

Figure 2-1: GWC assessment

Fill in the name of each PM, then rate them on the three parts of the GWC assessment: gets it, wants it, and capacity to do it. You'll simply mark each box next to the name of your PMs with a check mark, an X, or a question mark. Here's what those different ratings mean:

✔ This is a definite YES

✗ This is a definite NO

❓ You're uncertain and need to get more data

You can add any comments you like in the boxes at the far right of the assessment form that you have created. Now, let's see what we can do with the results of this exercise.

In my experience, not getting it or not wanting it are usually deal killers and you'll need to find another position for your employee when that is the case. (The only exception is if we are talking about a colleague that has recently joined and you did not take the time to explain the role properly!) If they don't have the capacity to do the job for some reason, this can often be resolved. If a person has the mental capacity to work as a PM and is just lacking some know-how to do their job—say, they need to do more forecasting and their Excel skills need improvement—this can easily be fixed with training.

However, if they are having mental/emotional capacity issues— maybe they're under a lot of personal financial pressure, or they're going through a divorce or other family or relationship turmoil—then you should consciously decide to give them a bit more room to breathe and for sure *not* assign them to the next bigger challenge.

You can probably see that I am advocating for one thing here: If you draw an X somewhere in this table, the first thing you should do is reflect on whether *you* are part of the problem. Have you done whatever you can to set up your PM to be successful in their role?

Use Your Insights to Navigate This Book

Now that you have filled in your quick team assessment form, here's what to do next. Take a look at your ratings and reflect on the overall place of each PM on your team. How do they stack up against other PMs?

✔ Jackpot! Your PM is doing well. You're getting what you need from them, and what they're doing for you is aligned with their career and life goals. You can give them more detailed feedback, coaching, and advice using the PMwheel as a guide. Read Chapter 7: The Power of Coaching to learn more.

✗ Your PM is lacking in some way and needs an upgrade. If you rated this a "no" in the *capacity* dimension, then this can likely be fixed through training, coaching, or by waiting a bit for the PM to recover from whatever issues are creating turmoil in their life. Please make it your mission to help them to get back to a check mark. Don't leave them alone! However, not *getting* it or not *wanting* it are usually deal killers (unless it's an onboarding issue), and you should be looking for a different seat or role for this person. Read Chapter 6: Identifying and Closing Product Manager Gaps to help your PMs in the best possible way.

? Observe the PM more, use the PMwheel to reflect, ask peers for their input, and talk to the person. Turn to Chapter 8: Monitoring Performance and Giving Feedback to do this well.

Assessing the members of your team isn't a one-and-done thing. Be sure to periodically assess your people to see if they are improving, maintaining the status quo, or falling behind. The feedback you get from these assessments will help you plan and budget your ongoing employee-development efforts.

CHAPTER 3

THE ROLE OF PRODUCT MANAGERS

- What is a product?

- What is a product manager?

- Key product manager activities

You may recall that, in Chapter 1, I explained what *your* role is—the role of the head of product. Since you're an HoP, I'm certain you already know what product managers do. However, the big question is this: Are you able to describe the role of the product manager to your PMs in a way that they will understand how *you* view it? Believe me—there's a difference between generally knowing what something is and being able to describe it in detail to others. It's the difference between an implicit understanding and an explicit role description.

With so many smart books and articles about product management, written by some very smart product people, when asked how you define the role of a PM, it's tempting to just say, "Wait a second and I'll Google it," or "I have a copy of *Product Leadership* on my bookshelf—let me see what it says." That's all well and good, but as head of product, you should be able to roll off an accurate description of what a product manager is and does when asked—anytime and anyplace.

Before you read any further in this chapter, I would like you to first find a highlighter and have it handy. Then, as you read through the text, highlight everything you agree with. After you finish reading the chapter and doing your highlighting, take a moment or two to write down a definition of what a product manager is *in your own words*. Make sure this definition is something easy to remember and easy to repeat/explain to people. It's superimportant for your product team to have a leader who has a clear idea what they should be doing and what they should not be doing. Not just in their day-to-day job, but also in a team, company, and industry context.

Before we dive deeper into the role of the PM, let's first define what a product is.

What Is a Product?

I'm sure you know what a product is, right? Surprisingly, I have seen many companies (and HoPs and PMs) that struggle with what should be a simple thing to define. I routinely talk with product managers who are responsible for 26 different (what I would call) *things* that they call "products." And they wonder why they are constantly struggling with prioritizing their work.

Then there are companies with backend product managers, and frontend product managers only delivering the shop front, and they're fighting hard to get any value to their customers. I really urge you as head of product to take a moment to think about what a product really is, and if this thing you've got is really worth being managed by a PM.

So, then, what is a product?

A product is something **created** and **made available** to somebody that brings **value** to customers/users (the market).

It's that simple.

In addition to that basic definition, a product should support the needs and constraints of a business/organization to keep production going so that more consumers/users can experience its value. That is, it should generate enough value to be sustainable over the long run.

Products can be all sorts of things, including physical goods (from laundry detergent to the book you hold in your hand to a Tesla), fully digital products (such as your Netflix streaming television service or an online course), or technology-powered products that merge together physical and digital products. And, many things that we call tech products today are a combination or bundle of services provided online (such as Facebook and Salesforce) or the use of the internet as a marketing/selling/distribution channel (think Uber or e-commerce platforms such as Etsy).

So now that we know what a product is, let's explore what a product manager is.

What Is a Product Manager?

The simplest definition of *product manager* is someone who is responsible for all facets of product development. However, in my experience, this simple definition doesn't really get to the heart of what a product manager truly is.

When I describe what the one major responsibility of a product manager is in just a few sentences, I use Marty Cagan's definition: It's the product manager's job to come up with a product solution that is valuable to the user, usable by the user, buildable by our engineering team, and still viable from a business perspective. It's all about finding a balance between these four dimensions. If you overly obsess on one or the other, chances are high that your product will fail.

As you can see from the diagram below, each of these four PM responsibilities represent risks that must be addressed and overcome:

1. *Value* risk (whether customers will buy it or users will choose to use it)

2. *Usability* risk (whether users can figure out how to use it)

3. *Feasibility* risk (whether our engineers can build what we need with the time, skills, and technology we have)

4. *Business viability* risk (whether this solution also works for the various aspects of our business)[8]

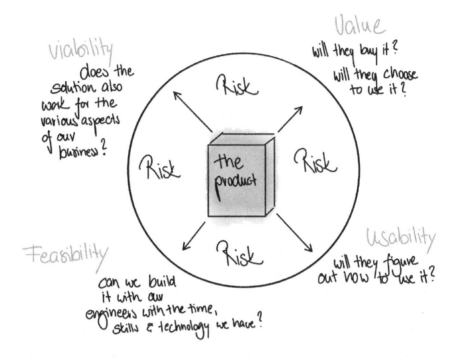

Figure 3-1: What I draw when I have to explain
the job of the product manager

So, who is *not* a product manager by this definition?

- Someone whose only job is to maintain a backlog for the Agile development team—not making any decisions

- Someone who only collects requirements from all across the company—putting them on some roadmap—and who sits in meetings, designs by committee, and doesn't make any decisions

---

8   https://svpg.com/four-big-risks/

- Someone whose job it is to write concepts while a team somewhere else works on it far later

Key Product Manager Activities

To find this sweet spot of product development, a PM must be able to perform these specific activities:

- Listen to their users/customers/market to understand their problems and how they could possibly solve them (That is generating the value!)

- Conduct several experiments and prototypes to test their assumptions/hypotheses and various solutions before they actually build the product (To minimize the risk of building the wrong thing in a beautiful way)

- Deliver value and test if people are actually using/ buying their product (product-market fit)

- Maximize value but minimize the effort to build the actual solution *and* make sure the winning solution(s) can be built by the team in a reasonable amount of time

- Deliver the product and optimize (or even innovate on) it based on customer feedback

In the product world, you'll find that these product manager activities are given all sorts of fancy names, including *design thinking, product discovery, user research,* and more. However, in the end, it all boils down to what product managers do.

I have created an assessment called PMwheel that measures eight key PM activities. We'll explore this assessment in detail in the next chapter but, for now, let's take a look at the activities themselves as illustrated in the following PMwheel graphic:

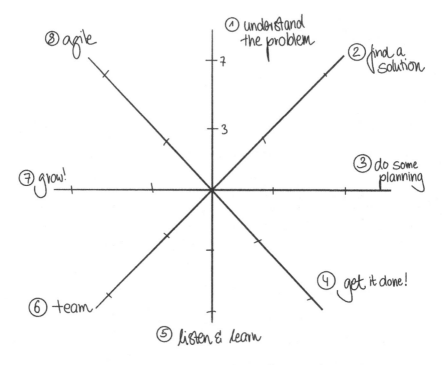

Figure 3-2: Key activities in the PMwheel

Here are the key activities in the PMwheel—I'll provide detailed descriptions of each activity in the next chapter:

1. Understand the problem

2. Find a solution

3. Do some planning

4. Get it done!

5. Listen & learn

6. Team

7. Grow!

8. Agile

Activities 6, 7, and 8 can't be tied to the product-creation process. Instead, they represent the know-how that a PM needs to work with her team (such things as motivation, Tuckman's stages,[9] and so on), the know-how she needs to personally grow and learn new things, and the know-how required to work in an agile environment.

No matter what the background of your PM is, it's his or her job to limit the risk of building the wrong thing in a beautiful way, and to upgrade the life of their users by delivering products these people actually want to use. And it's also their job to figure out what it takes to get this value delivered within the given constraints and their given product development team while earning some money to keep the organization running.

And now, on to the next chapter, where we'll dive deeper into the various tasks and skills a product person needs to thrive in the context of your company. I will also help you come up with your own definition of what a Good PM looks like. Please review your definition, optimize it, and make sure you recall it if somebody asks you.

Further Reading

- Martin Eriksson—an oldie but goodie: https://www.strongproductpeople.com/further-readings#chapter-3_1

- Behind every great product—Marty Cagan https://www.strongproductpeople.com/further-readings#chapter-3_2

- Good Product Manager, Bad Product Manager—Ben Horowitz: https://www.strongproductpeople.com/further-readings#chapter-3_3

- Jeff Patton—Product management in an agile environment: https://www.strongproductpeople.com/further-readings#chapter-3_4

---

9   Wikipedia (n.d.). Tuckman's stages of group development. Retrieved from https://en.wikipedia.org/wiki/Tuckman%27s_stages_of_group_development

- The Role of the PO—Henrik Kniberg: https://www.strong productpeople.com/further-readings#chapter-3_5

- 15 things you should know about product people: https://www.strongproductpeople.com/further-readings #chapter-3_6

- The evolving product management role: https://www .strongproductpeople.com/further-readings#chapter-3_7

- Books:
  - *INSPIRED* by Marty Cagan
  - *Product Management in Practice* by Matt LeMay

CHAPTER 4

DEFINE YOUR GOOD

- Why it's important to define your good

- Putting your system in place

- Some ideas to get you started (PM essence, PMwheel)

- Put it all together and start using it

In the previous chapter, we explored exactly what a product manager is. In this chapter, we'll take a close look at what it takes to be a "Good PM"–the kind of person that you want on your team.

You might think that defining your *good* would be a straightforward exercise. However, like most everything else in the product world, there are lots of opinions about what makes someone a Good PM. Here's one possible measure to consider, according to Marty Cagan:

> *The only true measure of the product manager*
> *is the success of his or her product.*[10]

Of course, what Marty says is true. But are there any other aspects determining whether or not a product manager has what it takes to

---

10   https://svpg.com/measuring-product-managers/

excel in their job? And is there a good way of providing PMs with the feedback and guidance they need to improve? Is there one framework HoPs can use for assessing them? I think the answer to the first two questions is clearly *yes,* and the answer to the last question is a definite *no.* There is no one-size-fits-all solution to that. Every HoP has to create their own definition of a Good PM, taking industry, company, team, and product aspects into account. So, this chapter will help you to come up with your own definition of *good.* And it will explore frameworks you can use as a starting point for inspiration. But it's still on *you* to come up with your very own definition of a Good PM.

Unfortunately, I personally know too many companies that for one reason or another do not have a written definition of what makes a Good PM, much less what their main tasks and responsibilities should be. In the absence of this definition, how do you as an HoP know that your product managers are Good PMs, or have the potential to become Good PMs? And, perhaps even more important, how do your PMs know?

Still not convinced? If you haven't defined your good, how do you...

- Make sure your PMs know what they are expected to do?[11]

- Make the right hiring decisions?

- Talk about your/the company's expectations when onboarding new PMs?

- Define if someone is falling short of standards or not performing?

- Show PMs their necessary areas of personal growth?

Defining your good provides you with a compass to help you navigate each one of these situations with your product managers, as well as many others. They are on display for everyone to see and a part of

---

11   This is the first part of the GWC assessment in Chapter 2: Gets it

every conversation you have with your PMs. Your people will know exactly what is expected of them and they will also know that your expectations and standards are the same for everyone on the team.

Yes, there will be a significant investment of time on your part to define your good. You might even need to create different goods if you're working in a very large product organization. However, it's something that will pay off for you—not just in your current position, but throughout your career. You can take it with you and make minor adjustments when you start a new role in your current company, or if you decide to make the move to an entirely new company.

How to Get There from Here

So, how exactly do you go about creating a framework for defining your good? You can come up with your own approach, or you can adopt one that someone else has already developed. Here's my own approach for your consideration:

1. Define your PM essence. These are the personality traits you're looking for in your product managers. Keep in mind that, since they are hard to change—they're usually already baked into someone's personality—they're most useful in the hiring process. Here are the components of PM essence that I personally look for:

- Curiosity
- Emotional intelligence
- Wants to make an impact
- Intellectual horsepower
- Adaptability
- Nice to spend time with

Let me explain why I've picked those particular traits.

If someone is **curious** about the world in general, and wants to learn all kinds of things just because she loves learning, that is a good thing for a product manager to have. Curious people want to learn more about the business space the company is operating in, the product itself, the user and how they are spending their time, and this new technology. And they don't complain if they have to learn a new methodology or work on a different problem space. In fact, they embrace these opportunities.

I've picked **emotional intelligence** because the term covers many other aspects. If you are in touch with your feelings and recognize the feelings and needs of others, you will feel the pain of users struggling to use your product and will, therefore, start easing this pain by improving the way it works. And high-EQ people will want to help that one team member who never gets a chance to speak up in a meeting. They help you to spot toxic behavior in the company/product organization. They will be a great partner in the hiring process because they can tell if a person works well with the existing team.[12] And they might even be great in partner management and negotiations because they can tell what the other party is interested in.

But I have seen curious people with a high EQ struggling in a product role, and I've figured out that there are some more things needed to make a great PM:

They need to **want to make an impact.** This means being focused on getting things done and focused on delivering real value to users while earning the money required to keep the organization up and running. They need to love the feeling of launching, finishing, optimizing, or improving something. And if they are smart and intelligent (that is, having the **intellectual horsepower** to understand complex correlations quickly) they will be well equipped for the job.

The cherry on this cake is being **adaptable**—are they comfortable with change in any form or way? If the answer is yes, that's a big plus!

---

12 Kate Leto, *Hiring Product Managers: Using Product EQ to go beyond culture and skills,* Sense & Respond Press (2020)

And last, but not least, I think it is essential that the PM himself is someone people like to work with, to **spend time with**, to hang out with, to talk to or consult with. I have included some additional sources of inspiration regarding the PM essence in the Further Reading section at the end of this chapter.

So, now it's on you: start filling out the canvas in Figure 4-1. What are the six main personality traits you want to see in *your* PMs?

2. Define PM responsibilities, skills, and know-how that matter to you. This is where we get into the actual product management process and what it takes to get the job done well. The PMwheel—which I introduced in the previous chapter—is a very useful framework for defining PM responsibilities, skills, and know-how. We'll take a detailed look at this framework in the next section.

3. Add company values and other company-wide factors. These are the core values and principles of your company, such as Amazon's 14 Leadership Principles[13] or Procter & Gamble's 5 corporate values.[14] It is important to add them to your definition just to make sure your PMs—and you yourself—are checking back on them every once in a while.

My definition of a good PM		Petra Wille	strongproductpeople.com
PM Essence Personality traits you think a Good PM needs to have	Curiosity Emotional intelligence Wants to make an impact	Intellectual horsepower Adaptability Nice to spend time with
Skills, Know-How, Responsibilities All the things that sum up to a Good PM. What are their main tasks? What do they need to know? What do they need to be good at?		See PMwheel for all the details. In short it´s: Finding and understanding user problems worth solving, finding solutions to these problems and identifying the best solution to implement, figure out how to build it with the given team and get it done in an effective way. Once released listen to the user feedback, see how the product is doing and iterate. Do all of this with your Team in an agile way and make sure you learn along the way and are spending some time on personal growth.
Values Add your company's and/or product team's values here		Earn trust. Deliver results. Invent and simplify. Take ownership. Put the customer first.

Figure 4-1: A framework for defining your good

---

13   https://www.amazon.jobs/en/principles
14   https://us.pg.com/policies-and-practices/purpose-values-and-principles/

Once you have your compass, then share it with your PMs, use it for coaching and feedback in your 1:1s, and make it a part of your hiring and onboarding process. In short, use it with your product managers all the time, in every way you can. When you create a structure for defining your good, it will make your life—and the life of your PMs—both easier and more effective.[15]

I know that this may seem like an overly complex approach, and I'll be the first to admit that it's not simple. It takes work to dig deep into the qualities that are required for your PMs to be Good PMs. People are complex, and if you go for a superficial approach that just skates along the surface of your product managers' personalities and competencies and skills and know-how, then your efforts will not be as effective as they could be. I strongly suggest that you take the time to put a system like this in place in your product organization.[16] I've seen this work in many companies, and the outcomes have been uniformly stellar.

The PMwheel

As I mentioned above, a key part of my own model for defining your good is to define PM responsibilities, skills, and know-how that matter to you. To help you accomplish this task, I created a tool that I call the PMwheel. The PMwheel allows you to graph the extent to which someone has what it takes to be a Good PM. Please keep in mind that you can use my version of the PMwheel, or you are welcome to tweak it and make it uniquely your own. It's all fine so long as you have some sort of framework you can use for hiring, onboarding, coaching, feedback, and so on.

---

15 Please keep in mind that no two PMs are alike, and that's a good thing. You don't want all your PMs to be the same. One might be brilliantly creative, while another might be an execution wizard, while yet another might be really strategic. The team will benefit from having all these different PMs contributing in their own ways.

16 If you're working in a large organization, I recommend aligning with other product leads on this.

There are eight buckets in the PMwheel:

1. **Understand the problem.** Are your PMs aware of the underlying problems the users are facing? Do they understand the motives, issues, and beliefs of the target audience? And have they thought about what the needs of the company/organization are?

2. **Find a solution.** They found some good problems to solve? Great! Can they partner with the team and stakeholders to come up with some possible solutions and an experiment for testing which of them is worth building?

3. **Do some planning.** No matter if you are a fan of good old roadmaps, or you know the latest agile planning tricks, a PM must have a plan and a story to explain what's next.

4. **Get it done!** Every PM needs to know how to work with her product development team to get the product out to the customer.

5. **Listen & learn.** Once you've released something new, you will want to observe if and how people are using it and iterate on the learnings to improve the current status.

6. **Team.** How good are the PMs when it comes to teamwork? What do they know about lateral leadership and motivation of teams?

7. **Grow!** Are they investing some time in their personal growth as a product person?

8. **Agile.** Are they just following what others exemplify as an agile way of working or do they fully understand Agile values, principles, and ways of working?

The first five buckets listed above are specific parts of the product-development process, while the remaining three are more general and not specific to product development. There is a detailed version of this on my website with many guiding questions that you might find very helpful.[17]

Here are 4 examples of the 17 questions in the "understand the problem" bucket of the PMwheel PDF:

- Is she able to project the user needs onto product value and onto potential revenues made? (Business case)

- Can she conduct insightful user interviews? Does she know about the things you CAN and CAN'T figure out with interviews?

- Is she aware of user biases and the psychology of people?

- Is she the trusted party when it comes to "being the advocate of the user?"

I have created the following graphic for the PMwheel, with each of the eight buckets (or *factors*) assigned to its own spot:

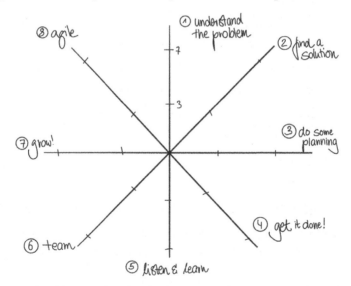

Figure 4-2: The PMwheel—the key part of my Good PM definition

---

17   https://www.strongproductpeople.com/pmwheel

No matter whether or not you like the PMwheel, you have to come up with a definition as precise and extensive as that to make sure your definition of a Good PM is a solid one. If for some reason you don't like the PMwheel, I've added a few more PM role definitions to the Further Reading section at the end of this chapter.

Start Using Your Definition of Good

Now that you have reflected on your good, you should start using it. I suggest doing a quick dry run: use it to reflect on each person on your product team, checking in on personality traits, skills, know-how, responsibilities, and values. Does the new definition of good work for you? Are you gaining more clarity when using it? Will it help you structure your 1:1s? If not, please make sure you refine it until it does.

And remember that people are *complex*. So, even if your definition of good is complex, like the PMwheel is, it will never be able to capture a person in all their different aspects. I have personally found that, when I use the PMwheel, it's like snowflakes—no two assessments for different PMs will be alike. Some product managers will be stronger in one area, while others will be stronger in another. So, please keep this in mind.

When you assess your PMs (we'll talk about how to do a collaborative assessment later), you'll rate them on each of the factors on a 0-7 scale (we use 0-7 because there's no mean value). If your PM has absolutely nothing to offer in, for example, "Get it done!" then he'll rate a 0. If, on the other hand, he is the most amazing person ever in "Get it done!" then he'll rate a 7.

After you have subjected all product managers to this assessment, it is important to look at the entire team again and make any necessary adjustments: Are all those who got a 6 in "do some planning" similarly good?

The Initial Assessment Meeting

So, now that you've defined your good and done your dry run, what's next?

There's one thing I haven't yet talked about that I will introduce to you now: the initial assessment meeting. It's where you'll present your definition of good to your PM and then conduct their first collaborative assessment session together. To make this initial assessment meeting as helpful and effective, both for you and for your PM, I suggest taking the following approach:

- Explain your framework and how you developed it.

- Invite your PM to conduct the first collaborative assessment session. Ask them to rate themselves on each of the eight buckets in the PMwheel (you will also be prepared with your own PMwheel assessment of the PM) and reflect on the team and company values.

- Present your own ratings to the PM and explain why you selected those particular scores. By the way, it's pretty common for PMs to rate themselves lower than their bosses do. (Don't just highlight shortfalls—be sure to let them know where you think they are already doing a great job!)

- Identify one area of improvement in this first session. Something small, something easy to learn or to change. You want them to succeed.

- Ask them if they would like to do this more often, and if so, how often?

- Encourage comments and even pushback on your approach. Your PM might have valid points on how to improve your Good PM definition right away.

Putting It All Together

The goal in doing all of the work in this chapter is to first create an ideal of what a Good PM definition should be, and second, to compare your product managers against this ideal that you have created. I have found that doing this in the most effective way possible requires five specific steps:

Step 1: Get to know your PMs. Spend time with your product managers! Learn all about their strengths and areas for development, what they want to achieve in life, how they learn, and the extent of their PM know-how. You can also learn a lot about your PMs by talking with their peers.

Step 2: Reflect on what you've learned and map it to your ideal. Take what you've learned and create your own PMwheel assessment of what you think your PM's strengths are—and where there is room to grow.

Step 3: Ask your PM to assess themselves using the PMwheel or the framework you have decided to use. Compare this assessment with your own assessment and discuss. What areas require further development?

Step 4: Ask yourself: Can I help this PM get better in their development area? If not, who can you tap to help your PM improve? This step is an important one because few things are more frustrating for your PM than being told, "Your time management could improve," without giving them some direction on where to start their journey.

Step 5: Sit down with them and ask how they think they're doing. This is perhaps the most important step of all. Explain to them the reflection you see (think of yourself as a mirror—reflect, don't patronize). Talk about what they are doing well and together decide development areas for them to work on. Your PMs usually already know their areas for potential growth and what would be most helpful to them to improve—in their current role or toward the next, bigger challenge.

Remember: Structure makes it easier to talk about development topics with your PMs. Structure also makes sure everyone gets the same kind of feedback—making the entire process fairer and more transparent.

Further Reading

- Learning from other companies:
  - How We Developed a Talent Growth Plan at Almundo https://www.strongproductpeople.com/further-readings#chapter-4_1

- Other PM skill models:
  - The PM Daisy: https://www.strongproductpeople.com/further-readings#chapter-4_2
  - Marty Cagan's PM assessment: https://www.strongproductpeople.com/further-readings#chapter-4_3
  - Shaun Russell's adaptation of the Spotify model: https://www.strongproductpeople.com/further-readings#chapter-4_4

- Key PM personality traits:
  - Ten Traits of Good Product Managers: https://www.strongproductpeople.com/further-readings#chapter-4_5
  - 638 Personality Traits: https://www.strongproductpeople.com/further-readings#chapter-4_6

- Books:
  - *FYI: For Your Improvement 5th Edition* by Michael Lombardo and Robert Eichinger

PART II

MANAGE YOUR TEAM—
FIND YOUR VOICE

As a head of product, you should have more than a passing familiarity with the art and science of *management and leadership*. It's through others, after all, that you get things done. In this part, we'll dig deep into what it takes to be a great boss and how to identify and close product manager gaps. We'll explore how great managers use coaching to up their games and how to monitor employee performance and give feedback. Finally, we'll consider the importance of employee motivation and alignment in building an outstanding product organization, and how to help your PMs find the time they need to do their jobs well.

I call all this "finding your voice" as a manager, which means doing the inner work required to be able to express yourself—your ideas, views, philosophies, principles, and more—both in words and in practice.

CHAPTER 5

BEING A GREAT BOSS

- Your "great boss" blueprint

- Feedback from your employees (and peers)

- Feedback from a mentor and coach

When it comes to the art and science of management, there is one simple truth: no one is born a great boss—it's a journey. This means that *anyone* has the possibility of becoming a great boss. Just as great products are the result of a deliberate process of experimentation, learning, and improvement, so too do great managers develop their own skills and experience through the very same process. In the words of former U.S. Secretary of State, Colin Powell, "Effective leaders are made, not born. They learn from trial and error, and from experience."[18]

Of course, many of us find ourselves placed into management positions quite literally overnight. One day we're building products, and the next day we're leading a team of people building products. The problem is that many of us receive little or no training from our

---

18 (November 30, 2005). Effective leaders made, not born, Colin Powell says. Retrieved from https://news.stanford.edu/news/2005/november30/powell-113005 .html

employers in the skills necessary to manage others, much less be a good boss. In fact, research conducted by leadership development consultants Zenger/Folkman reveals that people don't receive formal management training until they have already been a manager for 10 years—at an average age of 42 years old.[19]

I am often asked if I believe that it's possible to be a good head of product without ever having worked as a product manager. The answer is: it depends. It helps to have the experience of working in a development team, and whether as a designer, QA person, developer, or product manager is irrelevant. It is essential to have contributed to something that customers can touch and use. The countless steps that are necessary to release a product, the endless team discussions, the 1,000 compromises made. Whoever has seen this firsthand is going to be a better HoP.

But I also know HoPs without previous product experience who do their job well. In my experience, they all have one thing in common: they acquire the necessary background knowledge but don't make a secret of the fact that their lack of product knowledge is a weakness. So, they play to their strengths—they are empathic, they trust their PMs, and they look for good people within the company or, if necessary, externally.

What exactly is it that makes a great boss great? The results of a study of 300,000 leaders indicates that the top-five leadership skills most important for success are: inspires and motivates others, displays high integrity and honesty, solves problems and analyzes issues, drives for results, and communicates powerfully and prolifically.[20] How do *you* measure up against that ranking?

---

19   Jack Zenger (December 17, 2012). We Wait Too Long to Train Our Leaders. Retrieved from https://hbr.org/2012/12/why-do-we-wait-so-long-to-trai
20   Peter Economy (March 30, 2018). This Study of 300,000 Leaders Revealed the Top 10 Traits for Success. Retrieved from https://www.inc.com/peter-economy/this-study-of-300000-businesspeople-revealed-top-10-leader-traits-for-success.html

So, assuming you want to be a great boss, how exactly can you do that? In my experience, there are three main things you can do to improve your management skills and they are the focus of this chapter:

The first thing you need is a clear picture of what you are aiming for—what you think it is that makes an ideal boss.

The second thing you need is feedback from your employees—maybe even your peers.

The third thing you need is feedback from an external mentor or coach who you can exchange ideas with, but who doesn't work in your current company.

Let's take a closer look at each of these.

Your "Great Boss" Blueprint

There is a lot of material out there—articles, papers, books, videos, and much more—that explains the characteristics of great bosses. Instead of simply copy-and-pasting from one of those many resources, I would much rather highlight five aspects of great bosses that I have personally found to often be neglected or underestimated.

1. The human touch. The classic definition of "manager" is someone who gets things done through others—that is, they depend on their employees to accomplish their goals, and the goals of the organization. Managers align the members of their team to work together toward accomplishing these common goals. As such, the very best bosses understand that management is all about *people* and building strong relationships and trust. Great bosses are deeply human—they care about their employees, customers, and communities in which they do business. And this human touch is especially important in times of turmoil and uncertainty.

So, be very *human*. Show your fears, doubts, and vulnerabilities—along with the passion and joy you feel when things go right. Show your people that you care. Get to know who they are outside of work—do they have a significant other, kids, hobbies? Appreciate people with all their differences and assume positive intent in the actions they take (in my experience, people don't come to work hoping to do a bad job that day). Be open to their concerns and spot interpersonal tensions—and react to them appropriately—early, before they erupt into major issues. Acknowledge and reward good performance, creating appropriate rituals and ceremonies, and provide your people with opportunities to shine.

2. Opinionated but adaptable. It may seem somewhat surprising, but something I see in many heads of product is that they don't take a strong stance on issues affecting their organization, their product(s), or their people. So, for example, I'll ask an HoP, "What do you think about motivating your people? Do you think it is possible to influence the people who work for you to become more engaged in their work?" In return, I often get a response along the lines of, "Well, I never thought about that."

Great bosses have strong opinions about the topics that affect the workplace, including such things as motivation, incentives and rewards, ethics and moral business decisions, the benefits of diversity,[21] leadership vs. management, common product management topics, and more. At minimum, you've got to educate yourself enough to have an opinion on whatever the topic might be. But, at the same time, you must be willing to adapt and flex your strong opinions when you have new information on the topic that changes your basic assumptions or knowledge. The world is always changing around us, so we need to be willing to change our minds—perhaps even have fun in being wrong.

3. Lead by example. When you're the boss, the people who work for you keep a very close eye on how you behave and whether or not you do the things you ask (or demand) your people to do. For example, do you set a time for a weekly meeting with your team, and then arrive late—sometimes just a few minutes, and other times many more than that—week after week? This kind of behavior sends a clear message to your people—that you don't value their time, and between the lines, that you don't respect *them*. And if you don't respect them, then why

---

21 https://hbr.org/2013/12/how-diversity-can-drive-innovation

should they respect *you*? (Chances are, they won't!) They will also, of course, learn that it's okay for them to be late too.

Great bosses set a great example for their people to follow. Stay organized and know your stuff. HoPs need to know a lot about what product managers do, and how they do it. Be on time for meetings, share your know-how, focus on users and outcomes, be positive, delegate authority and responsibilities, be collaborative, communicate, and don't hesitate to make decisions when necessary (but make sure people see how you came to your conclusions).

4. A healthy attitude toward work. I personally think it's extremely important for each of us to have a life outside of work and not just make our jobs the central focus of all we do. When we adopt an unhealthy attitude toward work—allowing it to take over every waking moment of our lives—we may find ourselves stressed out, which can lead to some very real physical problems, including anxiety, high blood pressure, sleep disturbances, and more.[22]

Think about your own attitude toward work and what you are modeling to those who work for and with you. Is your attitude a healthy one? If not, what can you do to change it? Take care of yourself. Get out of the office—give walking 1:1s a try. Don't sweat the small stuff and know that working more hours doesn't necessarily lead to better results—work smarter, not harder. Make a point of looking for signs of burnout in the people who work for you and then taking action to help diffuse it.

5. Impact on the organization. If you've got strong opinions (and I hope you do), then you've got to make sure they trickle into your organization. Create a safe place for your people to work while fostering collaboration and alignment with your organization's values. Ensure that information flows in all directions—from the top down, bottom up, and sideways throughout the organization. Find and remove obstacles

---

22 (October 2019). Coping with stress at work. Retrieved from https://www.apa.org/helpcenter/work-stress

to motivation and sources of excess stress in the workplace, including toxic people, badly designed processes, and bad task management.

In summary, be human, have strong opinions but be adaptable, lead by example, maintain and model a healthy attitude toward work, and have an impact across your organization. Do that, and you'll be well on your way to becoming a great boss.

Feedback from Your Employees (and Peers)

So, now that you have a blueprint for leading your organization, how can you be sure that you are actually putting it into action? How will you know if you're doing a great job in certain areas, and in others you need to put in additional effort? The only way you can know for sure is to get feedback from the people around you.

The first place to look for feedback is from your direct reports. Encourage this feedback constantly by making this one of your standard 1:1 questions and by sending out a feedback form to your direct reports once a quarter. However, it's not enough to just encourage feedback and get it; you've got to show your people that you are willing to act on at least some of it. Check your progress against the different parts of your blueprint for being a great boss. If there are areas where you need to improve, then put your focus there.[23]

Here's a survey created by Google to enable employees to provide feedback on their managers. I have made a few modest tweaks to the questions. Answers should be given in the form of a Likert scale: strongly agree, agree, neither agree nor disagree, disagree, and strongly disagree. I have found that this survey works well with a team of five or more.[24]

1. I would recommend my manager to others.

2. My manager assigns stretch opportunities to help me develop in my career.

---

23 I address how to deal with feedback in Chapter 8: Monitoring Performance and Giving Feedback.

24 When a team is fewer than five people, the feedback isn't really anonymous. With such a small sample, you can usually tell who gave you which answers.

3. My manager communicates clear goals for our team.

4. My manager gives me actionable feedback on a regular basis.

5. My manager provides the autonomy I need to do my job (i.e., does not "micromanage" by getting involved in details that should be handled at other levels).

6. My manager consistently shows consideration for me as a person.

7. My manager keeps the team focused on priorities, even when it's difficult (e.g., declining or deprioritizing other projects).

8. My manager regularly shares relevant information from their manager and senior leadership.

9. My manager has had a meaningful discussion with me about my career development in the past three months.

10. My manager has the domain expertise (e.g., technical judgment in Tech, selling in Sales, accounting in Finance) required to effectively manage me.

11. The actions of my manager show they value the perspective I bring to the team, even if it is different from their own.

12. My manager makes tough decisions effectively (e.g., decisions involving multiple teams, competing priorities).

13. My manager effectively collaborates across boundaries (e.g., team, organizational) and fosters alignment.

Optional additional questions:

1. What would you recommend your manager keep doing?

2. What would you have your manager change?[25]

---

25 (n.d.). Tool: Try Google's Manager Feedback Survey. Retrieved from https://rework
.withgoogle.com/guides/managers-give-feedback-to-managers/steps/try-googles-
manager-feedback-survey/

Feedback from a Mentor and Coach

People outside of your organization are particularly good sources of feedback. There's a saying in German: *"Ein Auto, in dem man sitzt kann man nicht anschieben,"* which loosely translates to "A car you sit in can't be pushed by you." When you are a part of a system—your company or team—you may have a hard time recognizing your own behavior, both good and bad.

Not only do coaches and mentors know you well, but also they will bring with them an external perspective—helping you to see areas for personal development. A good mentor will provide you with good advice—explaining how they approached similar issues and making suggestions for you to consider along the way. And a good coach can help you create a development plan and then hold you accountable for progressing in your leadership journey.

When you're ready to find a mentor, I highly recommend you follow the advice that Gibson Biddle published in a series of 12 tweets (for example, "The simple advice: take a loose connection and slowly build on it.").[26] And when you're ready to find a good coach, I suggest you ask your network, ask your boss, and ask your community. I have found that the best coaches are most often recommended and referred by colleagues and they are usually booked solid. Regardless, good coaches are always happy to meet people who are ready to make real change in their management. So, have courage and don't hesitate to reach out—you may very well ignite a spark!

No matter where you get your feedback from, keep in mind that it's something you should make a point of actively seeking out. I guarantee that when you do—and you put into action—you'll be a better boss as a result.

---

26   https://twitter.com/gibsonbiddle/status/1258038802494316544

Further Reading

- On having a healthy attitude toward work:
  - Fire the workaholics by David Heinemeier Hansson: https://www.strongproductpeople.com/further-readings#chapter-5_1

- Personal growth:
  - To increase your self-control, start by shifting your mental state in order to "see" certain tasks as less effortful. Indeed, studies suggest that, by mentally framing a task as amusing or beneficial, we can reduce our perceived effort. https://www.strongproductpeople.com/further-readings#chapter-5_2

- What makes a great boss:
  - A talk worth watching on reasons for burnout and a personal story on how you can cope with it by Cate Huston: https://www.strongproductpeople.com/further-readings#chapter-5_3
  - Amazon's Leadership Principles: https://www.strongproductpeople.com/further-readings#chapter-5_4

- Coaching and mentoring:
  - How to find and keep a mentor by Gibson Biddle: https://www.strongproductpeople.com/further-readings#chapter-5_5

CHAPTER 6

IDENTIFYING AND CLOSING PRODUCT MANAGER GAPS

- Identifying areas for product manager improvement

- Identifying needs for additional training/support and then providing it

- Creating the future self

Now that we've shined a light on what great bosses do, let's start to talk about doing it! First on our list: how you can help your PMs develop, learn, and prosper by working with them to identify the gaps in their expertise and knowledge, and then correct them. By putting the focus on correcting their weaknesses, they'll make their strengths even stronger.

In this chapter, we'll explore how you can identify areas for product manager improvement and then provide the support necessary to fill these gaps. Finally, we'll consider how you can help your PMs create their future selves.

Identifying Product Manager Gaps

We all have gaps in our knowledge and experience, no matter how accomplished we may be, how many years of college we have under our belts, or the number of training classes we have attended. Some of these gaps may be obvious to us, and others we may be blind to. So, why is it so important to identify product manager gaps?

It is important because someone can only improve things if they know that these things need improvement. Or, in other words, they need to be consciously aware of their gaps and they need to be willing to close them. And in your role as HoP, you can help them identify their gaps, help them understand why learning a new skill or acquiring new knowledge would be beneficial for them and the team, and you can support them as they close the gaps they have identified.[27] Now, let's dive into some more theory here:

- Why people don't see their own gaps

- Why PM maturity matters

- Kicking-off your gap-identification process

People do often see some of their gaps, usually by comparing themselves to their peers. "He must know a lot more about creating and tweaking customer onboarding processes because his funnels always have superhigh conversion rates!" Or they see gaps because team members have told them (luckily, developers often do so) that they need to improve a certain skill. "Sorry, William, but the acceptance criteria in your backlog items are just bad. Could you maybe ask Susan to help you because she writes really good acceptance criteria?" What they don't usually know, however, are the gaps that fall

---

27 If you have never worked as a product manager yourself and are, therefore, struggling with this, make sure to find someone who can help you. This can be a senior product manager or even an external product coach.

closer to their own core personality. Here's a nice little model that explains this phenomenon:

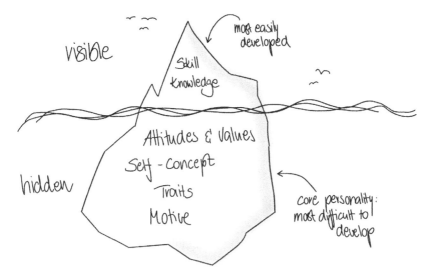

Figure 6-1: Spencer & Spencer iceberg model—the iceberg shows what competencies are visible and most easily developed, and those that are hidden and most difficult to develop

The Spencer & Spencer diagram above shows that it's hard to see gaps that are related to your motives, attitudes, or values–they are hidden below the surface and you'll need someone else's help to see them.[28] You can expect some resistance from people to opening up if you start working with them on these more personal topics. As you dive deeper into your PMs' personalities, it's increasingly difficult to develop them–you'll need some coaching skills to do so.

As you work with your PMs to identify gaps, you should always try to broaden the horizon. If your picture of the PM, and their own picture of themselves, don't have much overlap, help them to see some of the things you see. These things will include what they should be learning or getting good at to be better product people.

---

28 Lyle Spencer Jr. and Signe Spencer, Competence at Work: Models for Superior Performance, John Wiley (1993) p. 11

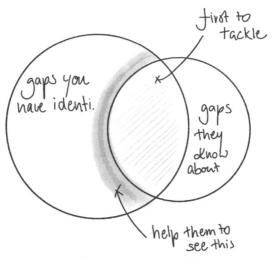

Figure 6-2: Identifying and tackling PM gaps
to help PMs broaden their horizon

Let's take a moment to consider the role of PM maturity in this gap-identifying exercise and why it matters. PM maturity matters because it tells you a lot about how urgent it is to help someone close a gap. There is a difference between getting a PM to competence versus further PM development. For a skilled HoP, the gaps are rather obvious, and they have their tactics at hand for how to get their PMs to competence. But further career development is much harder. To do this, the HoP has to listen much more attentively, has to ask what each individual PM has in mind for her future, and often has to open the eyes of the PMs for their potentials and possibilities.

Taking a closer look, the careers of product people generally evolve in the same way. They start as newbies, then they progress to becoming PMs able to keep a product development team busy with meaningful work. They then become competent product managers able to come up with a solid product strategy and to tackle whatever issues they might face along their product life cycle.

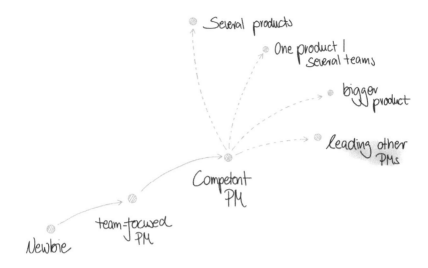

Figure 6-3: PM typical career progression

After that, there are a variety of different ways they can proceed. Some will work on a bigger product than the product they worked on before. Others will be assigned to manage several products, while others will manage multiple teams working on one product. Yet others will be chosen to lead other product managers.

This is a typical career path for most product managers. They first started working with a cross-functional team *and* managing the workload of two or three sprints or Agile iterations. And once they are capable of this, they usually learn to do more discovery work and work that is more outcome oriented—work that focuses on delivering as much value as possible to their users while having a positive result (for example, increased revenue) for the company. They learn how to create a strategy and the vision for their product, and how to share this vision with others.

This is the big-picture part of product management, and once someone has mastered all of these things, I would call them a competent product manager. Not only can they handle a development team, but they can also see and express the big picture while guiding their people toward it.

Now, let's circle back to the urgency of closing gaps. If you have a long-term team member—a PM who has been with the organization for several years—and you think she is not a competent team PM, then it is your responsibility to address this situation as quickly as possible. Talk with the individual about your expectations for a competent team PM and offer your help to get them there in a reasonable time frame. It is *not* okay to ignore this any longer. As Steve Gruenert and Todd Whitaker say in their book, *School Culture Rewired*, "The culture of any organization is shaped by the worst behavior the leader is willing to tolerate."[29] Everyone is watching to see what the lowest level of PM performance is that you as HoP are willing to tolerate.

The same thing applies if the company has been working with cross-functional, empowered product teams for quite some time[30] and your PMs are not performing at the competent PM level. This is because "being able to handle the backlog and the team" is not what it takes to thrive in such an environment. Empowered teams need competent PMs to deal with whatever is necessary to deliver value to users and make money for the company. If your PMs aren't performing at the competent PM level, then you should deal with this issue immediately. If your company is in a transition phase from feature teams toward empowered product teams, it's okay for gap closing to take a bit longer because everyone needs to understand the new world and then work on their own shortcomings.[31]

Last but not least, you also need to support the development and progression of your competent PMs who are ready to take the next step in their career. Urgency in this case is defined by your concern

---

29   Steve Gruenert and Todd Whitaker, *School Culture Rewired: How to Define, Assess, and Transform It,* ASCD (2015) p. 36

30   See https://svpg.com/product-team-faq/

31   More about the difference between these two types of teams here: Marty Cagan (August 29, 2019) Product vs. Feature Teams. Retrieved from https://svpg.com/product-vs-feature-teams

about them being bored (and maybe leaving the company as a result). If this is the case, then hurry up and work with them over the course of the next few months to identify the next gap to close and the next step in their careers.

Now that we have considered why it is hard for your PMs to see their own gaps and why PM maturity matters (because it helps you to prioritize which gaps need to be closed most quickly), we can start with our initial gap-identification session.

Initial Gap Identification

As we discussed in the previous chapter, coaching should always start with an assessment of the situation of the person being coached. And a good start to reboot your personal growth initiative with your PMs is a one-hour, 1:1 session.

Start by considering the answers to these three questions:

- **Can they describe their *now?*** What will they deliver over the next four weeks?

- **Can they describe their *next?*** What will they be working on over the next five to 12 weeks?

- **Can they describe a long-term vision?** Can they articulate the bigger opportunities for their products, and when and how they will pursue them?

If they can't do all this in a one-hour session, then you know you have to develop these PMs toward competence. If they can, then you're ready to start a more detailed product manager assessment based on the "Good PM compass" you created after reading Chapter 4: Define Your Good.

Once these gaps have been identified, it's your job to provide product managers with the support, training, and opportunities that will develop them to competence.

Side note: If you're a seasoned head of product, it might seem odd asking your PMs some of these questions, for example, "What are you currently working on and what will your next task be?" As head of product, I suspect you already think you know the answers to those questions for every member of your team. Chances are, however, that you can't answer these questions for all of your product people without actually consulting them. So, it's a good exercise to go through, even if you've been managing your people for quite some time. And if you explain to them why you are doing this, and that you want to invest more of your time in their personal growth, they usually like this exercise.

Now, let's sum this all up: As someone who leads product managers, you should reflect on what you think the right product person is made out of and is capable of doing. Think about the maturity of each of your product managers. What is their current career level and how competent are they as product managers? Observe your PMs and give them specific feedback. Talking with someone about their gaps is usually a hard conversation—it helps a lot if you have specific feedback, including feedback from others in the organization. You should also encourage your product managers to gather feedback from their peers to gain a bit clearer picture of what they are actually capable of doing.[32]

Closing Product Manager Gaps

So, once you determine that one of your product managers has a gap—then what? You'll want to work with your PM to close that gap—usually by learning something new. One thing you should be aware of is learning something new requires a lot of energy, and people naturally want to avoid wasting it. But they will put energy into learning something new when they realize that it is energy well invested.

---

32   We take a close look at feedback in Chapter 8: Monitoring Performance and Giving Feedback.

Most of the time, people are happy to have the opportunity and the support to learn new things. In this case, they are what we call *intrinsically* motivated to learn something new, and that's the perfect place for them to be. If this is not the case, however, you should try to foster the intrinsic motivation within your PM by explaining why it's relevant and meaningful for her to learn this something new.

It is very important to offer your PMs ways of learning that each individual personally enjoys and responds to. Not everyone loves reading books, for example, or is enamored with attending an offsite training.

Understand that, just because you're a leader, that doesn't mean you can force people to learn something—you can't. They might say they will, even if they think it's a bad idea, just because you're the boss and they want to please you. But brains don't learn if they are stressed and being forced to sit in the training that they think is not relevant—it's just a waste of everyone's time and money. Instead, find ways to convince them that it's a good idea and to gain their interest and engagement. You want to draw them toward competence through their own volition, not push them.

So, what can you do to support your PMs and encourage them to close their gaps?

The usual reaction for heads of product when faced with a PM who needs to learn something new is, "Let's get them a training!" In my experience, however, a training is probably the least effective way of helping people to learn something new. Let me explain.

When exploring how best to help PMs learn something new, the first thing we need to do is differentiate what it is they need to learn by determining their competence. Competence is being able to take a skill and apply it in any given on-the-job situation. Is it something just to be recalled later—which we call knowledge—or do they need to learn something to *do* something? That's a skill.

In the first case, to gain knowledge, a training might be a good option. There might be, for example, some new laws or regulations that your product managers need to hear about. Super—get them a training.

But, it's usually not so easy. If they need to pick up new skills, these can be learned only by performing the action, inspecting the outcome or results, and adapting the action to improve the outcome. Do, inspect, adapt; do, inspect, adapt; until the desired outcome is good enough.[33]

So, if there is a gap, it's not enough to just let the person know that there is a gap. As a good head of product, you will help them understand what should change—the desired outcome. And once they start their journey to learn a new skill, you will help them visualize the "good-enough" point. The more junior your PM, the more important it is to actually let them explicitly know this. You might say, "Your time management is not where it should be. And once you are good in time management, this is what I will see that will let me know you have improved." (For ideas, see the list of common ways to learn something new or acquire a new skill at the end of this chapter.)

When working with PMs to help them close their gaps, I like to use something called the *future self*, a supersimple framework to give the conversation a definite structure. I learned about this framework in the book, *FYI: For Your Improvement,* published by organizational consultancy Korn Ferry.[34] The future-self framework takes the form of a document that PMs draft and it has four parts:

- **As-is.** This is the PM's current situation.

- **To-be.** This is how the PM sees himself after he has worked on or gained competency in a particular skill.

- **Actions.** This is a list of actions that will help the PM get closer to his future self.

---

33 Inspect and adapt are basic scrum concepts. See this article for more about what these terms really mean: Dan Ray (June 18, 2019) What does "Inspect and Adapt" really mean? Retrieved from https://medium.com/serious-scrum/what-does-inspect-and-adapt-really-mean-c9c61897027d
34 Michael Lombardo and Robert Eichinger, *FYI: For Your Improvement 5th Edition,* Korn Ferry (2009)

- **Time frame.** This is the number and interval of follow-ups, something like: "May to September, 10 follow-ups, approximately twice a month."

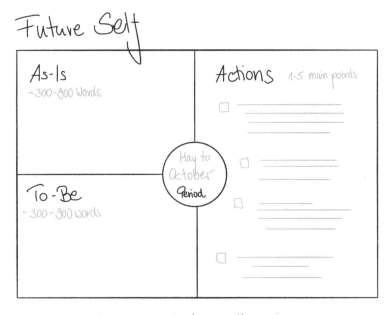

Figure 6-4: The future-self template

Be sure to check for interest on your PMs' part as you work with them to create the future-self document—get to know them! Understand their learning type, prior knowledge, and past experience. Here are some checklists to guide you through a two-session, future self-exercise with your PMs:

Future Self—Session One

- Make sure you are both on the same page. What is the gap you are going to address? Use this as the document headline. (I assume you gave them your detailed input why this is a thing in the initial gap-definition session.)

- Explain the differences between skill vs. competency vs. knowledge and why they matter

- Explain the four-part template and ask your PM to create a first draft version. Explain that there will be a second session and that you will help them to make this one really good.
  - As-Is should be around 10 sentences minimum. Suggest they ask 3–5 of their peers about the status quo for the As-Is part.
  - To-Be should be as precise as possible. What are the things other people will recognize in a few weeks or months from now? What has improved?
  - Ask them to list 3–5 actions, not more. If you are familiar with BJ Fogg's concept of tiny habits, applying this may be very helpful.[35] If it's a superbig thing they want to learn/change, maybe agree on a follow-up version of the future self and start small. In my experience, it's hard to keep up the spirit for change for more than 3–4 months at a time. Tell them that they should list whatever they think would help such as additional training, even if that would cost some money. You'll discuss this in Session Two.
  - Offer your help for follow-ups and nudging. Ask them how much support and friendly reminders they think they need, and ask them for a realistic time frame. Remember to consider daily work, unforeseen complications, holidays, and so forth.

- Agree on a date for your follow-up sessions—one or two weeks out

---

35 More about tiny habits here: https://www.tinyhabits.com/

- Ask them to send the draft document to you two days before your next session

Future Self—Things to check once you've received the draft

- Write down your feedback!

- As-Is: Check to see if your input made it into the description and if they made an effort to ask others. If not, you will end the Session Two meeting before it starts and tell them why you think this is key.

- To-Be: Check to see if it's precise and if it creates a picture in your mind about what the PM's future self will look like. Reflect on if you think learning a new thing is what it's all about or if it is more unlearning some old behavior that the PM needs. (*Unlearning* things is a powerful concept and there is an entire book focusing on the topic. Check out Barry O'Reilly's book *Unlearn* for some tips in this area.)[36]

- Actions: Check for small steps—things that can be ticked off on a weekly or biweekly basis. Check if they have picked appropriate learning methodologies. Check if there are better alternatives. Sometimes a training can be supplemented with a book, an online course, or a mentor and it's a much better way to learn.

- Timing: Make sure they've planned enough time. The brain needs time for subconscious processes to work when learning complex things, and your PM will need time for at least two inspect-and-adapt cycles. If a new habit needs to be created, it will take exactly 66 days to

---

36   Barry O'Reilly, Unlearn: Let Go of Past Success to Achieve Extraordinary Results, McGraw-Hill (2018)

do this.[37] Being patient and granting them the necessary time is where you can show your PMs that the company values learning!

- Feeling stuck? The book *FYI* offers suggested action items for specific competencies—consider using it as an inspiration.

Future Self—Session Two

- Ask them how it felt to use the template. Which parts were easy to complete, and which were harder? This will provide you with some additional insights to tailor your upcoming feedback.

- Tell them what you have reflected about their future self and then consult on some changes. Ultimately, it's their decision if they want to follow your advice. Research shows that having and making meaningful choices when it comes to learning new things makes a difference!

- Budget-related things might be your call. Make sure you explain if you need to change an action item, such as changing a training to an online course.

- Ask them if they know their learning type ("How do you learn best?") and if they think their future self reflects that.

- Encourage them to find other peers to collaborate with. If they can participate in, for example, something like a small study group, they will influence each other in a positive way and success is more likely.

---

37   James Clear (n.d.) How Long Does It Actually Take to Form a New Habit? (Backed by Science). Retrieved from https://jamesclear.com/new-habit

- Ask them if they think their future self has the right balance of being challenging, but not stressing them too much. Balance is key here!

- Agree on your next follow-up sessions—hold them accountable!

When you have completed the future-self template with your PM, it should look something like Figure 6-5.

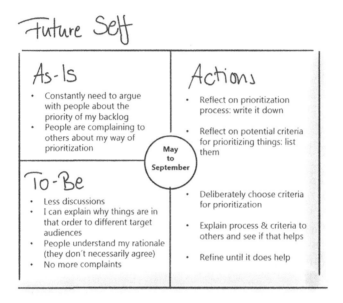

Figure 6-5: A completed future-self template

Common Ways to Learn Something New or Acquire a New Skill

There are many different ways for your PMs to learn something new or acquire a new skill. Some people learn while reading a book—and imagining the change this will bring—and this is enough to initiate the change process. Others learn while applying new methods in their day-to-day work, while yet others learn by training others. The possibilities are endless.

Here are some of the most common ways to learn something new or acquire a new skill—what other ways have you found to be successful when working with your PMs?

To gain knowledge/competency/skills

- Online course

- Read books

- Watch talks

- Do side projects

- Learn by doing (+ extra time to make it easy to inspect and adapt) and/or by working with a mentor (most likely one from your own organization)

- Peer-to-peer learning

- Training (right timing for training is after some initial efforts while thing is ongoing)

- Training and follow-up coaching sessions

To deepen knowledge/competency/skills

- Write a blog post or article about the topic

- Do a talk about it (internal vs. external)

- Teach others

Various combinations of these approaches are possible and should be tried. Keep in mind that the bigger the change, or the more complex the skill to be learned, the more time and money you should expect to invest in your PM. And don't just set it and forget it. When you make a learning assignment, be sure to follow up with your PMs. At minimum, ask them how it's going.

Further Reading

- If you want to learn more about human biases (book): *The Art of Thinking Clearly* by Rolf Dobelli

- Why it's relevant and meaningful for PMs to learn something new: https://www.strongproductpeople.com /further-readings#chapter-6_1

- A bias that comes into play if you want to work with people on their personality: the Kruger-Dunning effect: https://www.strongproductpeople.com/further-readings# chapter-6_2

- On the cost of tolerating underperforming employees in your organization:
  - Robert Half International, News Releases, Survey: Managers Spend Nearly One Day a Week Managing Poor Performers https://www.strongproductpeople .com/further-readings#chapter-6_3
  - Society of Human Resource Management, HR Magazine: One Bad Apple https://www.strong productpeople.com/further-readings#chapter-6_4
  - The Wall Street Journal: How a Few Bad Apples Ruin Everything https://www.strongproductpeople .com/further-readings#chapter-6_5

- If you like the idea of the future self, vision writing might be something else you could try:
    - https://www.strongproductpeople.com/further-readings#chapter-6_6
    - https://www.strongproductpeople.com/further-readings#chapter-6_7

CHAPTER 7

THE POWER OF COACHING

- Coaching: A head of product's superpower

- How to start your new coaching habit

- A playbook for your first coaching session

Countless studies show that investing in the career development of the people who work for you pays off. In fact, it's probably the single most powerful tool you have to drive employee retention, engagement, productivity, and results. In just one example, the 2019 Workplace Learning Report published by LinkedIn Learning revealed that 94 percent of employees say they would stay at a company longer if it invested in their learning and development.[38] Why is this the case? Because your people will feel more valued (and they will *become* more valuable to your organization) if you care about them and their personal development and you invest a bit of time and money in them.

This is, in fact, something that makes the job they're currently in supersticky. When your people have a place where they can grow and

---

38 LinkedIn Learning (n.d.). 2019 Workplace Learning Report. Retrieved from https://learning.linkedin.com/content/dam/me/business/en-us/amp/learning-solutions/images/workplace-learning-report-2019/pdf/workplace-learning-report-2019.pdf

become better product people, they will want to stick around. And as your product people get better at their jobs, your products will get better too, which directly benefits your company and your users.[39] At the same time, hiring talented product people gets easier because your company or your product team will earn a well-deserved reputation for being a great place to develop product management skills and personally grow. Your people will tell their friends about the great company they work for and some of them will decide to apply for jobs at your company too. It's a virtuous circle.

How do you make all these good things happen? You do it through *coaching*—ongoing, quality one-on-one conversations with your employees to help them reach their full potential.

Sure, these quality conversations can take place in your office during the course of a formally scheduled performance review. However, they can also take place informally in the breakroom during lunch, or a little feedback given while walking down the hallway after a dev team meeting, or really most anyplace anytime.

You don't need to master the Art of Coaching or get a coaching degree from a top university to be a good and effective coach. In fact, I find that erroneous belief to be superblocking for a lot of people. They'll say, "Hey, how can I coach my people? I have no clue about how to coach—no degree, no training classes, no nothing. So, I don't do it at all."

But formal coach training or certificates or degrees are not necessary. Ultimately, it all boils down to one thing: You need to care about the people you are managing, and you need to make an effort to help them develop. Let me be perfectly frank: If this is something you're not up for, then your product organization will *never* be a great place to work and your team will never have the opportunity to live up to its full potential. So, you have a choice: Master this fundamental management skill or prepare to watch as your best people leave for better opportunities and your organization begins its inevitable decline.

---

39   See the soap bar empire story in Chapter 1: Your Role in This Game.

As an HoP, coaching starts with having a solid understanding of what makes a good product manager—the topic we addressed in Chapter 4: Define Your Good. Then you need to have a vision for your PMs' development as employees—where do you see their careers two years from now? We discussed this in Chapter 6: Identifying and Closing Product Manager Gaps. And, finally, you'll consider whether or not they are ready for their next bigger challenge, which we explored in Chapter 1: Your Role in the Game, and what that next bigger challenge might look like.

Before we dive deeper into how to be a better coach, let's first consider exactly what it is that coaches do.

What Coaches Do

You can look at coaching as a four-part cycle with a clear beginning point that progresses from step to step during the course of the quality conversations we have with our people.[40] This cycle is ongoing—people continuously improve as they pass through the cycle, over and over again. This is what coaches do if you hire one to work with you:

Step 1: Gain clarity. The number one thing coaches do is help the people they coach—their *coachees*—gain clarity. This is usually accomplished in the first couple of coaching sessions where they and their coachee get to know each other, decide if they can work together, and then define the topics and goals of the coaching. In *your* setting, the cycle usually starts with feedback: feedback your PM got from her team, peers, or stakeholders, or some feedback you provided. This could be anything from a career-development topic to a learning goal to any other improvement the PM needs to make. You can help your coachee define the coaching engagement by asking her to answer these questions:

---

40 Based on Kate Peyton's "How Coaching Works" https://www.katepeyton.org /how-coaching-works

- What's important to me right now? (Example: Getting some to-dos off my list.)

- What's this really about for me? (Example: Too many moving parts and no one to delegate to!)

- What needs to change? (Example: Somebody should take one of my topics.)

Step 2: Create a strategy for success. Once you've agreed on the goal for your coaching, then the next step is for you to help your PM come up with tactics to put it into action—a strategy for success. As a coach, you will help your PM see what success looks and feels like and get new perspectives and fresh possibilities.

Step 3: Act. When your PM has a strategy for success, it's time to put it into action: first steps, next steps, commitment, and follow-up. A coach doesn't do the work—she helps her people find ways to put themselves in action to reach their goals. A coach provides the guardrails that help keep her coachees on track.

Step 4: Evaluate progress. A good coach will hold you accountable, often through follow-up meetings and checking results. You will evaluate your progress, adjust your tactics if necessary, and perhaps move onto a new coaching topic or goal. Good coaches ask the right questions at the right time—that's the magic superpower that coaches bring with them to their organization. They ask questions that challenge their PMs, that initiate action, and that in the end foster change. And a good coach will help her PM reflect on the whole process to make sure the PM's personal growth toolbox gets an upgrade as well.

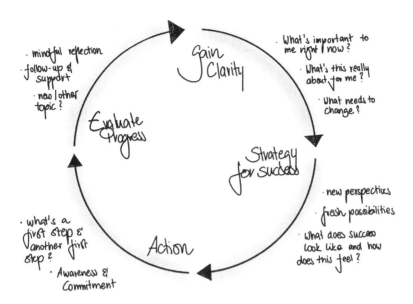

Figure 7-1: The coaching cycle[41]

As head of product, you cannot only ask questions as most coaches do. You need to provide some bits and pieces of advice here and there, but not in a way that tells your people what to do or how to do it. You need to find a balance. Figure 7-2 shows the progression from telling to asking.[42] When you tell your coachee what to do and solve the problem for him, he won't develop as an employee. When you challenge your coachee's thinking by asking the right questions, you build long-term development.

---

41   Based on Kate Peyton's "How Coaching Works" https://www.katepeyton.org/how-coaching-works

42   Based on: J. Preston Yarborough (March 25, 2018). The Role of Coaching in Leadership Development. Retrieved from https://onlinelibrary.wiley.com/doi/abs/10.1002/yd.20287

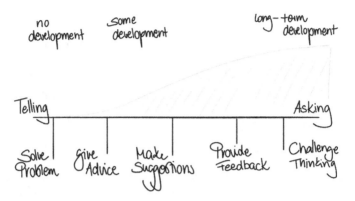

Figure 7-2: Telling versus asking in coaching[43]

So, what else is different for you as head of product when you're coaching your product people? As already briefly mentioned, when it comes to picking the coaching topic, you cannot be precisely as neutral as an outside coach is. Coaches paid for by the coachee or brought in from outside the organization because a coachee has reached a certain career level where it is part of the journey into leadership are solely focused on *the coachee*. And they can work on whatever the coachee wants to work on. That's simply not something you as head of product can do—you are in a different position.

First of all, your people haven't picked you personally to be their coach, except perhaps in the case of an employee who joined the company because of its reputation for legendary people development and product work. And you always have to keep the company in mind, which means you can't (and shouldn't) be 100 percent dedicated to coaching your people on whatever topic it is they would like to be coached on.

As head of product, it's up to you to figure out if your PMs lack the skills and knowledge they need to be competent PMs, and then you have to work on this together. So, you have a say in what your

---

43 Based on: J. Preston Yarborough (March 25, 2018). The Role of Coaching in Leadership Development. Retrieved from https://onlinelibrary.wiley.com/doi /abs/10.1002/yd.20287

next coaching topic could be, and I hope you explain this well to your PMs by defining your good, using your PMwheel, and by following some of the advice I provide in Chapter 8: Monitoring Performance and Giving Feedback.

How to Start Your New Coaching Habit

Like anything else, you can learn how to be a good coach, and the more you do it, the better you'll get at it at the same time as your confidence grows. Here's how you can start your new coaching habit:

Commit yourself to it! The first step is to commit to developing your people through ongoing quality conversations. Once you make that commitment, then you can actually start the work. If you're not already doing 1:1s, then start doing them—dedicating a decent amount of time during the meeting to helping your PMs improve and develop.

Make an effort and show you care. Next, you really need to make an effort and show your PMs that you care. I have personally found that the Rule of Never Miss Twice helps a lot. If, for example, I have a weekly 1:1 scheduled with an employee, my rule is never miss twice. Sure—something may come up, and I may not be able to make a scheduled meeting. It can happen. But this is something that should never happen twice in a row. And you can also show your PMs that you care by being fully prepared for your coaching or 1:1 sessions.

Work on your listening skills. While this should go without saying, far too few managers *really* listen to their people. They nod their heads a lot and smile, while their brains are many miles away. Make a point of listening to be alert to and understand the little invitations from your people to be coached—things like: "Preparing for this presentation kept me up all night," or "I don't know why this slipped—I really tried to get it right. Maybe I was too focused on this other thing." Follow up on these little invitations by asking the question: "Do you want to tell me more about that?" Then get comfortable with silence as you draw out your people in conversations.

Focus on competence first. As I mentioned earlier, before you start to coach your PMs for performance improvements or further career coaching, you need to first focus on getting your PMs to competence.[44]

Find good questions to ask. You need to find good questions to ask that will have an impact on your people. Good questions provoke insight, constructive discomfort, ideas, and actions in others. Keep the focus and ownership for development on your PM and demonstrate that you respect and value her. There are plenty of online sources for good questions, but for some well-tested suggestions, be sure to check out my 52 Questions card deck[45] and the coaching playbook at the end of this chapter.

Tame your advice monster. It's natural for HoPs to want to tell their direct reports *how* to get things done instead of letting them work it out for themselves because they *love* to give advice and are always focused on getting results ASAP. Make a point of identifying your advice monster and taming it. The next time your PM asks, "Hey, what do you think I should do about this?" put your advice monster back in his cage and don't fall into the trap. Instead of offering advice with a quotation mark attached (for example, "Have you thought of...?") ask him first what *he* thinks he should do, then tell some stories or give some examples and ask if that gave him some new ideas.

Keep the dialogue going. It's superimportant that you keep the dialogue ongoing—following up is really essential. If you set up a goal with your people and then never ask about it again, that's actually the worst thing you could do. Figure out how to follow up with your coachees without ending up doing the task yourself, or as project management trainer Mike Clayton suggests: "Don't take on their monkeys."[46]

---

44 I cover closing these gaps in Chapter 6: Identifying and Closing Product Manager Gaps.

45 https://www.petra-wille.com/52questions

46 Mike Clayton (March 27, 2018). Monkey Management—William Oncken Jr.'s Great Insight. Retrieved from https://www.pocketbook.co.uk/blog/2018/03/27/monkey-management/

Learn to be patient and ditch the "why." Being patient is superhard for product people, which means you as a head of product. Focus on addressing just one thing at a time. Understand that it takes time to forge new habits and change behaviors, so you need to learn to be patient with people.

There's another big shift that needs to happen for you as a coach. We, as product people, are trained to ask "Why?" when stakeholders or customers say, "This is not working the way I thought it would be working. And I would love to have it this way around." We always ask "Why?" to understand the underlying problems.

This is nice if you're talking to customers and stakeholders, but if you're in a coaching situation, asking "What?" is a much more powerful word to use. You can ask, "So, *what* do you think about this?" It's a much more open-ended question and it will give you more insights. "Why did you do that?" needs to become "What were you hoping for here?"

A Playbook for Your First Coaching Session

All great journeys start with the first step. In the case of coaching your PMs, the journey starts with your first coaching session. Even if you have been the line manager of your PMs for quite some time, but you previously haven't invested much in coaching, there still needs to be a coaching kickoff. If you frame the kickoff right, your people won't be confused about your new emphasis on coaching. Just tell them that you are committed to doing more coaching from now on, and that this is the first of many interactions like this to come.

Oh. And by the way, the 1:1s following this first coaching session should follow a similar pattern. As mentioned above, it's a constant cycle.

Keep in mind, however, that there can (and should) be more moments of coaching than just these formal sessions. This most often means small, informal pieces of coaching here and there throughout the workday. But if it is a rather formal session—something scheduled, such as a 1:1—then it can follow this pattern.

I think of this coaching journey as a story with a hero (the PM), a destination or calling, and a villain (often *themselves*—the inner critic they constantly battle as a victim of the imposter syndrome)[47] or obstacle that gets in the way. Your PM heroes can overcome the villain or obstacle by getting active, using their talents, living up to their values, and mastering their fear. Figure 7-3 illustrates this journey, and you could use this as a template for your first session. Draw the PM journey on a flip chart during your first session and help your PM fill in the blanks by asking the right questions.

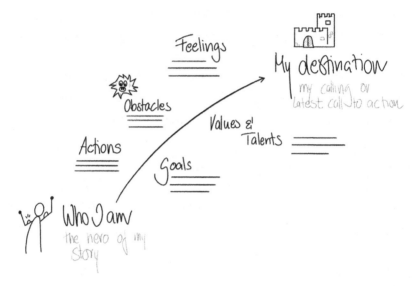

Figure 7-3: The PM journey

Step 1: Check in. Start building a connection by asking some personal questions and getting in the listening zone. Questions like:

- What have you been reading lately?

- Been anywhere for the first time recently?

47   Learn more about how PMs can overcome imposter syndrome here: Martin Eriksson and James Gadsby Peet (November 2, 2018). Embrace Your Imposter Syndrome. Retrieved from https://www.mindtheproduct.com /embrace-your-imposter-syndrome/

- What have you been excited about lately?

- How have you been feeling since our last 1:1? Why?

Step 2: Find/agree on today's topic. When coaching your PMs, the hardest part is usually finding a coaching topic that makes a real difference. Focus on *real* problems, not on the first problem that comes up in the conversation. If you're stumped for questions to ask that will reveal good coaching topics, my 52 Questions card deck can help, or I like these questions—based on the book *The Coaching Habit*:

- What's on your mind? And what else? (You'll end up with a few topics if you are patient.)

- If you had to pick one of these to focus on, which one here would be the real challenge for you?

- If XYZ is your topic, what do you want related to that?

Some other good questions include:

- What was the best idea you have had in the past 12 months? When and how did this idea come about? How can you get into this mode easier/more often?

- If we (company/team/department/...) could improve in any way, how would we do it?

- Are you happy working here? Tell me about the things you enjoy most.

- What have you been wanting to learn more of, get better at, and improve on?

- Is there an area outside your current role where you feel you could contribute?

- If you could design your ideal role in a company, what would it look like?

- Is there anything stopping you from doing good work?

Step 3: Explore the topic. Take some time to explore the topic a bit more—talking about opportunities, changing perspectives, and alternatives. These questions can help:

- What else could you do or what different kinds of options do you have to achieve this (goal)?

- What are the principal advantages and disadvantages of each option?

- If I handed you a magic wand what would you do with it?

- If you worked for the perfect organization, what would you do?

- How do you stay true to your principles while working to reach your goals?

I have found two concepts to be particularly useful when exploring the topic of your coaching—employees need to be allowed to think this way:

- **Love it, change it, leave it.** It's okay to leave something behind, but only after you have tried to change the situation and you figured out you can't, or it's above your capacity/out of your hands.

- **Disagree and commit.** It's okay to not always agree with other people's decisions. That's just normal. But you should still be able to contribute and work toward a common goal.

Step 4: Focus on one action and ask if you can help. Now that your PM has her coaching topics to explore, it's time to pick one and then focus on action and commitment. This is facilitation business as usual: stack rank, dot vote, select. The idea is to be as precise as possible and really find something they can act on right away. Make sure you create some momentum. All of this can be framed with the following questions:

- Which option will you choose to act on?

- When are you going to start the first action?

- What would you like to have as a first result? (one first next step, a new strategy how to tackle this, the solution)

- What's one thing you could do today to help you with your long-term goal?

- What is your goal related to this issue?

- When are you going to achieve it?

- What are the benefits for you in achieving it?

- Who else will benefit in what way?

- What will it be like if you achieve your goal?

- What will you see/hear/feel?

The "How can I help?" question could be framed like this:

- What can I do to support you better? What can I do more or less of? Why?

- What can I do to help unblock you? Where can I support you best? Why?

Finally, do a bit of a reality check:

- If you're saying yes to this, what are you saying no to?

- What do you think: Will this fit your daily routine?

And make sure they are committing themselves to something:

- How committed are you on a scale of 1–10 to taking each of these actions?

- If it is not a 10, what would make it a 10?

- What will you commit to doing? (Nothing plus review later is an option)

Step 5: Check out. At the end of your (first) session, you'll want to seal your agreement on what your PM will be accountable for when you have your second follow-up session. Make sure you end the meeting on a positive note. Here are some questions to ask:

- What can I hold you accountable for next time we talk?

- What can I be accountable to you for the next time we talk?

- What was most useful for you?

The second follow-up coaching session with your PM will focus on evaluating progress. You can do this by asking the following questions:

- In our last 1:1, you raised your concern about XYZ. How do you see that now?

- What has been going well, what hasn't? Why?

- What action have you taken so far?

- What is moving you toward your goal?

- What is getting in the way?

A Coaching Example

Let's go back for a moment to our future-self example from Chapter 6. In this example, the PM wanted to move from her As-Is current self, to a new, To-Be future self. She filled out the future-self template (Figure 7-4), listing some actions she planned to take over the course of five months, from May to September.

A completed future-self template is a perfect tool to use in upcoming coaching sessions with your PM. First, you would ask things like: "Did you already take your first action?" If the response is yes, then the PM is on course and you don't need to dig any further. However, if the response is no, then you'll need to dig a little deeper. You could ask, "Why not? What would you need to change to make it happen?"

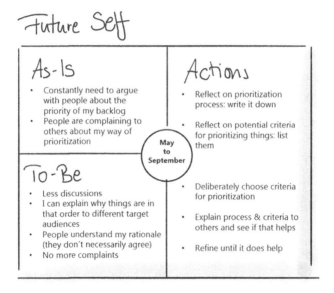

Figure 7-4: A completed future-self template

To coach the PM in Figure 7-4, you can offer your support if they have reflected on the prioritization process—it's best, however, that you don't help them *outline* the process. Instead, help them understand what things they need to know to achieve their initial goal of fewer discussions and no more complaints.

Keep following up throughout the next month. You could ask questions along the lines of, "On a scale of 1–10, how committed are you to taking your next action?" If their response is not a 10, then you could follow up with: "What would make it a 10?"

Finally, once they have reached their goal, help them reflect on what they have achieved and how they have achieved it. Ask, "What has been going well? Why do you think that is the case?"

As you can see, coaching is not rocket science. It's mostly a matter of asking your PM the right question at the right time.

If You Want to Dive Deeper

I hope this chapter has sparked some interest in coaching within you. If you would like to dive deeper into the coaching topic and go beyond just mastering the basics, there are some very effective things you can do.

First, you can get your own coach. This helps a lot because you can observe how they work with you and learn quite a bit from this interaction. And, as a side benefit, they can help you with one or two of your own personal-development topics.

Self-reflection is a powerful tool and you can reflect on how you can best help your PMs, when you need to get out of their way, and when you might need to bring in another person (a mentor, coach, peer, etc.) to help them. I have three questions to get this started:

- Think about the most interesting and engaging conversations you've ever had. Note two and explain why these conversations have had an impact on your professional life. Try to apply this to your conversations with your PMs.

- Think about the most career-changing experiences you've had. Note two of them and explain why these experiences made a difference. Try to apply this to your conversations with your PMs.

■ Who do you admire? Why? What could you learn from this person?

One thing I see a lot is that it is hard for some HoPs to assume good intent in every employee. It seems like there are always one or two people on our team we don't like as much as the others. But you can work against this bias and assume good intent, and always come back to this truism: It's not necessarily the *person* that is the problem; it might instead be the *role* we put them in that is the problem.

Keep experimenting with different aspects of your coaching: the setting (for example, less-formal settings vs. more-formal settings), the frequency of your coaching sessions, different questions, approaches to follow-ups, different coaching frameworks, and so on. Take some time to reflect on what works best, then do more of that.

Learn more about the art and science of coaching. Read about the GROW model (or even better, listen to Christina Wodtke's podcast on how she's actually using it),[48] and study psychology, ego development, neuro-linguistic programming (NLP), biases, creating new habits, and related topics. See the Further Reading section for suggestions on related books and other coaching resources.

Coaching is your most important tool when it comes to employee development and it's not too hard to learn or something you need a degree for. You, as HoP, can coach your PMs. It is all about **ongoing, quality 1:1 conversations with your employees to help them reach their full potential**. No magic, no spells. You just need to commit yourself to these quality conversations, make an effort, and show you care about each and every person on your team. You can do this by working on your listening skills and by finding the right question to ask at the right time. If you tame your advice monster and you learn to be patient while keeping the conversations relevant to the PMs, you will be impressed by how far they can come.

---

48   https://www.mindtheproduct.com/leading-teams-to-success-christina-wodtke-on
     -the-product-experience/

If I could recommend only one thing for you to do starting today, it would be to start creating a vision for every PM on your team and think about a good first step on this journey. Having this **inner picture** will immediately change the way you see and treat them. If, for example, one of your PMs lacks some time management skills and you picture her being brilliant at these skills four months from now, that initiates the change process right away just because you want to make her successful and want to support her in reaching this goal! You will ask the right questions and you will assign her to the perfect "next bigger challenge."

And, ultimately, that's what a good coach does.

Further Reading

- People from all around the world sharing their favorite coaching questions: https://www.strongproductpeople.com/further-readings#chapter-7_1

- Brandon Chu on managing and developing PMs: https://www.strongproductpeople.com/further-readings#chapter-7_2

- The GROW Model (coaching framework): https://www.strongproductpeople.com/further-readings#chapter-7_3

- Become a better listener: https://www.strongproductpeople.com/further-readings#chapter-7_4

- The leader as a coach: https://www.strongproductpeople.com/further-readings#chapter-7_5

- On 1:1s:
  - Marty Cagan on 1:1s: https://www.strongproductpeople.com/further-readings#chapter-7_6
  - Ben Horowitz: https://www.strongproductpeople.com/further-readings#chapter-7_7

- Marc Abraham on 1:1s: https://www.strongproduct
    people.com/further-readings#chapter-7_8
- Books:
    - *The Coaching Habit* by Michael Bungay Stanier
    - *Help Them Grow or Watch Them Go* by Beverly
      Kaye and Julie Winkle Giulioni
    - *Trillion Dollar Coach* by Eric Schmidt, Jonathan
      Rosenberg, and Alan Eagle
    - *Empowered* by Marty Cagan
    - *Tiny Habits* by BJ Fogg
    - *The Team That Managed Itself* by Christina
      Wodtke
    - *Banish Your Inner Critic* by Denise Jacobs

CHAPTER 8

MONITORING PERFORMANCE AND GIVING FEEDBACK

- Creating a healthy performance culture

- How to deal with poor performance

- Giving and receiving feedback

Good employee performance is critical to the success of an organization and the products it builds, and feedback is one of the most important factors in employee performance. For good reason. As management professor Christine Porath points out in *Harvard Business Review:* "High-performing teams share nearly six times more positive feedback than average teams."[49]

Even so, it's hard to talk about performance in many companies—there always seems to be one of two possible extremes. In some companies, performance is all that matters, and employees who don't constantly give 110 percent of themselves are viewed with suspicion or derision. This is superexhausting for everybody. In other companies, measuring, assessing, and quantifying the performance of employees

---

49   Christine Porath (October 16, 2016). Give Your Team More-Effective Positive Feedback. Retrieved from https://hbr.org/2016/10/give-your-team-more-effective -positive-feedback

is done rarely, if ever. "We are a family and we are here enjoying our time, hanging out together, and sometimes doing some work." The concept of performance doesn't fit into the "We are a family" ideology of these companies.

In reality, both of these extremes lead to a work environment that is unsatisfactory, and ultimately demotivating for employees. In the first case, employees are worked to the point of exhaustion and burnout, and performance suffers. These burned-out employees underperform or simply leave. In the second case, motivation suffers because mastery, autonomy, and purpose are not being served.[50] Employees become disoriented, unfocused in their efforts, and just muddle their way through the workday.

Sure, the first kind of company may be successful for some time, but this success is fleeting. Products built by these companies usually lack soul because no one has time to work with users and find innovative solutions on their behalf. Stress and employee turnover are high, leading to bad products and stagnating or declining revenues as a second-order effect. On the other hand, the second kind of company never becomes successful in the first place. In an organization where performance doesn't count, nothing significant gets delivered and good, ambitious employees quickly look for—and find—more challenging (and more satisfying) organizations to work for.

The solution? Create a healthy performance culture.

Creating a Healthy Performance Culture

Creating a healthy performance culture means finding a beneficial balance when it comes to employee performance. You want to set up your system in the right way, as illustrated in Figure 8-1—a balanced approach that prevents overwork and burnout while demanding and acknowledging good performance. Ultimately, this is more about fixing the *system* than about fixing the *employee*.

---

50 Daniel Pink, *Drive: The Surprising Truth About What Motivates Us*, Riverhead Books (2009)

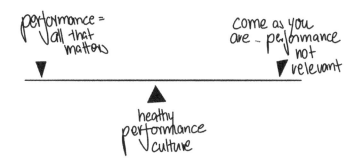

Figure 8-1: A balanced, healthy performance culture

I have found that it usually helps to explain to everyone exactly what a company is all about. A company is a group of people who have committed themselves to, and are aligned with, a shared goal. And the shared goal is solving customer problems so well that they will pay you enough money in return so your employees can earn a living and you can invest in the future of the company.

What a company is *not* is a family. Yes, we may be friendly with one another, may meet after work for drinks or dinner, and the CEO may sometimes act like a proud parent of her employees. But families don't typically have a common goal—especially not an economic one. A company cannot function without common goals, and these goals in many cases ultimately lead to economic outcomes. Companies are all about creating value together, and every employee who receives a salary must make a real contribution to this effort.

So, if your performance culture is out of balance, my advice is to fix the system first, then work with employees to improve *their* performance. Companies that have a healthy performance culture are set up in a way that:

- Value creation is a shared goal and the expected growth rate for things like revenue is appropriate/not crazy (e.g., not driven by greedy shareholders). Everyone knows what the company is up for and why.

- The resulting performance obligations must be distributed as evenly as possible over a reasonable number of shoulders.

- Roles must be clearly defined, communicated, and understood.

- Expectations for the individual contributions of each employee must be clearly communicated.

- Managers (and the company) must support employees in meeting expectations.

- Employees who do not live up to expectations must be supported to improve. The motto is: "It's hard to get better if you don't know what better looks like." The manager himself needs to have a clear picture of what better means and must support employees on this journey as a tour guide.

Figure 8-2: It's hard to get better if you don't know what better looks like[51]

---

51   Based on a comic by Joshua Howard: https://www.slideshare.net /MrJoshuaHoward/career-development-in-a-boxgdc-2011

This brings us back to the idea of *defining your good*.[52] Heads of product need to have a clear definition of what a competent PM looks like, and they must share this definition with their product teams—working with their product teams and individual PMs to improve.[53]

One more important aspect essential to a healthy performance culture is *feedback*—both giving and receiving it. Only when feedback is mutual and possible in all directions (upward to management, sideways to colleagues and stakeholders, and inward to the team) can everyone in a company learn, grow, and improve together. We'll talk more about feedback later in this chapter.

How to Deal with Poor Performance

If your people aren't performing up to standard, you've got to do something about it—*now*. In addition, some employees will for whatever reason fail to align with your company culture, values, and goals. This also must be dealt with. Allowing poor performance or misalignment to continue unchallenged is a sure way to demotivate your high performers (encouraging them to move on to other organizations) while delivering lackluster products that don't solve customer problems.

You have put your heart and soul into every employee on your team, helping them along their career paths and sharing their struggles and sorrows, their ups and their downs. Sometimes, our employees become our friends, which makes it even more difficult to engage in difficult conversations over performance. Unfortunately, many leaders try to ignore the issue of poor performance and hope it will go away.

But there is something else you can do that is in between ignoring and ultimately firing somebody: You can actually really try to help them. This might be by helping them find a new position outside your team that plays to their strengths, or by helping them understand what they need to improve. I personally believe that you should try to help

---

52 As addressed in Chapter 4: Define Your Good
53 See Chapter 7: The Power of Coaching for ideas on how to best accomplish this.

them for a variety of good reasons, not the least of which is economic. It has, in fact, been estimated that replacing an employee–including sourcing a replacement, interviewing prospective candidates, onboarding the new hire, and the loss in productivity as you bring the new hire up to speed–can cost an organization more than $65,000.[54]

Needless to say, it makes more sense to keep your people motivated and happy in their jobs than to continuously replace them. Invest a significant amount of your time providing your people with feedback and coaching them, and invest some money for training that will improve their skills and further develop their careers.

Remember: A high work standard starts with the example *you* set for others to follow. Any difference in the expectations you set for your team compared with the expectations you set for yourself will be duly noted and seen as hypocritical.

And if none of this helps to improve employee performance, you will have a reason and examples to share and discuss with HR or your boss. If you are providing your people with regular feedback (which you should be doing), then discussing your performance concerns with them won't be a surprise. The key is continuous feedback, which just happens to be the topic we'll explore next.

Feedback: The Breakfast of Champions

Every one of us needs continuous feedback–delivered direct and unvarnished–to perform at our very best. It's no wonder that feedback has been called by some "the breakfast of champions." But how do you create a good feedback culture, what kinds of feedback are there, and how can you give and accept feedback that may be perceived as negative?

Again, continuous feedback is key–it really does make a difference in the performance of your people. It's not possible to have a good

54   Jason Evanish (May 5, 2015). The Hidden Costs of Replacing an Employee that Total Over $65,500. Retrieved from https://www.linkedin.com/pulse /hidden-costs-replacing-employee-total-over-65500-jason-evanish/

feedback culture, however, if people don't feel safe. You need to create an environment of trust so that they are comfortable enough to show their vulnerability, admit and accept their errors, and say, "I'm sorry." There needs to be psychological safety.[55]

And if you are having a hard time giving feedback that could be considered negative, focus on what your people need—not just in their current role, but also in their future careers. The bigger picture helps, even if you find it superintimidating to give them the feedback. If you don't, then they won't have the information they need to change for the better. To get in the right frame of mind for delivering performance-related feedback, be sure to read Kim Scott's book, *Radical Candor*. As she points out, you have to care personally and challenge directly.

Be sure to give feedback, both praise and criticism, as close to the triggering event as possible. Be liberal with praise—catch your people doing things right and let them know you appreciate it. But avoid delivering what is known as a "compliment sandwich," where you first praise an employee, then offer some criticism (the actual reason for your feedback), and then close the conversation by again praising the employee. This approach tends to be seen as fake by those who receive it.

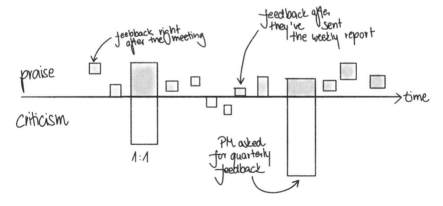

Figure 8-3: Delivering praise and criticism—constantly

---

55   To learn more about psychological safety, go to this chapter's Further Reading.

When you deliver feedback, Julie Zhuo—former VP, Product Design at Facebook—suggests that this feedback will generally fall into one of two categories, either task-related feedback or behavioral feedback.[56] Here are a couple examples of task-related feedback:

- "I liked the management summary you added to the last email you sent. That helped me quickly understand the main points and saved me a lot of time!"

- "The report you sent to us yesterday had some mistakes in it. The problem is that, if people are making their decisions based on the report, those decisions will most likely be wrong. In the long run, this will harm the company. I think this happened because you started to compile the report just one hour before you had to send it. Is that correct? What could you do to avoid that in the future?"

And here's an example of behavioral feedback:

- "When you gave your presentation in yesterday morning's team meeting, you were uncertain about two of the slides and jumped back and forth. I noticed how the meeting attendees began to question everything you said from that point on. I'm worried that this may negatively affect your reputation here because many senior execs attended the meeting. I would love to support you. What do you think would help you best avoid this the next time you give a presentation?"

---

56 Julie Zhuo, *The Making of a Manager: What to Do When Everyone Looks to You,* Portfolio (2019)

5 Steps to a New Feedback Culture

If your feedback culture needs some work (and this is the case in many companies), there are some definite things you can do right now to improve it. Here are five steps to creating a solid feedback culture in your organization:

Step 1: Ask for feedback and learn how to receive it. As an HoP, your PMs look to your example to decide how they will behave. So, if you want your PMs to consistently ask for and receive feedback—and to do the same with their people—then *you* need to model the right way to ask for feedback and learn how to receive it.

First, find your question—the question that will trigger the kind of candid feedback you need to do a better job. It has to be authentic and something you can ask in every 1:1. I like to ask, "What could I do or stop doing that would make it easier to work with me?"

Then, you need to learn how to take the feedback, which may not always be positive. Embrace discomfort—remain calm and fight the natural instinct to become paranoid or defensive. Count to six before you respond. Listen to understand, not to just react, and reward your PM for her candor.

Here are some specific tips on how to receive feedback:

- **Listen.** Keep an open mind. Everyone makes mistakes, and we can all use improvement in some areas. Resist the temptation to argue or make excuses.

- **Consider the source.** Does the speaker have the authority, knowledge, and expertise to give you this feedback? Does he or she have an ulterior motive? (Be careful not to invent one, though, just to make yourself feel better.)

- **Ask for specific examples.** Don't accept generalities such as "poor," "disappointing," or "lousy." Politely ask the speaker to tell you exactly what is wrong. Questions like, "Exactly what was wrong with the presentation?" or a request such as, "Help me to understand what you mean by 'poor'," should help you get some useful feedback.

- **Evaluate the criticism.** If the feedback is valid, accept it gracefully and with a positive attitude, and thank the person giving the feedback. Tell the speaker you appreciate his or her comments and be enthusiastic about your willingness and ability to use the suggestions to improve your performance.

- **Keep the useful information but let go of the negative feelings.** Don't dwell on the embarrassment of being criticized. Hold your head up high and move on.

Remember: Always assume that the feedback you get from your people is given to help, not hurt you. As Indra Nooyi, former chairman and CEO of PepsiCo, suggests, "Whatever anybody says or does, assume positive intent. You will be amazed at how your whole approach to a person or problem becomes very different."[57]

Step 2: Create a habit: collect and prepare. Creating a feedback culture requires that you and your people make it a habit—something you do continuously. As you create this habit, you'll want to focus your efforts in two areas: collecting your feedback and preparing to deliver it.

When collecting feedback, find the triggers that will make it a habit. For example, "Whenever I enter a room for a meeting where one or more of my PMs is attending, I'll get out a pen and paper to collect some feedback for them." In addition, track your collection efforts to reinforce the habit—making notes in a small journal is enough. You'll also need to plan how you will get back on track if your feedback collection habit starts to slacken: "When this happens I will…"

57 https://archive.fortune.com/galleries/2008/fortune/0804/gallery.bestadvice
    .fortune/7.html

Preparing positive feedback is easy: simply note the task or behavior you want to praise and how it made a positive contribution to the team, organization, or customers. Preparing negative feedback, however, takes a bit more work. Here are some specific things you should do to prepare for delivering negative feedback:

- Check to see if the expectations where clear—if not, change this first!

- Make a list of what's not working.

- Focus on the patterns—the recurring issues are the ones you'll want to focus on with your PMs. Fixing these recurring issues will yield the greatest improvement overall in the shortest amount of time.

- Map it to something they know: role description, PMwheel, and so on. The feedback will be taken less personally that way.

- Plan to discuss in your next 1:1
  - Think about how the feedback could be misinterpreted. As Kim Scott puts it, "Measure at the other person's ear."[58] Keep cultural and personal differences in mind.
  - I like to use the Situation-Behavior-Impact (SBI) feedback tool, developed by the Center for Creative Leadership to help managers deliver clear, specific feedback.[59] It requires you to describe the exact *situation* you want to talk about, the *behavior* the other person showed in this situation, and what negative/positive *impact* this might have on them, the team, or the company.

58   Kim Scott, *Radical Candor: Be a Kick-Ass Boss Without Losing Your Humanity*, St. Martin's Publishing Group (2017)
59   https://www.mindtools.com/pages/article/situation-behavior-impact-feedback.htm

○ Don't make it personal—instead of "you" ("You screwed this up!") use "this" ("This requires a different approach.")

Step 3: Ask if they want it. Did your PM ask for feedback? Yes? Great, then give it! No? Then ask if they want feedback. This may require asking some specific questions that elicit feedback about work performance:

- "Would you like more or less feedback on your work? Why/why not?"

- "Would you like more or less direction from me? Why/why not?"

- "On what aspect of your job would you like more help or coaching?"

- "What's a recent situation you wish you handled differently? What would you change?"

Step 4: Give feedback (praise *and* criticism). Start your new feedback habit by giving praise. Not only is it easier to give, but positive feedback encourages people to change their negative behaviors while keeping the positive ones. Remember: You get what you reward! Once you've given some praise, then work your way into giving critiques as well. As shown in Figure 8-4, it's important to say the right things (content) clearly with the right attitude in an appropriate setting and in a timely manner.

But please don't be the party pooper. For example, if the team is celebrating a big product launch, that is not the time to single out people to deliver negative feedback about how they could have done better. Please save that for your 1:1 improvement discussions.

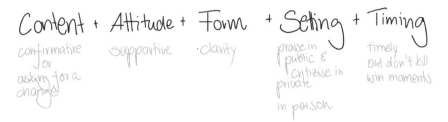

Figure 8-4: Content, attitude, form, setting, and timing

Here's a step-by-step approach to giving feedback to your PMs:

1. **In the meeting, get context first.** Someone's poor performance could be due to problems at home or work, being overwhelmed, not enjoying the work they are doing, changes in their goals and interests, burnout, or any number of other reasons. You want to find out the source of the poor performance before you jump into your feedback.

2. **Then say it right away.** You are prepared, so there's absolutely no reason to beat about the bush. Don't make room for assumptions—explain exactly where you are coming from. Ask and say the obvious, for example, "I think X is the reason why, is that correct?" Reference back to either the PM's role description, the definition of your good, or the PMwheel.

3. **Transition to coaching.** Talking about a problem is not enough. Make sure it's clear what needs to be different going forward, and that your PM understands why his work was below standard. Your specific examples and explaining how the issues affected others can paint a more vivid picture that helps him understand your coaching more clearly. Tell people what success regarding the feedback topic looks like. (For junior employees, it might be necessary to say something like, "This is the issue in my view—here's a suggestion on how to fix it. What do you think about that?")

4. **Offer help.** You need to support your employee who may feel overwhelmed for a variety of different reasons.

5. **Agree on next steps.** Ask your PM to email you the agreement. (In their words, did your feedback resonate with them?)

6. **Follow up.** Did the feedback you provided lead to the change you would like to see? (If not, ask yourself: Am I giving feedback often enough? Am I highlighting positive things often enough?)

And remember the words of Kim Scott, author of *Radical Candor:* "Don't focus on what you fear, focus on what they need."

Step 5: Make sure you're not the only source of feedback. Your PMs will take your feedback more seriously if they also hear it from others, so don't be the only source of it. Encourage peer feedback and make sure everyone knows how to give—and receive—it.

Ultimately, it's up to you as head of product to create a culture in your organization where feedback is valued and happening on a continuous basis. Model the behavior yourself and provide the resources and support your people need to do it themselves without your constant prodding or intervention. Giving feedback should be as easy and invigorating as taking a breath of fresh air.

Further Reading

- Situation-Behavior-Impact (SBI) feedback tool: https://www.strongproductpeople.com/further-readings#chapter-8_1

- Joshua Howard has written a lot about engineering role expectations—his "There Is No Them" blog contains many tips on how to make sure employees know what the expectations are: https://www.strongproductpeople.com/further-readings#chapter-8_2

- If you have to discipline or let an employee go, this article presents many alternative approaches: https://www.strongproductpeople.com/further -readings#chapter-8_3

- Jeff Gothelf wrote this excellent article on psychological safety: Without Psychological Safety There Is No Learning and There Is No Agility: https://www.strong productpeople.com/further-readings#chapter-8_4

- This article on psychological safety by Laura Delizonna has good advice on how to create it: High-Performing Teams Need Psychological Safety. Here's How to Create It: https://www.strongproductpeople.com/further -readings#chapter-8_5

- Books:
  - *Radical Candor* by Kim Scott (or watch her video: https://youtu.be/f-TcrOT9Tyw)
  - *The Making of a Manager* by Julie Zhuo
  - *The Team That Managed Itself* by Christina Wodtke

CHAPTER 9

MOTIVATION DO'S AND DON'TS

- Theory X and Theory Y

- 14 ways to demotivate your employees (and how to avoid them)

- What you can do to help keep your people motivated

One of the great mysteries of the art and science of management is the topic of motivation. Where does motivation come from? Is it something we heads of product must somehow pound into the brains of our PMs, or is it instead something that is already there—just waiting for the right environment to emerge and flourish?

In my own experience, it's most definitely the latter.

But first, a definition. *Employee motivation* is defined as the level of energy, commitment, and creativity that a company's workers bring to their jobs. As an HoP, over the course of your career, you have certainly encountered people who were highly motivated go-getters, and others who were supremely unmotivated do-nothings. So, what is the fundamental difference between employees who are highly motivated and those who are not? Let's explore this question together now.

One of the most pervasive myths in management is that it's *your* job as a manager to motivate your employees, most often by offering them incentives such as rewards and recognition, or—what I consider to be more helpful—by ensuring employee involvement and empowerment. I personally believe that you don't need to motivate people—they are already motivated when they show up for work each day. They have joined your team or your organization for a reason.

What you *do* need to do as a manager is to avoid *demotivating* your people. And, unfortunately, demotivating them is exactly what many managers and organizations do each and every day of the week. Managers demotivate through their actions—or inactions—and organizations demotivate through poorly designed and implemented rules and processes. So, please "never push loyal people to the point where they don't give a damn," as management guru Peter Drucker once cautioned.[60]

Theory X and Theory Y

It's probably no big surprise that managers have many different beliefs when it comes to what motivates their people and what demotivates them. These beliefs are greatly influenced by the basic assumptions managers have about their people, and these assumptions determine in great part the way they treat them.

In the 1960s, management professor Douglas McGregor developed Theory X and Theory Y to explain how managers' beliefs about what motivates their people can affect their management style.[61]

According to Theory X, people dislike work, have little ambition, and are unwilling to take responsibility. Managers with these assumptions try to motivate their people using a rigid, "carrot-and-stick" approach, which rewards good performance and punishes poor performance.

On the other hand, Theory Y proposes that people are inherently self-motivated and enjoy the challenge of work. Managers with these assumptions have a more collaborative relationship with their people

---

60 https://wist.info/drucker-peter-f/39723/
61 https://www.mindtools.com/pages/article/newLDR_74.htm

MOTIVATION DO'S AND DON'TS | 121

and motivate them by allowing them to work on their own initiative—giving them responsibility and empowering them to make decisions.

Which of these theories do you personally ascribe to? How do your assumptions about the people who work for you affect how you manage them? What about your team members? And how would you rate yourself? Are you a Theory X or Theory Y person?

I ask the last question quite often in trainings and coachings, and HoPs usually tell me that their team is 50:50 Theory X and Theory Y. And if I ask them about themselves, about 99-100 percent of people answer that they are Theory Y. Let that sink in for a moment. If everyone thinks they are Theory Y, how can it be that there is a 50:50 ratio of X and Y in their organizations? It's the manager's *perception*—not what people are actually bringing to work!

If you find yourself micromanaging the work of your PMs, and you're not sure you can trust them to do their jobs, then you're probably leaning toward Theory X. If you believe your people enjoy their work, and you trust them to get the job done—and they do—then you're probably leaning toward Theory Y. I know it's not easy to change this mindset. But if you believe in Theory X, I would strongly encourage you to take a moment and think about the gains you could achieve by shifting perspective.

14 Ways to Demotivate Your Employees

While there are an almost unlimited number of ways a manager can demotivate her people, I have found that 14 in particular are most often the case in a product organization. How do you think your people would rate you on each of the following?

1. The manager/company has an old-school management style (e.g., they are micromanaging).

2. The manager/company fails to recognize employee/team achievements.

3. The manager/company tolerates poor performance or toxic behavior.

4. The manager/company doesn't encourage personal development and/or does not offer opportunities for growth.

5. The manager doesn't follow through on her own commitments.

6. The manager doesn't care/is disinterested/isn't present.

7. There's no clear direction or communication.

8. Chaos reigns (vs. a rapidly changing environment, which is okay if well managed).

9. Everyone is treated equal (vs. fair—people don't want the same salary; they want fair compensation).

10. Pay is too low to make a living.[62]

11. The "wrong" people are hired and promoted.

12. The workload is unrealistic.

13. Boredom is widespread.

14. People feel a lack of job security.

I recommend the following exercise: Take the two demotivating factors from the above list that you think you are most guilty of and make a note of five things you will start doing tomorrow to stop engaging in them. Keep this list visible and don't let it get buried by your other to-dos. Put it in a calendar entry and make sure you get reminded of it every now and then.

Let's Talk About Ego

Now that we have had a look at you and your organization's role in the motivation game, let's focus on the individual PM. One question that undoubtably drives motivation—and it's a question people always

---

62 See the article in this chapter's Further Reading about how PayPal CEO Dan Schulman and the company closed its pay gap.

ask me—is this: What's in it for me? If all motivation is ultimately *self*-motivation, then it makes sense that this question is top of mind for every one of your people.

Ultimately, the answer to the question: "What's in it for me?" depends on one's stage of ego development, of which there is a definite progression. American psychologist Jane Loevinger developed a widely accepted, nine-stage model of ego development. According to Loevinger's model, as we mature, we consecutively pass through each of these stages. Problems occur when people get stuck at one of the earlier, self-focused stages of ego development and fail to progress any further.

Here's a quick summary of Loevinger's nine stages of ego development:

1. Pre-social: Infancy, essentially no ego

2. Impulsive: Driven by emotions—the world is "good" if it meets his needs and "bad" if it does not.

3. Self-protective: Perceives the world in terms of punishments and rewards, but tries "not to get caught"

4. Conformist: Becomes aware of society and the need to belong to a group

5. Self-aware: Becomes self-critical and envisions multiple possibilities in life events (according to Loevinger, this is the model for most adult behavior)

6. Conscientious: Has internalized the rules of society but understands that there are exceptions and special contingencies

7. Individualistic: Has a respect for individuality in himself accompanied by a tolerance for the individual differences in others

8. Autonomous: Achieving a feeling of self-fulfillment becomes important

9. Integrated: A fully formed and mature ego that favors individuality in self and others[63]

In our context, let's apply this to our product organizations: people strive for some very specific things. When they are missing, employees will most likely be unhappy, unmotivated, and may seek a new employer that will provide them. These things include:

- Quality of life upgrade,

- Mastery/learning and growing,

- Autonomy/empowerment,

- Creativity and innovation, and

- Purpose.

And which of these things they consider to be most important depends on their ego development stage. Somebody at Stage 4 does everything to be accepted by the team he belongs to and really suffers if the team's mood is bad. Somebody at Stage 7 is not that attached to what's going on in her team and her motivation is not influenced by these "basic things." She might be more affected by a massive cut in the people-development budget because she had plans to learn something new.

As an HoP, it's your job to figure out which of these things matters most to each of your PMs—different people want different things—and then ensure that you're not acting as a barrier to their achieving them.[64] Just get out of their way or even support them to get to new motivation highs!

---

63 Thomas Armstrong (January 31, 2020). The Stages of Ego Development According to Jane Loevinger. Retrieved from https://www.institute4learning .com/2020/01/31/the-stages-of-ego-development-according-to-jane-loevinger/

64 The Moving Motivators card deck can help you discuss motivators with your PMs: https://management30.com/shop/moving-motivators-cards/

What You Can Do Right Now to Support Your People

There are some things you can do right now to support your people and help ensure they don't lose the motivation they bring with them to their jobs. First, here are some specific things that we dig deeper into throughout this book:

- Really care about your people! What are their individual goals in life? (Chapter 7: The Power of Coaching)

- Create room for personal and professional improvement (throughout the book)

- Not tolerating poor performance (Chapter 8: Monitoring Performance and Giving Feedback)

- Foster autonomy and empower people (Chapter 10: Building Individual and Team Alignment)

- Lead by example (Chapter 1: Your Role in This Game + Chapter 5: Being a Great Boss)

- Provide direction (Chapter 15: Help Your Product Managers Create a Product Vision and Set Goals)

- Ensure good communication within the organization (Chapter 20: Communicating Directly and Openly)

At a more global level, some of the most effective ways to ensure your people remain motivated is to create a favorable environment for those in the team who are motivated, recognize good performance, and focus on psychological safety—fear of losing a job is more common than you might think! If you're convinced that: "I know what motivates me, so I therefore know what motivates others," you're probably wrong. Motivation is very much an individual thing, and what motivates one person may not motivate someone else.

Show teammates how their work contributes to the success of the organization ("What our customers say...") and challenge your people (sometimes) so that they get to feel personal mastery, but be careful that they don't work *too* hard over a prolonged period of time. Know that there is a fine line between rapid change and chaos—make sure you apply enough structure and process to ensure that your organization doesn't cross the line into chaos.

Paying your employees a fair wage is important—figure out what employees need to make a living in their particular location. This is your minimum pay! At the same time, do not tolerate pay inequality based on gender and other factors. If, for example, women are paid less than men for the same job and the same performance, then you are a part of the problem. And if you believe in Theory Y as much as I do, then get rid of your bonus systems and individual incentives. (Stock ownership is different—this makes employees owners and gives them the opportunity to participate in the organization's success.)

Create your own framework for measuring employee performance (for example, the PMwheel), make it transparent, use it on everyone, and act on it. Finally, never, ever break your organization's rules or norms. If promotions only take place twice a year—say, in March and September—then don't promote your superstar developer in July just because. You'll do more harm to the motivation of your employees than good.

Further Reading

- PayPal CEO Dan Schulman on how his company closed its pay gap: https://www.strongproductpeople.com /further-readings#chapter-9_1

- How you can ensure your workers are not just surviving, but thriving: https://www.strongproductpeople.com /further-readings#chapter-9_2

- Books:
  - *Illuminate* by Nancy Duarte and Patti Sanchez—a book that shines a new light on managing and motivating people through speeches, ceremonies, stories, and symbols: https://www.duarte.com /illuminate/

CHAPTER 10

BUILDING INDIVIDUAL AND TEAM ALIGNMENT

- The two types of clarity you need for alignment

- The process of aligning: Starting discussions and seeking transparency

- What if two parties can't align?

All of the work we do today requires a tremendous amount of communication and collaboration because we do things in teams. And if people aren't aligned when they are working together, things tend to go wrong. When I talk about *alignment,* I mean that people are working *with* one another—they are all pulling together in the same direction to achieve common goals.

When your people are not aligned, you'll notice that outcomes are not as you expected, resources—including time, money, brainpower, and so forth—are wasted on the wrong things, and employees become frustrated. Misalignment causes organizational friction that results in inefficiencies all around. Consider the example in Figure 10-1 (based on a drawing by Henrik Kniberg) of two teams pursuing a common goal of getting from one side of a river to the other, but that aren't aligned in their approaches to achieving this goal—leading to surprise and frustration.[65]

Figure 10-1: The mission was "Cross that river"— the sad side effects of misalignment

Before we dive deep into how to get to alignment in your organization, there are three key things you can do to make sure your people are aligned:

- Provide **clarity of intent**—the underlying thinking of initiatives.

- Ensure **discussions** on the tricky questions—the ones that need alignment—take place as early as possible.

- Make the results of the alignment process **transparent** to get everyone on the same page.[66]

65   Henrik Kniberg (June 8, 2016). Spotify Rhythm—how we get aligned (slides from my talk at Agile Sverige). Retrieved from https://blog.crisp.se/2016/06/08 /henrikkniberg/spotify-rhythm and https://blog.crisp.se/wp-content/uploads /2016/06/Spotify-Rhythm-Agila-Sverige.pdf

66   A framework you could use to get everyone on the same page https:// auftragsklaerung.com

Gaining Clarity of Intent

Let's take a close look at the first of these three key things: clarity of intent. In his brilliant talk, "Clarity in Collaboration," my friend and colleague Arne Kittler, VP Product, XING, explains that there are two kinds of clarity to focus on:

- **Directional clarity:** Clarity provided by management, including vision, strategy, and goals

- **Situational clarity:** Clarity provided by the people for the people[67]

As an HoP, providing your people with directional clarity is your job, and it's something you should be actively working on. If there is no vision, create one. If there is no strategy, design one. If there are no goals, make some. If, however, these things exist but they are not well communicated or widely understood, then figure out how to change this. And if you've done all this but you're not getting the expected alignment, chances are you have skipped the discussion part of the alignment process. Go back and reopen your discussions on the tricky questions.

Situational clarity, on the other hand, is something that occurs hundreds of times a day in every organization. It helps people who are working together to better understand what everyone is working on. This is something you should actively engage in and help your PMs to understand. For example, instead of saying in a meeting, "Someone should be testing this backlog item," one could say, "I will be testing this backlog item today."

There's one more kind of clarity to consider in addition to directional clarity and situational clarity: *role clarity*. Everyone has specific roles in an organization, but if these roles aren't clearly defined, then misalignment will be the certain result. This becomes evident

---

67 Arne Kittler (May 2, 2019). Clarity in Collaboration. Retrieved from https://youtu.be/T5Ta6TJtQKs

when someone is disappointed by how someone else behaves—the role expectation they had for the other person is not fulfilled. And if this misalignment is not brought up as an issue, perhaps out of fear of damaging a relationship, then the other person will have no chance to improve and no opportunity to create alignment.

There are a variety of tools you can use to help create role clarity with your people. I'm a big fan of The Manual of Me (https://manualofme.co/), which "is a handy guide for others to help them get the best of you from work."

In addition, I have found that having your people fill out this role worksheet can help everyone gain the clarity they need to create alignment with one another, and with the organization:

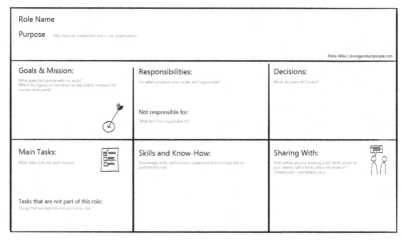

Figure 10-2: My role definition canvas—it helps teams align on everybody's roles and responsibilities[68]

Remember: It's everyone's job to bring more clarity to the work environment. Tell your PMs not to rely on others and to talk about this with their teams. Don't use buzzwords or jargon—make yourself clearly understood. It's okay to ask others for clarification or to double-check.

---

68 https://www.strongproductpeople.com/download

And keep the words of comedy writer Jerry Belson in mind: "Never ASSUME, because when you ASSUME, you make an ASS of U and ME."[69]

Starting Discussions for Alignment

In addition to clarity of intent, you need to have discussions on the tricky questions—the ones needing alignment—as early as possible. As you start having these discussions, it's important to understand that, according to Arne Kittler, there are three dimensions of alignment in any organization (see Figure 10-3). There's the upward dimension, which represents management. There's the lateral dimension, which represents peers and partners. And there's the inward dimension, which represents teams.

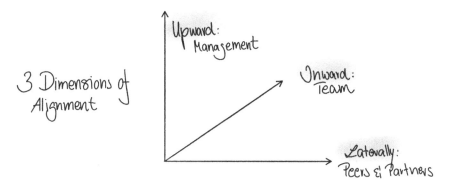

Figure 10-3: Three dimensions of alignment

To get to a place of complete alignment within the product organization, each of these three dimensions must be addressed. Here's how to do that:

- Get all the relevant people on board.

- Start a dialogue.

---

69   https://en.wikipedia.org/wiki/Jerry_Belson

- Talk about the tricky questions early.

- Get people to externalize their thoughts.

One example of an approach for getting discussions going is *planning poker*. It's a good example for explaining alignment to your PMs because we're all familiar with it. I know—some of you believe that planning poker is an Agile thing that's all about getting an estimate from a development team: A product person describes what she thinks the team should build and what the user actually wants this feature to do. Then the development team raises cards with their individual estimates of implementation complexity—say, one with a 5, one with an 8, and one with a 13—and then they start their discussion, unless everyone on the team agrees that it's a 5 or an 8 or a 13. However, the real value of planning poker isn't the estimates, it's the discussions it fosters and the clarity and alignment it brings.

There is one other framework for collaborative alignment developed by product people at XING, which they call *Auftragsklärung* (in English, this word translates to *order clarification* in a military context). There are two parts to this framework: structured writing and dialogue. The people who developed this framework make a point of explaining that the value of the process is not in filling out forms or creating documents that are just filed away in a drawer. Its true value is in having dialogues and discussions. Here's a summary of the framework, and you can learn more about it on the respective website:[70]

---

70 https://auftragsklaerung.com/

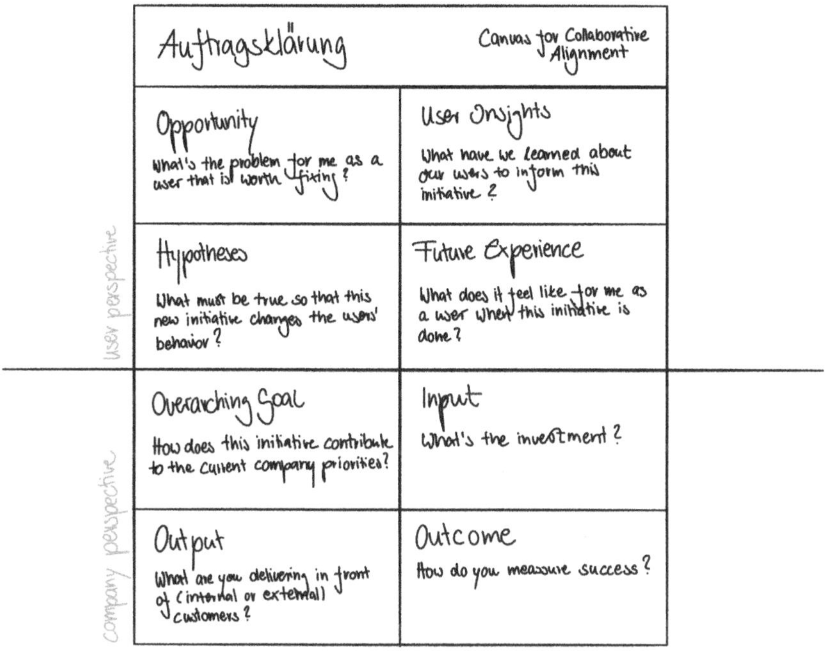
Auftragsklärung
Canvas for Collaborative Alignment
Opportunity
What's the problem for me as a user that is worth fixing?
User Insights
What have we learned about our users to inform this initiative?
Hypotheses
What must be true so that this new initiative changes the users' behavior?
Future Experience
What does it feel like for me as a user when this initiative is done?
Overarching Goal
How does this initiative contribute to the current company priorities?
Input
What's the investment?
Output
What are you delivering in front of (internal or external) customers?
Outcome
How do you measure success?
user perspective
company perspective

Figure 10-4: The XING framework for collaborative alignment

Discussions Resulting in Conflict

Conflict is common in any organization. However, so long as the parties in conflict are respectful of each other—and their opinions—conflict can be a positive thing. This is what I call *positive friction.* We can debate ideas and give them a thorough working out without attacking the people who have them. There is, of course, also a negative side to conflict.[71] However, I want to add a few aspects here that are closely related to alignment.

It's not uncommon for conflict to keep two teams or two people that want to align from being able to do just that. In my experience, in about 90 percent of the cases, this is because of conflicting goals. As a result, the parties can't agree on one particular solution or outcome

71 I deal with conflict in great detail in Chapter 28: Handling Conflict

or direction. But what do you do in those situations when, even when you're encouraging your people to resolve conflicts on their own, they reach a deadlock and can't get past it?

In these cases, you need a mechanism to solve this: an escalation. An *escalation* is when teams or individuals in conflict delegate the decision upward—usually one level up in the hierarchy, perhaps the line manager—and ask for help.

Arne Kittler mentions XING's handy "Clarification Manifesto" in Figure 10-5—make sure your PMs know that escalation is an option and that there's nothing wrong with it:[72]

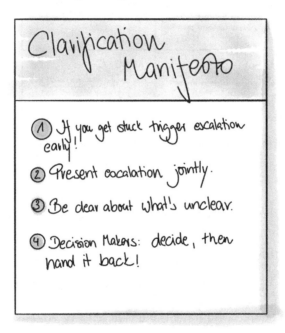

Figure 10-5: The Clarification Manifesto[73]

72   In this video from Mirror Conf 2018, XING's Arne Kittler discusses Clarity in
     Collaboration: https://youtu.be/T5Ta6TJtQKs
73   https://youtu.be/T5Ta6TJtQKs

Making Your Results Transparent

After you have gone through the process of clarifying the intent of an upcoming initiative and having discussions about it, then—to gain full alignment—the results must be made transparent, that is, they must be widely communicated to all the people you have identified who play a role in the alignment process. Write a summary of your results and then pass it around your people to get their reactions and feedback. Do they agree with what you've written? Did they hear the same? Something different?

Only after everyone has had the chance to review something tangible—the filled-in Auftragsklärung canvas, or the written summary of the alignment process—and they don't have any additional comments, can you be sure alignment has been achieved.

Further Reading

- Arne Kittler on Clarity in Collaboration: https://www.strongproductpeople.com/further-readings#chapter-10_1

- Auftragsklärung website: https://www.strongproductpeople.com/further-readings#chapter-10_2

- Collaborative Alignment for Product Managers: https://www.strongproductpeople.com/further-readings#chapter-10_3

- Henrik Kniberg on "Spotify Rhythm—How We Get Aligned: https://www.strongproductpeople.com/further-readings#chapter-10_4

- Janice Fraser on how to assess team buy-in: https://www.strongproductpeople.com/further-readings#chapter-10_5

- Books:
    - *The Art of Action* by Stephen Bungay

CHAPTER 11

HOW TO FIND THE TIME

- Finding time for people development as an HoP

- Understanding if you really care about your PMs

- Finding time for people development as a PM

As you may have already noticed, this book is full of things that you as a head of product can and should do to build a more effective product organization. But, there's just one problem: how to find the time to do all these things—particularly when it comes to developing your people and yourself. It's something that often gets put onto the back burner, much like exercising or eating properly. We know it's a good thing to do, and we know we should do it, but other things keep getting in the way.

Allowing other priorities to get in the way of working with your people to develop themselves and their careers is a big mistake. Why? Because career development is your most powerful management tool. Numerous studies show that it drives employee retention, engagement, productivity, and results.

So, why then don't we do it? Ask any HoP, and the answer you'll likely get in return is "I just don't have the time." This chapter is all about helping you find the time you need to move people development onto the front burner.

Finding Time for People Development (the HoP Edition)

Finding time for people development isn't so much about doing less of your other responsibilities—it's more about engaging in people development in a much more effective and efficient way. Let's take a look at what you as an HoP can do to up your people-development game.

Focus on small, meaningful conversations. You don't need to do a two-hour, 1:1 session with each of your people every week to guide their development. Much more effective are small, short, dedicated 1:1s plus meaningful conversations—10 minutes here, 10 minutes there—on a frequent and ongoing basis. Provide instant feedback on the good things (right after a meeting) and find a formal setting for feedback on the bad and the ugly things. If I'm heading into a meeting and one of my PMs is there, I'll get out a piece of paper, write down some positive feedback, and give it to her right then and there.

Make it a habit. Bad habits are hard to break, and good habits take time (and hard work) to develop.[74]

Use timeboxing for preparation. It's important that you reflect on each person on your team before meeting with them. You can make this happen by adding a weekly slot to your calendar for this—10 minutes per person should be enough, but even five minutes is better than nothing. Think about what feedback you want to give them, what their next development step is, and what your one main question/topic is going to be for the next conversation. Find a framework that you can use to help prepare—the PMwheel, my 52 Questions card deck,[75] or chapters in this book.

Find a way that you love doing it. Your chances of turning this into a habit are greater if you find a way of making the people-development

---

74 For tips on creating a new people development habit, see Chapter 8: Monitoring Performance and Giving Feedback.

75 https://www.petra-wille.com/52questions

process more enjoyable. You don't have to be stuck in your office when you do 1:1s—try walking 1:1s outside the office, catching some fresh air with your PM on a balcony or in an outdoor café or restaurant, or walking phone calls.

If you're still struggling with finding time to do people development, maybe the problem is deeper than just getting organized or starting a new habit.

For example, maybe your team is too big. I recently spoke with a head of product who told me that he has 40 PM direct reports. Frankly, it's impossible to do proper people development if you have 40 PM direct reports. My recommendation to this HoP was to restructure his organization to reduce the number of direct reports. (To me, more than six direct reports are too many.)

You should also reflect on why it's important to do people development. Connect the process to the big picture—if you don't do people development, you'll lose good people, and hiring replacements takes time and money (plus you lose the time and money you've already invested on the employees who leave).

Connect people development to your bigger work and life goals: "If I spend more time on coaching, my people are more likely to stay, and the results of the teams will improve. With people being more experienced and knowing what they are doing, we won't be in firefighting mode all the time, and I can spend more time with my family or playing guitar in my band or doing whatever it is I want to do." (Leo Babauta calls this "making a vow" in his book, *Essential Zen Habits*.)

Do You Care? Really??

If you've done all the above and you're still struggling with finding the time you need for people development, I'm going to tell you something that I suspect no one else has had the courage to tell you: You don't really care about your PMs. Either they're simply not important enough to rate your attention, or you routinely forget that you care as you deal with the day-to-day demands of running a product organization. I know that may be hard to hear, but it's the truth.

Don't believe me? Here's what Marty Cagan says about this important topic in his book, *EMPOWERED*:

> *By far the biggest reason I see that people don't develop and reach competence is because so many managers either don't like developing people, or they don't view it as their primary responsibility. So, it's pushed off as a secondary task, if that, and the message to the employee is clear: You're on your own.*[76]

If you don't care about your people, you and your organization won't be successful until you do. You don't have to be their friends, but you do need to care about them as fellow human beings—with aspirations and dreams, the same as you. Sure, your people can develop themselves into competent PMs. However, it will take a lot longer than if you make time on a regular schedule to help them develop. Your outside perspective and experience will help them see themselves in a new light. And, through your example, they will make time for this critical task in their own busy calendars.

Sometimes, it's good to be reminded why we should care about our PMs. We may know that exercise is good, but we may not really care about doing it until after we have a heart attack. We may know that protecting the environment is good, but we may not really care about it until one of our children becomes sick after swimming in a lake that is tainted with industrial pollution.

Imagine, for a moment, the following conversation between a cost-conscious CFO and a performance-conscious CEO. The CFO asks the CEO: "What happens when we invest all that money in the development of our employees and they leave us?" The CEO replies by asking the CFO her own question: "What happens if we don't do it and they stay?"

---

76 Marty Cagan with Chris Jones, *EMPOWERED: Ordinary People, Extraordinary Products*, Wiley (2020)

You can use this same logic to understand why you should care and apply it to your own situation. Here's a canvas I created to help you do just that. The canvas is based on four reasons why you should care: good for them, good for you, good for us, and good for all. Figure 11-1 is an example of the canvas with responses filled in.

Why I should care about people development   Petra Wille | strongproductpeople.com

| good for them | They feel seen, they tend to stay if they are developing, they are |
| What will change for the better if you invest some time in people development? | motivated, they want to learn more if they see the positive effects |

good for you	Less hiring and onboarding efforts if people stay
What will therefore change for you to make your life easier?	Less escalations if people get better
	Better products if they know their craft

good for us	Teams are achieving better results with a motivated product manager
What are the positive effects of people development even beyond our organization?	-> their positive energy will influence the whole team
	More value for the customer if PM knows more about his craft and
	ultimately more revenue for the company

good for all	Company will come closer to its vision of making the world a better
What are the positive effects of people development even beyond our organization?	place faster
	My family will see me more because of less firefighting and overtime
	hours

Figure 11-1: The "Why I should care" canvas—completed example[77]

Finding Time for People Development (the PM Edition)

Keep in mind that your PMs may have the same challenge you're facing: they can't find the time to develop themselves. If this is the case, then you need to help them understand why it's good for them to invest in themselves—it's good for the PM, it's good for you as HoP, it's good for the team and organization, and it's good for all beyond the organization. Make it clear to your PMs that you and the organization value self-progression.

More specifically...

---

77   You will find a blank version of this canvas, ready for you to fill out at: https://www.strongproductpeople.com/downloads

- Always refer to how this learning will help move your PM forward and toward their career goal.

- Ask them to set aside time for personal development during their working hours. Just 20 minutes a week is a good start. Consistency beats intensity! And tell them to never miss twice!

- Be their friendly reminder.

- Ask them to figure out how they learn best (time, location, medium).

- Make sure they know about the different ways of learning: consuming, applying, reflecting, contributing (see Figure 11-2).

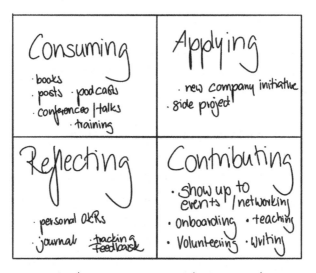

Figure 11-2: The various ways to learn something new

We learn by *consuming* books, blogposts, podcasts, and so on. We improve our skills by *applying* what we have learned to our daily work, or to a side project we're working on. *Reflecting* helps us make sure we're investing our precious development time wisely. And *contributing* to the product management community (no matter whether it's your company's tribe or the global community) helps you to see how much you have already learned. Similarly, onboarding a new colleague allows you to see your methods, tools, and ways for working through a new set of eyes, which can help you switch perspectives.

Further Reading

- Books:
  - *The Power of Habit* by Charles Duhigg
  - *Mindsight* by Daniel Siegel
  - *Immunity to Change* by Robert Kegan and Lisa Lahey
  - *The Dip* by Seth Godin

PART III

FIND AND RECRUIT GOOD PRODUCT MANAGERS— ATTRACT THE BEST PEOPLE

Every great product organization needs great product managers. This requires first finding and attracting the right people to your organization, then interviewing, assessing, and hiring them, and finally, taking the time to effectively onboard them so that they become fully contributing and engaged members of your team as quickly as possible. In this part, we will explore each of these critical areas in detail. In addition, we will consider how HoPs can use the PMwheel assessment introduced in Part I to help better navigate and execute the hiring and onboarding processes.

CHAPTER 12

WHERE TO FIND GREAT PRODUCT MANAGERS

- Active and passive sourcing

- Job ads

- Candidate profiles

Every organization has to hire talented people to do great work and deliver the very best products to their customers. Ironically, many leaders consider hiring to be a problem—a troublesome burden that needs to be solved. If this is how you feel, I suggest that you consider adopting a different perspective. Hiring is not a problem to be solved—it is your golden opportunity to influence the future of your team, your products, and your company. And if done right, you are creating an environment where people solve meaningful challenges and enjoy going to work every day.

To be perfectly honest, hiring is not always the most effective or the fastest way to get great people. Developing the people you already have—providing them with the training and opportunities they need to progress in their job skills, experience, upward career movement—is usually the better approach.

Sound ridiculous? In Germany, where I live, it currently takes about nine months to hire a decent product manager—that's the average across the entire country and across all industries and companies. And once you've got your new employee recruited, selected, and hired, then onboarding takes another three months or so. So, from beginning to end, you're looking at an entire year to get your new hire fully functioning in your team or organization.

Now, think about what you could accomplish with your current product people if you devoted those same 12 months to providing them with the support they need to improve their skills and become more valuable employees. However, since this chapter is about hiring, let's focus on that for now.

Active and Passive Sourcing

In general terms, there are two types of candidates that you should be interested in:

- **Active candidates.** The ones actively looking for a job.

- **Passive candidates.** The ones who could be convinced to leave their current positions if they get approached by someone with the right offer in hand.

So, which of these two kinds of candidates should you focus on? Both.

Active candidates are browsing job boards, talking with people in their network, attending meetups, and more in search of a new job. So, you need to make sure there *is* a job ad out there for them to find, that as many people as possible know you are hiring, and that your employees are aware of referral bonuses if you have such a program. Ideally, you will post the job ad on a variety of different platforms and you will optimize your career website for search engines. This is called *passive sourcing* because it's mainly a sit-and-wait-until-the-candidate-applies type of game.

Active sourcing (for passive candidates) requires a totally different set of HR skills. You need to come up with a detailed candidate profile that helps identify the right candidates. You then need to think about where to find these candidates, how to contact them, and how to convince them that they should consider your company as their next employer. Stellar companies are doing this all the time. Even if there are no open positions at the moment, they actively build talent pools and lists of candidates they can start talking to when the perfect position is available.

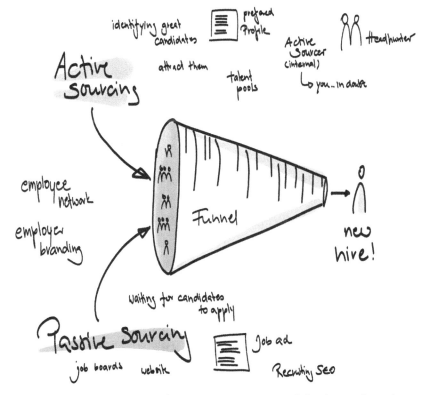

Figure 12-1: Active and passive sourcing and the hiring funnel

Let's have a look at two parts of this process: the job ad and the candidate profile.

The Job Ad

To create a great job ad, start by reading some job ads published by your company and also those of other high-performing companies. As you write the ad, put yourself in the ideal candidate's shoes—think about what you like and what you don't like. What should you include to help the candidate decide to apply for your opening?

One warning: Don't just do the copy-and-paste thing. I know that this might seem like the most efficient way to go, but believe me, you can do better. Define what you are looking for, and that's easy to do with the PMwheel assessment.

Make sure the candidates are able to get an idea of the company they will be joining, the product they will work on, and the people they will be creating the product for. Include your company values or purpose. And be sure to reflect whether or not the position really requires 10 years of experience or an MBA.[78] So many companies include requirements like this, and they miss out of some very bright talents who might not apply as a result. I often hear from women, for example, who tell me that a job required three years of experience, so they didn't apply because they only had two. This is in contrast to men, who will readily apply when they fit 70–80 percent of the requirements. So, my tip is to create a prioritized list of your main criteria you will filter the CVs by and not include too many of these criteria in the ad.

Be careful about how you present your company benefits—you don't want the PMs to join your company just because you serve Blue Bottle coffee or free lunch. I suggest that you say something like, "Great company benefits including a development budget." And since we're talking about filling product positions, I suggest that you test the ad before you run it. Show it to your product managers and the team

---

78   https://www.quora.com/Why-are-MBAs-looked-down-upon-in-Silicon-Valley

you are hiring for and see what resonates with them the most. Based on their feedback, you may decide to adjust the ad before you run it.

Which brings us to where to post the ad. It should, of course, always be on your website. And it should be posted on job boards for product people—such as the one for Mind the Product (https://jobs.mindtheproduct.com)—which are also a good place to look for PMs. Some job boards don't charge a fee to post ads while others do. There are also the big job boards such as Monster, Indeed, LinkedIn, and others. And don't forget to share your open positions with your employees—some may want to apply themselves or maybe they know someone who would be interested in the job. In any case, ask them to spread the news.

Announce the position via your company's social channels—Twitter and LinkedIn can be very effective recruiting tools—and mention on Meetups that you are hiring. You can also reach specific communities, such as Women in Product (https://www.womeninproduct.com) or Mind the Product on Slack.

The Candidate Profile

A great candidate profile will contain a definition of what you're looking for, based again on your definition of a Good PM (or the PMwheel assessment) and create something like a candidate persona. You know the drill—education, personal situation, willing to travel, key skills and experience, experience in remote work, and so on. Then there are desired traits such as great communicator, collaborative team player, good in dealing with ambiguity, and so forth. And you should think about how to identify them online, because you'll usually hand off this profile to your HR colleagues. You need to give them some ideas and guidance on how to identify these people. This includes job titles they should be looking for and certain skills and keywords in their social profiles. You may, for example, want to specify frameworks and methodologies such as OKRs, design sprint, and so on.

Geographical location is important because not everyone can afford to relocate their new hires. If you can afford relocation, then you can go global. You may want to search for certain company sizes—if you're a midsized company, for example, then it may not be perfect to get somebody from a supersmall startup. Last but not least, their current role is a superinteresting indicator of whether or not we should talk with them.

According to a study by LinkedIn, millennials change jobs on average four times in the first decade after they graduate from college, or once every 2.5 years.[79] So, if you want to do active sourcing, it's better to talk to people that are two years into their jobs, more or less.

You can source them by checking to see who they are following on Twitter because that says a lot. If they want to become thought leaders in their field, they're probably following a certain combination of product people on Twitter. And also meetups they might attend.

Always test your profile by taking the profile of some of your current product managers and checking to see if they would have ended up as candidates, using the candidate-filtering rules you've defined. And if not, then adjust the profile to more accurately reflect the reality of what makes a great product manager in your organization.

Unconventional Ways to Identify Candidates

There are always people in product organizations that I call "deputy product managers." Some product teams don't have a product manager, or not a real strong one, and in those situations someone else tends to step up and take on much of the PM role. It might be an engineer, a quality assurance person, or someone else on the team. These people are great candidates for your open PM positions—they're probably already doing the job, and they may have been doing so for quite some time. People in customer-care roles can be good candidates too

79 Guy Berger (April 12, 2016). Will This Year's College Grads Job-Hop More Than Previous Grads? Retrieved from https://blog.linkedin.com/2016/04/12/will-this-year_s-college-grads-job-hop-more-than-previous-grads

because they tend to be superempathic—they want to help the user. You can also consider hiring recent university graduates who show promise. But remember: Hiring junior people requires more coaching effort from your side!

In addition, you can target product people who work for your competition. This isn't always the best idea however. First of all, you don't want to copy what your competitors are already working on. Second, you may not want to bring their company culture into your own because there are often big culture differences between companies—even those competing for the same market.

Then there are consultancies and agencies which can be a good source of temporary product people. If they work out, you may be able to convince some of them to join your organization on a permanent basis.

Product management conferences are a great source of potential PM candidates. If you are looking to hire somebody with a lot of experience, check the list of speakers for interesting candidates. Some conferences publish attendee lists so you'll have those available to review and recruit from.

Blogs are another good source for product people. Look at who is commenting on popular online product discussions on Quora, Medium, or product-related blogs. Some blogs allow guest posts, so keep an eye on those too. And, guess who's commenting on product books on Amazon—books like Marty Cagan's *INSPIRED*? Right—product people.

This just shows you how creative you can be in finding candidates for your PM positions if you just step outside the box for a moment or two.

Of course, once you've identified a strong candidate, you've got to decide if they are really all they appear to be. As head of product, I suggest that you do as much up front communication with the candidates as you can instead of delegating it to HR or someone else. I know—it's a lot of work but you'll get a much better idea about just how good your candidate is if you do the scheduling and interviews yourself. How good are they at writing emails and how fast are they in responding? Make sure you are superresponsive when you're recruiting so your candidates know you value them.

If you're actively sourcing for a more senior role, I strongly recommend that the first contact they have with your organization should be *you* and not your HR people. Schedule for a less formal first session if they show general interest—a chat over coffee, if possible, or a casual phone call without any particular structure or process behind it.

If you're working for a larger company and hiring is an ongoing effort, measure and optimize your funnel. How many passive candidates do you need to speak with to get 10 applications? How many active candidates are applying if you're just posting a job on a particular platform and how good is the quality of these applications? How long is your hiring cycle? Develop metrics, track them, and then make adjustments to your approach based on your outcomes.

Employer Branding

You should also look into the art of employer branding. If you're lucky enough to work in a company with an HR department, they usually do a lot to make sure candidates get a positive image of your company when they start Googling it. The jobs section of the website will therefore be awesome, and they'll try to ensure that online discussions about the company are positive. The goal is to be sure candidates get the message that your company is a great employer of product people. Even if they're not actively searching for their next opportunity, they'll have a good impression of your company. What are your employee ratings like on Glassdoor or kununu? Are you proud of them, or do they leave something to be desired?

It's your job as head of product to at least think about the many different options available to you. You should be personally visible as your business's leading product person outside the company. Are you attending meetups? Are you hosting them? Are you maintaining a social media presence where you share your take on product-related topics? Does your company have a booth at conferences? Is the product team visible outside the company? It's not only you, it's your team as well. Encourage your team to share their learnings with the product community in a series of blog posts or during a talk on the local product meetup.

CHAPTER 13

INTERVIEWING, ASSESSING, AND HIRING CANDIDATES

- Building your team

- The hiring process

- Interviewing, assessing, and making a job offer

Once you find some promising PM candidates, you've got to decide if they are going to be the right people for the job. So far, you've only seen a resume or CV, and you have not yet had the chance to actually speak with the person to determine if they have the right mix of experience, smarts, and personality for your organization. This all changes when you actually conduct interviews, then use the data you have gathered to assess your candidates and make hiring offers.

Please keep in mind as you read this chapter that the actual process of interviewing and hiring a new team member differs significantly around the globe. In fact, I have never seen the exact same hiring and recruiting process in two different organizations—whether they are across town, or in an entirely different country. Local regulations and social norms will have an impact on how difficult it is to find great job candidates, how you approach them, and what you can say to these folks during the interview and hiring process. In addition, the reputation of your business, the attractiveness of your brand, and many other factors all have an effect on who applies for your PM positions.

Above all, keep in mind that there is no one-size-fits-all solution to interviewing, assessing, and hiring the very best candidates. There are, however, some basics—the lowest common denominator—that remain true no matter what your current situation may be. Use the information in this chapter as a stepping-off point but be sure to customize your approach to create your own, perfect hiring process.

Build Your Team Intentionally

Before you start the recruiting process, you first need to spend some time thinking about exactly what kind of team you want to build. My own personal best practice when building a team is to do an annual planning meeting with myself where I ask, "What would my ideal team look like 12 months from now?" If you decide to adopt this approach, then I suggest you reflect on:

1. Your current role (How much support can I give to my new PM? How much time do I currently have available for onboarding and coaching?)

2. Your definition of a Good PM (Skills, competencies, and knowledge you would like to see—use the PMwheel to assist you with this)

3. The shape of your product team and their designated product development team (What shortcomings can we tolerate skill-wise, because the team is already really good at it?)

4. The environment and culture in which they need to work (Stakeholders, the rest of the company, the industry as a whole)

Reflecting on these different aspects of what you would like your ideal team to look like 12 months from now will help you answer a variety of questions related to the PMs you plan to hire, including:

- How many people should you hire?

- Should you search for pioneers (people who are excited by building prototypes, who are pumped about the riskiness of the endeavor and creating something brand new in the world), settlers (much more focused on impact—they really care about reaching a lot of people, they're obsessed with growth and optimizing), or town planners (these are your platform managers who take over when it's time to build the infrastructure and systems necessary to handle scale and accommodate your product's use cases, current and future)?[80]

- What level of experience should you target? Senior? Junior/Associate? Something in between?[81] What fits your budget and your schedule? (Junior/Associate PMs are less expensive, but you'll need to invest more of your time in bringing them up to speed.)

- What experiences/personality traits should you look for to ensure alignment with your core values while adding new flavor to your company culture in a positive way? (Aim for more than cultural fit—aim for cultural add.)

- What experiences/personality would help increase the diversity of your team?

---

80   See this article for an explanation of these three kinds of product people: First Round Review (n.d.). The Power of the Elastic Product Team—Airbnb's First PM on How to Build Your Own. Retrieved from https://firstround.com/review/the-power -of-the-elastic-product-team-airbnbs-first-pm-on-how-to-build-your-own/

81   No matter how small your company is, the career ladder is something you'll need to define at some stage. This book holds tips on how to get there in Chapter 4: Define Your Good and Chapter 24: Keep the Senior PMs Engaged.

In the end, keep in mind that the very best product people do three things well. Todd Jackson, former VP Product & Design at Dropbox, suggests that you should:

- Articulate what a winning product looks like;

- Rally the team to build it; and

- Then iterate on it until you get it right.[82]

So, that's what you are ultimately looking for.

The Hiring Process

Every organization and every HoP will have a different hiring process. However, the basic steps are mostly the same. Here are the six steps in my own hiring process that take place after finding a great PM candidate:[83]

1. Scan applications.

2. Compare applicants. (Comparing applicants to candidates we've actively sourced, and deciding on whom to invite to our first interview.)

3. Do a profile check. (I tend to do this in a 25-minute phone interview.)

4. Assign take-home case. (I usually send them a case to prepare and present during the interview.)

5. Conduct a formal interview. (If candidate passes the profile check, then I usually invite them to an actual job interview.)

---

82 Todd Jackson (2019). Find, Vet, and Close the Best Product Managers. Retrieved from https://firstround.com/review/find-vet-and-close-the-best-product-managers -heres-how/

83 Addressed in Chapter 4: Define Your Good

6. Make the job offer. (If the candidate is a great fit, then we'll have a final conversation to present the job offer, negotiate the contract, and figure out the details.)

Let's take a deep dive into each of these steps in the hiring process.

Step 1: Scan applications

The question you want to answer as you scan your PM candidates is this: Does this person look like a *product* person?

Regardless of whether or not they have previously held PM roles, use your PMwheel assessment as a first check. Is there anything in their experience that talks about "understanding the problem" and "getting things done" with a "team?" If too many of the dimensions result in a "?" then you may want to remove that candidate from further consideration.

Every HoP has certain "no-way" rules, that is, factors that will automatically remove the candidate from further consideration. For example, certain companies may be on your hiring blacklist—perhaps your dying competitors. Another no-way rule might be that the role requires a degree in computer science or an MBA, so applications that arrive without these requirements will be removed from further consideration.

That said, please note that I am personally not a big fan of filtering people by their education. I have seen and worked with so many dedicated and hardworking PMs over the years who do not have the "right" degrees from well-known universities. In the interview section of this chapter, I describe what I really think matters.

I also look at the style and format of the application and the resume or CV. Is it easy to read and understand? Are they treating me as a "user" of the CV? These things tell me a lot about the candidate. For example, what name have they given to the files they sent? Have they even given thought to details like this?

Good: 2020_06_ROLE_COMPANY_THEIRNAME.pdf

Bad: My_Application.doc & My_CV.doc

Imagine these files in your hiring folder. The first one has all you need. The second one will have you wondering who the candidate is. We're looking for PMs who pay attention to detail and make an effort. On the other hand, if it has taken them ages to put the files together, but they are beautifully designed, make sure you check in on "done is better than perfect" during any interviews you do with these candidates.

Step 2: Compare applicants

After an intensive sourcing effort and scan of applications, you have some promising PM candidates—congratulations! The next step is for you to take a closer look and compare the qualifications of your candidates to decide who to invite first. Once you've decided who deserves to move to the next step, invite them to participate in a short, 25-minute phone interview (Step 3 in our process).

If you don't yet have any perfect candidates, but some show the possibility of potentially working out, consider doing a telephone interview with them anyway. It's a small investment to make on your part and the person may show promise once you dig a little deeper.

Step 3: Do a profile check

Before you get too deep into the interview process, you'll first want to verify that your PM candidate has the right stuff for the job. This is best accomplished by way of a call—via telephone, Zoom, Google Hangouts, Skype, or whatever communication platform you choose. There are two main reasons for doing a profile check:

First, some HoPs don't do a very good job filtering out PM candidates who clearly aren't qualified. So, they end up wasting everyone's time when an unqualified candidate is brought into the business for a round of interviews. Second, some HoPs have the opposite problem—they limit the number of candidates early in the process just because "I can't talk to that many people."

No matter which of these groups you belong to, a phone interview is a good idea. I divide the profile check into three parts:

Explaining the role (5 minutes)

- I explain why we are searching, our current setup, and what the role would be all about.

Questions for the candidate (15 minutes)

- Walk me through your CV/resume.

- Highlight what you think is relevant.

- Talk about your favorite product (no matter if it's a digital or physical product) and explain why you like it and how you would improve it.

Questions for you (5 minutes)

- Ask me anything.

After the interview session, I ask myself the following questions:

- Did the candidate manage her time well? (Did they respect the 15 minutes granted?)

- Was the candidate hard to follow? (If yes, that's not a good sign. PMs have to be great in communication. That's the main part of their job!)

- Did the candidate show interest? (Did they ask some great questions? Have they wrapped their heads around how their life might be at your company?)

If you stick to the suggested 25-minute format, you will end up with a much clearer picture about who to invite to the longer interview session. In addition, you'll gain some insights on what you should ask them once the day arrives. As such, it's helpful to take notes so you'll be able to prepare questions for the next interview and presentation of one or more cases.

If the candidate shows promise, then ask them to send you some past examples of similar work they have done. Ask if anything is publicly available.

Finally, explain to the candidate the next steps in the interview process.

Whether during this interview or any subsequent ones, be sure to deliver an amazing experience. This is important—even if you are not making an offer, because people tend to talk, and the interview process is something that sticks. People know that they are in a larger process but please make them feel like humans not like resources!

Think about the candidate experience every step of the way: Are they informed about the next steps? Are your email messages answering their key questions? Make it fast, make it personal. And if you need to say no to candidates, make sure they get a personal email as soon as you have decided to not hire them—including feedback that helps them to understand your decision. That's just fair!

One quick note: Sometimes you'll have too many candidates and it's just not possible to interview them all in one go. Alternatively, sometimes you may have only one candidate and you would like to wait a little longer until there are at least two, so you have the opportunity to compare. And sometimes a superpromising application lands on your desk right when you are in final negotiations with a candidate. These kinds of situations mean that candidates have to wait and that is never good. Always keep the candidate's experience in mind and try to keep it optimized. It's good business.

Step 4: Assign take-home case

Once I've narrowed down the list of candidates to the ones who I'll invite in for a formal interview, I'm a big fan of assigning them a "take-home" case that they can prepare in advance of the meeting. I usually also ask them to do an *ad-hoc* case in front of a whiteboard during the interview.

Ideas for the take-home case

Take something one of your product teams is currently working on—or has recently been working on—and see if you could use this for the interview. Let's assume you are working for a job board. My questions would be:

- Check out one of the job postings through the eyes of an applicant: What parts are most interesting? What is missing? What would you like to see? (Can they step into someone else's shoes?)

- Now, change perspective. As a product person, please have a look through the different parts of the site and walk us through why you think they are there. Highlight the ones that are particularly interesting for candidates, for the companies searching for somebody, and for our company to earn money with it. (Are they using state-of-the-art product lingo? Can they reverse engineer the product? Can they assume why things are there?)

- Talk about your current goals for this product. What's the current direction/strategy? Ask them to come up with some opportunities they see in this situation. What are their assumptions and solution-ideas, and how would they validate these ideas? (Are they able to come up with something? How are they structuring it? Are they using state-of-the-art methodologies such as story mapping, opportunity solution trees,[84] and so forth? How are they at presenting their work? Are they using storytelling techniques to explain their work? Clear communication? How would this person work with your development teams?)

Sometimes using a company-related case backfires because candidates (especially if you are taking their application down later in the process) have the impression that they are giving you free advice and getting nothing in return. If this happens to you a lot, you might want to come up with a company-independent case. In this case, I'd suggest you look to problems NGOs or public organizations are currently facing and create a case out of this.

Please make sure your PM candidates have sufficient time to prepare their take-home case properly. I always try to send it five days in advance, though three days is okay. Anything less is just rude.

Ideas for the ad-hoc case

When it comes time to do the ad-hoc case during the formal interview, I'll tell the candidate that we're going to spend some time creating a new product on the whiteboard. I'll then say, "In an area you're passionate about, walk me through the steps you would use to come up with a new product to build."

If they don't have an idea, try giving them an idea of your own. I'll say, "You are responsible for coming up with the new version of the website of your local airport. How would you start and what would the site look like?"[85]

---

84   More about those here: Teresa Torres (August 10, 2016). Why This Opportunity Solution Tree is Changing the Way Product Teams Work. Retrieved from https://www.producttalk.org/2016/08/opportunity-solution-tree/
85   This case is something I inherited from my former boss Jason Goldberg. Thanks, Jason.

Some other ideas might include:

- How would you design, position, and sell sunglasses for babies?

- How would you (re)design a grocery store for senior citizens—or introverts?

- How would you redesign your shower?

An airport is a nice case to use because so many user groups with so many different needs must be taken into account—from business travelers to families with kids to the airport and flight staff and more. Is the PM candidate thinking of all of them? Then, ask the main questions for this ad-hoc case:

- Imagine you are the sole owner of this product. You are responsible for getting it launched and successful as soon as possible.

- What product-development process would you use? Can you document the requirements, provide basic wireframes, and talk about your release plan?

Are they using a user-centered approach when they answer? Is there something like *their* preferred process? Do they think in assumptions, experiments, and iterations?

Finally, you can ask some follow-up questions:

- What metrics would you track? Why?

- What business model would you propose for this product?

Is your candidate used to working with metrics? Can they think business and not just product?

Each of these two kinds of cases tells me something different about the candidates:

The take-home case tells me...

- If they are making a real effort to get the job.

- If they are using known frameworks and tools (doesn't matter if they're the latest ones—I just want to see how they structure their work). My checklist usually comprises the PMwheel buckets. If they are talking about buckets 1-6, that's a good sign.

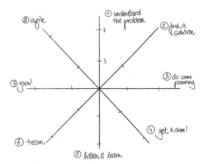

Figure 13-1: The PMwheel can be a helpful reminder to spark questions or take notes during the interview.

- Attention to detail vs. get it done.

- How good their time management skills are. I always say something like, "Please spend approximately two hours on the case." Good candidates indicate in the presentation how long it took them. (One thing: make sure your case isn't too big. If the candidate has to spend eight hours to come up with something solid to present, that's too big of an ask.)

- How good their presentation skills are.

- How they deal with critical questions regarding their proposed solution.

- If they can criticize our current product/solution and if they are able to do it in an adequate way.

In contrast to this, the ad-hoc case tells me...

- How their brain works.

- If they have already built their PM toolbox: Are they putting the user first? Are they working with hypotheses and would they use experiments (user feedback, etc.) to validate them?

- If we can get into the flow of working together. If they won't be working with me directly, I make sure to bring in some colleagues here! (How are they at dealing with other people's ideas?)

Step 5: Conduct a formal interview

So, your shiny new PM candidate has passed the first round of scrutiny—it's now time to schedule a formal interview at your office (or remotely, if that is mainly how your company works). Here's what you should do:

Before you start, be sure to prepare your interview questions and the ad-hoc case with your hiring plan, candidate profile, and PMwheel assessment in mind. Try to find the glint in their eye when their passion is sparked. Talk about your product—the problem it solves, its weaknesses, its potential—and see if that gets your candidate excited. If in doubt, ask about their hobbies or a pet project that they are passionate about. Look for signs of toxic behavior and for fit and alignment with your company values and culture.[86] Look also for signs of the ability to unlearn, that is, to be adaptable.

Should you include the team (developers, designers, HR, etc.) in the interview process? Yes—include the team, but don't obsess about

---

86 A Conscious Rethink (July 24, 2019). 30 Toxic Behaviors That Should Have No Place in Your Life. Retrieved from https://www.aconsciousrethink.com /3865/30-toxic-behaviors-no-place-life/

it. Only include them if they know how to interview people (if they don't know how, then train them accordingly).[87] Don't include too many people in the process.

Now that you have created some questions and decided on two or three interview participants, it's time to reflect on the personality traits you want to look out for. As mentioned in Chapter 4: Define Your Good, I have a set of six PM personality traits I look for in PM candidates during the formal interview:

- Curiosity: This is important because, if you are curious (and I mean the "I want to understand what makes the world go 'round" version of curiosity—not only the job-related, next-career-step curiosity) you are constantly learning, and if you are constantly learning, you can ask better questions and come up with better hypotheses. Both are necessary for stellar product work.

- Emotional intelligence: EQ is a particularly important thing if you want to understand users, convince stakeholders, and work with a team.

- Wants to make an impact: If you are finding all the other personality traits but this one is missing, your PM will never be a really successful PM. They might end up as a decent backlog administrator, but the hunger for making an impact focuses them on real outcomes.

- Intellectual horsepower: The world we are living in is pretty complex, and as a product person, you need to understand enough of it to come up with new ideas and creative solutions for the field your company operates in. This requires a sharp, acute mind.

---

87 You might want to have a look at Kate Leto's book mentioned in Further Reading

- Adaptability: Change is the only constant in life, and PMs need to be comfortable with this fact to be able to quickly adapt to a new situation.[88]

- Nice to spend time with: This one somehow overlaps with the emotional experience trait, but I still think it is important to mention. It's a massive plus if PMs are pleasant creatures and people like them to be around.

As Lea Hickman of SVPG says, "We want to make sure that, especially in product management, you bring people in who can get the best out of the people that are around them and really shine a light on that."[89]

Since we're talking about a formal interview, you'll need to structure the schedule for the interview day to make it as smooth as possible while obtaining the information you need about the candidate to make a good decision. Here's a typical schedule for a new PM hire:

9:15 a.m. Candidate arrives

9:30 a.m. Start the interview session:

- Do a quick intro on People, Product, Processes.

- Start take-home case presentation and ask your questions.

- Start ad-hoc collaborative exercise, ask analytical questions, and test for soft skills.

- If time remains, ask "Tell me about a time when..." questions (e.g., "Tell me about a time when your team has overcome a big dip in their performance/velocity.

88   Lucy King (April 1, 2019). Who Said Change Is the Only Constant in Life? Retrieved from https://medium.com/mindset-matters/who-said-the-only-constant-in-life-is-change-233fd9e27b87

89   Holly Hester-Reilly (May 14, 2019). The Lea Hickman Hypothesis: Product Management Is a Team Sport. Retrieved from https://h2rproductscience.com/ep015-lea-hickman/

How did they achieve this?" or "Tell me about a time you reached a big goal at work. How did you reach it?")

12:00 noon Lunch with two or three peers—you do not participate because you want to know if the team thinks they could work with this person. That's easier for them to figure out if you aren't in the room. Remember: You won't be in the room later, after you make the hire and the team is actually working together.

1:00 p.m. Closing (only you and the candidate)

- Ask if they have any questions.

- Get references if possible. This is not a big thing in all countries.

- Ask what they would consider to be fair compensation.

- Explain the rest of the process and timing.

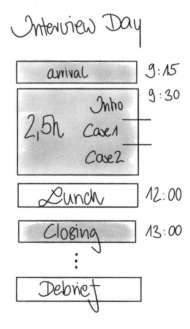

Figure 13-2: PM interview day schedule

The final part of the formal interview is to conduct a debriefing session with your team/HR. Your specific goal is to get feedback—it is not a group discussion or committee decision for hiring (this might be different for holocratic organizations). But team members should be always be able to say, "No way," and put in their veto.

Ask everyone who was involved in the formal interview to put up a hand and show their fingers: thumb up for HIRE, thumb down for NO HIRE, and high five for STRONG HIRE. I suggest you only hire PMs who rate as a STRONG HIRE. Ask people to go through their notes and then share your thoughts on how you would like to proceed.

To make the hiring decision, ask yourself:

- Does this person fit your current team?

- Do they fit your dream team for a year from now?

- What would onboarding look like for them? Any special things to take into account?

- Could I guide, inspire, develop, coach this person?

- Reflect on "Do I have a vision for this person?"

- What will it take to make this person a happy employee for the next 2–5 years?

Decide if you want to consult some of their references. In some industries, you'll need to conduct your final due diligence, particularly to discover if the candidate has any litigation pending.

Finally, make the decision whether or not to make an offer.

Note: Many companies require candidates to take a personality test, then they use the results as a factor in assessing the candidates.

I have consciously chosen not to mention personality tests because, for a variety of reasons, I'm not a fan of them.[90]

Step 6: Make the job offer

Once you've decided to hire a new PM candidate, you'll need to put together a formal, written job offer. (Before you make any job offer, be sure to check with your HR or legal department to ensure you follow your local laws and regulations.) Here's what you should be sure to include:

- Describe their role and responsibilities and what their title will be

- Working hours, remote, flex-hours, home office

- Compensation: salary + bonuses + shares

- Days-off: holidays, mental health days

- Training/development budget

- Social benefits

Send your candidate the offer, then follow up two days later to show your candidate how much you want them to accept it. Make sure they understand how they can have an impact on your products and offer a follow-up chat or lunch meeting (the clever HoP blocks out this time in her calendar). Help them understand your offer in detail—if they are negotiating, that's a good thing! Know your limits. Make sure the only task remaining is updating and signing the contract.

---

90 Merve Emre (September 20, 2018). Five myths about personality tests. Retrieved from https://www.washingtonpost.com/outlook/five-myths/five-myths-about -personality-tests/2018/09/20/3a57a8ee-b78a-11e8-a2c5-3187f427e253_story .html; Martin Luenendonk (October 6, 2019). Personality Tests Are Flawed: Here's What You Really Need to Know. Retrieved from https://www.cleverism.com /personality-tests-are-flawed/

Titles are, of course, important. Keep them as simple as possible and consistent with your company's title hierarchy and structure. Don't mess with titles just to get a certain candidate in the door, and don't tie titles to compensation. This limits your flexibility in upcoming discussions about compensation.

One thing: If your company still uses "Product Owner" as a job title, consider moving away from this. Being a product owner is the product manager's role in a scrum team and just a fraction of what a PM does.[91]

And compensation is also important. I'm personally a fan of fair compensation and *no* bonuses—I believe bonuses kill motivation in the long run.[92] If you are a fan of bonuses, at least be sure to tie them to the success of the PM's product or your company's main KPIs. Don't use personal objectives or activities ("Visit 5 customers next quarter"). Outcomes over outputs!

Further Reading

- Natalie Fratto on why adaptability is important: https://www.strongproductpeople.com/further -readings#chapter-13_1

- The Challenges of Product Manager Incentive Compensation: https://www.strongproductpeople.com /further-readings#chapter-13_2

---

91   If you want to learn more: I like Martin Eriksson's blog post on titles:
     Martin Eriksson (July 9, 2018). Product Management Job Titles and Hierarchy.
     Retrieved from https://www.mindtheproduct.com/product-management-job
     -titles-and-hierarchy/
92   Jurgen Appelo (August 13, 2013). The 6 Rules for Rewards. Retrieved from https://
     svpg.com/the-vp-product-role/https://svpg.com/managing-product-managers/;
     Daniel Pink, *Drive: The Surprising Truth About What Motivates Us,* Riverhead
     Books (2011)

- The Product Science Podcast: Lea Hickman – Product Management Is a Team Sport: https://www.strongproduct people.com/further-readings#chapter-13_3

- Video: Are you a giver or a taker? Adam Grant: https:// www.strongproductpeople.com/further-readings #chapter-13_4

- Tips for hiring PMs:
  - Our 6 Must Reads If You're Hiring a Product Manager: https://www.strongproductpeople.com /further-readings#chapter-13_5
  - How to Hire Great Product Managers by Jackie Bavaro: https://www.strongproductpeople.com /further-readings#chapter-13_6
  - 7 Tips for Hiring a Great Product Manager (and Avoid Hiring a Jaded One) by Shaun Juncal: https://www.strongproductpeople.com/further -readings#chapter-13_7
  - 7 Tips to Hire the Perfect Product Manager by Codrin Arsene: https://www.strongproductpeople .com/further-readings#chapter-13_8
  - How to Hire a Product Manager—the classic essay on the role of product management by Ken Norton: https://www.strongproductpeople.com/further -readings#chapter-13_9
  - Quora: https://www.strongproductpeople.com /further-readings#chapter-13_10

- More ideas for interviewing PMs:
  - Interviewing Product Managers—Questions and tips for interviewing product managers by Brent Tworetzky: https://www.strongproductpeople.com /further-readings#chapter-13_11

- The Ultimate Guide to Product Manager Interview Questions by Andy Jagoe: https://www.strongproductpeople.com/further-readings#chapter-13_12

- Hiring PMs—best practices:
    - Hiring Product Managers: what have we learned from three years of scaling the team by Galina Ryzhenko: https://www.strongproductpeople.com/further-readings#chapter-13_13

- Books:
    - *Hiring Product Managers: Using Product EQ to go beyond culture and skills* by Kate Leto
    - *Emotional Intelligence* by Brandon Goleman

CHAPTER 14

EFFECTIVE ONBOARDING

- The basics of onboarding

- My advice on onboarding

- A time-phased approach to onboarding

Once you have hired your awesome, new PM, you'll need to invest some time in bringing them onboard—and all the things you'll do with them afterward. It's at this point, however, that many product organizations—and the HoPs who run them—fall down. While I don't have statistics specific only to product organizations, here are some key numbers for onboarding in businesses as a whole:

- Organizations with a standard onboarding process experience 50 percent greater new-hire productivity.

- 69 percent of employees are more likely to stay with a company for three years if they experienced great onboarding.

- 22 percent of companies have no formal onboarding program.[93]

As you can see, organizations that properly onboard their new hires experience both higher levels of productivity from those new hires and a clear majority decide to stay with their employer for three or more years. This is clearly a win-win situation for the company, for the customers who get better products, and for the employees (and for the manager who has to juggle all these different balls in the air).

However, there's just one problem. As you can also see, almost one-fifth of companies have no formal onboarding program at all. And in my personal experience with product organizations, after HoPs devote a lot of time to recruiting and hiring great PMs, they often spend precious little time attending to the important task of onboarding them.

This, of course, is a mistake. In some cases, perhaps fatal for the organization and the products they deliver.

The Basics of Onboarding

First, let's make sure we're on the same page. According to the Society for Human Resource Management (SHRM), *onboarding* is "the process of integrating a new employee with a company and its culture, as well as getting a new hire the tools and information needed to become a productive member of the team."[94] When you onboard your new hire well, the end result is a PM who can have a significant impact on your ways of working, your product team, and the product they are responsible for. In the words of Steve Jobs:

---

93   Christine Marino (January 13, 2016). 18 Jaw-Dropping Onboarding Stats You Need to Know. Retrieved from https://www.clickboarding.com/18-jaw-dropping-onboarding-stats-you-need-to-know/

94   Roy Maurer (n.d.) New Employee Onboarding Guide. Retrieved from https://www.shrm.org/resourcesandtools/hr-topics/talent-acquisition/pages/new-employee-onboarding-guide.aspx

*"It makes no sense to hire smart people and
then tell them what to do."*[95]

When you properly onboard your new PMs—a process that takes up
to at least a full quarter, and sometimes longer—you're providing them
with a strong foundation for their future success in your organization.

My Advice on Onboarding

The good news about onboarding is that it doesn't have to be a
supercomplicated process. In fact, my advice on onboarding is actually pretty simple:

- Invest as much time in onboarding your new PM as you
  do in hiring them.

- Make a good first impression: prepare well for their first
  day (access, whom to contact on arrival, hardware, etc.).

- Think about what they need to learn or hear to get their
  "first educated decision" made as quickly as possible.

- Make this a program—don't reinvent the wheel for
  each person joining! (Involve other people such as peer
  product people to be their onboarding buddy.)

Let me explain why this is important. As head of product, you want
to secure the investment you have made on behalf of your organization. Recruiting and hiring product people is a large financial
investment for any business, and once you have them on board, that
investment continues to grow. You don't want to lose this investment
when a promising PM decides to leave—or underperforms—after a
poor onboarding experience.

---

95   Steve Jobs, *Steve Jobs: His Own Words and Wisdom,* Cupertino Silicon Valley
     Press (2011)

In addition, you want to constantly shorten the time to value—represented by the "value-add" zone in the graph below. A good onboarding program will shorten the amount of time it takes to get your new PM up to speed and fully functioning in their new role.

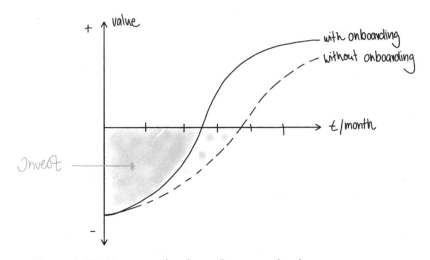

Figure 14-1: Hiring and onboarding somebody is an investment and you want to get to the value-add zone as fast as possible.[96]

Finally, as an HoP, you need to be *human* (a.k.a. not an asshole) and have empathy for your new PM, who is trying to figure out your company and team culture, build new relationships, and master the organizational dos and don'ts. Helping your new hire overcome this awkward time is a deeply human act on your part—it shows them that you care, and it sets the tone for all your future interactions.

I have found that most heads of product do a phenomenal job recruiting and finding the right candidates to fill the pipeline. Hiring in their organizations is often a well-structured process and they have the right rigor around interviewing and deciding who to hire. However, the minute the new PMs show up for their first day of work, the HoP forgets about them—leaving their new PMs to their own devices.

---

96   Michael Watkins, *The First 90 Days: Proven Strategies for Getting Up to Speed Faster and Smarter,* Harvard Business Review Press (2013)

Let me walk you through an onboarding routine that works for me. Please feel free to adapt it to your needs.

A Time-Phased Approach to Onboarding

As I said at the beginning of this chapter, onboarding is a process that can take at least one quarter or more. As time goes on, and your new PM progresses through the onboarding process, he or she will become more proficient, productive, and fully integrated into your team. This process naturally lends itself to a time-phased approach. I suggest that you consider dividing the onboarding process into four parts:

- Day 1
- Week 1
- Month 1
- Quarter 1

Let's consider each of these parts in more detail.

Day 1

The first day of work for your new PM is a very exciting one. As the old saying goes, you only have one chance to make a good first impression, so make sure it's a good one!

At the beginning of your first meeting with your new hire, open your calendar and show them that you've already blocked out meeting times for the two of you going forward. First daily meetings, then every other day, then your usual 1:1 rhythm. Put your new PM in the driver's seat from day one. For example, tell them that they are responsible for picking the main topics for the next week's check-in meeting.

Make sure they get customer exposure as early as possible. Preschedule some exercises for them that get them this exposure, such as spending two or three days in the call center, or answering first-level support questions, or sitting in a usability test, or conducting some initial customer interviews.

Next, introduce them to their onboarding buddy—a coworker who you have designated to help your new PM learn the ropes. Having an onboarding buddy is, I think, key to the ultimate success of your process. This person provides practical guidance (such as, where to go to get a pen and notebook, or where the lunchroom is) and answer easy admin questions (such as, how sick leave works and what the rules are about holidays).

In addition, be sure to talk about your overall expectations for the position. Be superprecise—it's better to do this now than later, when patterns of behavior are already locked in. It's a bit like hiring a personal trainer. The trainer will explain what people usually want, what they can usually achieve, and how much effort they usually need to put into the training if they want to see results. It's not personal at this level—it's information that can highlight traps and pitfalls right away while providing you some general guidelines.

The rest of this first onboarding meeting will be devoted to a discussion of three specific topics: company, communication, and collaboration.

Company

- Review your organization chart and where your PM fits in it.

- Vision, mission, strategy

- Values, culture, codes, dos and don'ts (see Figure 14-2, the culture pyramid)

- The PM's playground: their product, their users, their business case, their team

- Their roles as PM (use the PMwheel assessment as a guide)

- Important peers

Communication

- Tools and rules (e.g., Slack and how people are using it)
- Email (read on to learn more → building efficiency)
- Meetings (read on to learn more → building efficiency)

Collaboration

- Meeting their product development team
- Meeting main stakeholders
- Time management basics for your organization

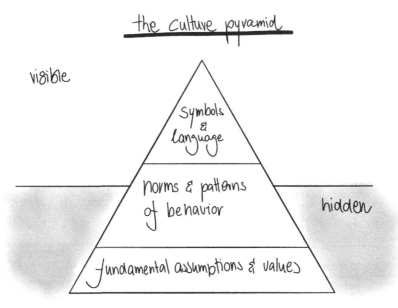

Figure 14-2: Reflect on how you can help them to see/ explore some of the hidden things—the culture pyramid[97]

97   Michael Watkins, *The First 90 Days: Proven Strategies for Getting Up to Speed Faster and Smarter,* Harvard Business Review Press (2013)

Finally, I ask new PMs in a Day 1 meeting to take some work off my desk soon, or if a larger team, to take some work off their colleagues' desks. There is always something small they can start right off with. I also discuss the goal of "first educated decisions made." It's okay to back up most decisions they make with peers or a line manager, but in the right way. They should say something like, "I've learned XYZ and that's why I would go for ABC. Do you have any advice from your side on that?"

What new PMs tend to say when facing a situation/problem is:

- "The team says X, the data says Y, and stakeholders are telling me to do Z. Tell me what to do, boss."

What I *want* new PMs to do is:

1. Describe the situation/problem.

2. Describe solutions.

3. Ask for advice on which solution to pick, or even better, explain what they will do/which solution they've picked.

4. Offer a veto option and advise on deadline (If I am totally against the proposed solution, I can withhold my veto until this deadline.).

Week 1

Throughout the first week, I like to do daily check-ins. Then I'll move to check-ins every other day, and finally to my usual 1:1 rhythm.

You'll cover the same topics with your PM as you did in your Day 1 meeting, however, you'll start going into much greater detail dependent on the experience level of your PM. I suggest adding a deep dive on discovery topics and user-centered design, delivery topics and getting things done and shipped, and a session on personal efficiency.

Here's some additional detail on some topics that I think can make the greatest difference in your PM's first week, along with some more thoughts on onboarding that you can use to foster your first few sessions:

And additionally, for rather junior PMs...

1. Tell them to start with some quality assurance work. Have the PM meet with the team or, if there is a QA person, go sit with them and observe what they are doing.

2. Make sure they get going with some backlog work. Ask them to read some of the specifications—making sure it all makes sense to them—and then starting the usual sprint work.

3. Have them prepare the sprint and estimation meetings, plus go-live stakeholder and release management.

4. Assign them to listen to and learn from user feedback and support tickets.

5. Make sure they wrap their heads around reporting, OKRs, goals, key performance indicators, and how the product is doing.

6. Guide them through doing their first pieces of discovery work.

7. Ask for their first attempt in roadmapping—planning ahead for longer periods of time.

Building efficiency...

During the course of Week 1, coach your new PMs in how to have more effective meetings. We will explore three different meeting types—update, brainstorming, and decision—in Chapter 18: Time Management for Product People.

Foster effective email skills that waste less time while building more effective connections with coworkers and customers.[98] Here are some tips you can offer:

- Pick recipients wisely.

- Subject: Should always say what you expect the other person to do and by when you need an answer.

---

98   This may seem too basic, however, this continues to be a problem in many organizations.

- Open with a management summary on top. This includes a brief summary of the issue or need and your recommendation.

- Then provide full details that the reader can refer to for more information.

In addition, give guidance to your PM on how the company/team uses chats, wikis, email, Slack, and so forth. Talk about response time expectations and communication protocols—the unwritten laws of communication in your organization.

Important aspects of onboarding...

The book, *The First 90 Days*, has some good tips about how to look at onboarding. I like to use it as a kind of checklist for my HoP onboarding responsibilities: Did I help my PMs work on *focused learning* and *effective relationship building*? And did I make sure to help them with other important aspects of the PM's onboarding process, including:

- Making good decisions,[99]

- Building supportive alliances,

- Gaining early wins,

- Creating an informed strategy and vision, and

- Increasing credibility.

If the answer is no, and you did not do enough to help your PMs, think about a good format to talk about this with them, or what insights they should have in this case.

---

99   For more information on how to identify good decisions or supportive alliances, I recommend the book, *The First 90 Days* by Michael Watkins.

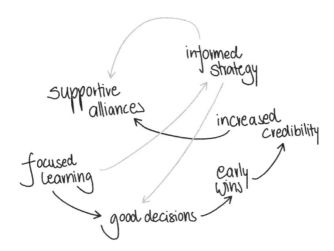

Figure 14-3: Goals for PM onboarding and how they benefit from one another (e.g., focused learning helps to come up with an informed strategy and that helps to form supportive alliances and make good decisions)

Month 1

Now that your new PM has survived their first week, the easiest and most basic questions have been answered, and the PM is now engaged in their job and quickly becoming a productive member of your team. It's time to have your first "how-is-it-going-so-far" session.

Use your Good PM description (or the PMwheel assessment) again throughout the first month to make sure the two of you have established a solid framework for ongoing onboarding discussions. These discussions should focus on the high-level buckets in the following diagram.

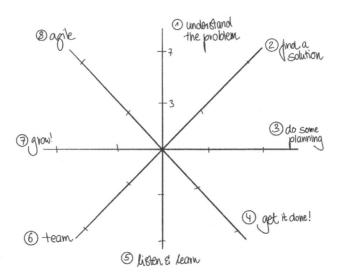

Figure 14-4: Use your PMwheel assessment throughout the first month.

This is your checklist: Do they truly understand the user's problem? Can you help them understand it better? How are they progressing with finding solutions to those user problems? Use the diagram to guide your discussions in your Month 1 meeting.

Be sure to also bring your own feedback to the table. Talk with some of their peers to gather feedback before the meeting. Observe how they work and gather some examples for task-related positive feedback, and helpful, actionable, task-related negative feedback if it exists.[100]

Quarter 1

Hard to believe, but your new PM is already wrapping up their first three months with your organization. It's now the perfect time to reflect on how far they have come. Are they already generating value? Have they become a productive team product manager, or even an effective and efficient product manager? Work through the PMwheel assessment again to foster these kinds of discussions.

---

100 See Chapter 8: Monitoring Performance and Giving Feedback.

While your involvement in the onboarding process has been winding down, your job isn't done yet. Have you thought about what's ahead for this PM—the bigger picture for this person? If not, do it now, and be sure to let them know what you've got in mind for them. They'll gain a greater level of comfort—and engagement in their work—when they know what lies ahead.

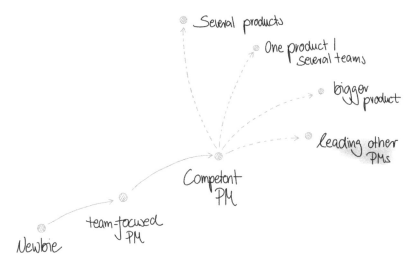

Figure 14-5: Typical PM career progression (not talking titles here)

And if they're not doing well in their PM job? Be sure to address the problem and not ignore it or hope it goes away. It won't. Talk about your expectations again and ask them why they think they're not performing up to them. Set a definite time frame for improvement, and if they aren't able to improve their performance, then you'll need to let them go while the probation period is ongoing.

If you've done your recruiting, hiring, and onboarding right, then chances are you won't have to worry about letting *anyone* go.

Further Reading

- Lessons from My First 90 Days as a Product Manager at a New Company: https://www.strongproductpeople.com /further-readings#chapter-14_1

- How to Spend Your First 90 Days as a New Product Manager: https://www.strongproductpeople.com/further -readings#chapter-14_2

PART IV

DEVELOP YOUR EXISTING PRODUCT TEAM—TRAIN FOR EXCELLENCE

One of the most important jobs of any head of product is developing the skills of the product managers who work for them. In this part, we'll explore the many different skills that you can and should develop within your product team, including such things as creating a product vision and setting goals, engaging in hypothesis-driven product development and experiments, balancing product discovery and product delivery, time management, working with cross-functional product development teams, communication, planning and prioritization, increments and iterations, product evangelization and storytelling, and keeping the senior PMs engaged.

The chapters in this Part do two things: they explain the core concepts *and* the plain basics—not because I think they are new to you. I do this to provide you with a nice summary you can quickly refer to before coaching one of your PMs on the topic—it's a shortcut that will hopefully save you a lot of time. And my hope is that these chapters will fill your mind with little stories, metaphors, helpful illustrations, and just the right amount of information to help your PMs in an even better, more sustainable, long-term way.

CHAPTER 15

HELP YOUR PRODUCT MANAGERS CREATE A PRODUCT VISION AND SET GOALS

- Product vision, strategy, goals, and principles

- The process

- A final note

For some organizations, product vision, strategy, goals, and principles are very scary things—so much so that they avoid creating some or all of them. In some cases, companies find it easier to simply pay an external consultant to create them on their behalf. And they get dropped into a slide deck that managers periodically showcase but that no one in the org actually puts to use.

There's really no reason to fear creating these things—in fact, they are essential elements of any product organization. Why does this fear exist? I believe in great part this is because people think that it's a complicated and difficult process. Let me tell you a story about my visit to a Mind the Product conference in London in September 2014. During a lunch break, I chatted with a fellow attendee who said something that has stuck with me ever since and explains the reason why. He said, "It's all about decision making. These things should help everyone make decisions faster."

Product vision, strategy, goals, and principles provide a framework—the guardrails—for making decisions faster, and I would argue, *better.* This realization provided me with a completely different perspective on the topic. "Creating a framework for better decision making? That's something I can actually do! That doesn't sound too complicated so long as I really focus on that!" This new perspective helped me create my own vision, strategy, goals, and principles documents when my organizational responsibilities called for them.

In addition to making better decisions faster, these elements do several more things. They make decisions *easier* because everyone has a clear focus on what they should be working on. They help you filter the noise, data, and questions you are looking into—or the assumptions you are creating—during discovery and delivery. And they help you pick the next, best action. It's not always about what we will be doing in three years, it's also about what we need to do today—right *now.*

And, whose job is it to come up with these essential elements?

It's the job of a *talented leader,* which in most organizations means *you* as head of product. In empowered product organizations, PMs may also play a role in coming up with these essential elements, and in this case, you might have to coach them on how to do so. That is why I've decided to put this chapter in this part of the book. It is *ONE person* (you or your PM) that needs to take the lead in creating the product vision, strategy, goals and principles—*not* a committee and not a consultant. When they're absent, then the result will be an organizational lack of focus and slow decisions.

Let's consider each of these essential elements in turn.

Vision

The vision you create for your part of an organization is about purpose and meaning, and it's about alignment and an audacious goal. It describes why we get up in the morning and what our contribution looks and feels like. And it's often easier to come up with a mission first to get to a full-fledged vision later. So, let's start there. Consider the example of athletic footwear, apparel, and equipment maker Nike, which adheres to the following mission:

Bring inspiration and innovation to every athlete* in the world.

*If you have a body, you are an athlete.[101]

As you can see, it's crystal clear who Nike serves—athletes—but then the company defines athletes as anyone with a body. So, everyone is ultimately Nike's customer and it's the job of the company's employees to constantly find ways to bring inspiration and innovation to customers. As long as employees do that, then they know they are aligned with Nike's mission.

Once you have your mission, you should start to create the company's product vision. This is a narrative that keeps everyone focused on the customer and explains what we are all hoping to accomplish together.[102]

If you don't know where to start when it comes to creating your product vision, I suggest using the product value pyramid developed by Eric Almquist, John Senior, and Nicholas Bloch at Bain & Company. The pyramid arranges 30 elements of value (such things as "provides hope," "makes money," and "attractiveness") in four categories of needs: social impact, life changing, emotional, and functional.[103] Reflect on which of these values your current product(s) is/are supporting and see if it makes sense to deliver on one or more of the other values as well.

---

101 https://about.nike.com/
102 See Marty Cagan's book *EMPOWERED* for an in-depth discussion about creating a compelling product vision. Also see: https://asana.com/vision for a great example.
103 Eric Almquist, John Senior, and Nicholas Bloch, "The Elements of Value," Harvard Business Review (September 2016). Retrieved from https://hbr.org/2016/09/the-elements-of-value

Strategy

It's great to have a product vision, but eventually we have to make it come true. Strategy provides us with the tools we need to do that. Ideally, strategy will address:

- The current situation we are all in (diagnosis);

- The hard and critical business problems we need to solve (first) to get closer to what we have described as our vision;

- How we might tackle these problems; and

- Some examples of things we therefore no longer will be doing or stop doing immediately.

I'm a big fan of the decision stack idea created by Martin Eriksson and illustrated in Figure 15-1.[104] Working down the stack, at each successive level you ask, "How?" Working up the stack, at each successive level you ask, "Why?"[105]

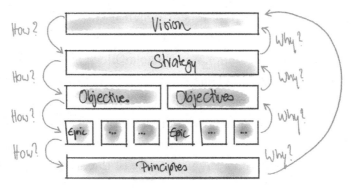

Figure 15-1: Martin Eriksson's decision stack

104 Martin Eriksson (May 22, 2019). The Decision Stack. Retrieved from https://speakerdeck.com/bfgmartin/the-decision-stack?slide=11

105 Also see the book, *Good Strategy Bad Strategy* by Richard Rumelt, referenced later in this section, about making decisions about what we will do, and what we don't do

To get a clearer picture of what needs to be done, I suggest that you reflect on the maturity of your current product(s)—the words in bold—and see if the following list might spark some ideas on where to start shaping your product strategy:

- **Research and development:** Understand the needs of your users and build the minimum viable product needed to meet them.

- **Introduction:** Test and refine your product with a small number of users, increasing resilience ahead of growth.

- **Growth:** Get your product into the hands of as many users as possible, focusing on sales/marketing/support/ communication/training/engagement.

- **Maturity:** Reduce the intensity of investment, incrementally optimizing your operational model and business model.

- **Retirement:** If your value proposition gets weaker and your business model ceases to be viable, it's time to end your product.[106]

In his book, *Good Strategy Bad Strategy*, Richard Rumelt reminds us that:

> *[Good strategy] does not pop out of some "strategic management" tool, matrix, chart, triangle, or fill-in-the-blanks scheme. Instead, a talented leader identifies the one or two critical issues in the situation—the pivot points that can*

---

106 Scott Colfer (November 21, 2019). 5 Product Management Hacks for Product Leaders. Retrieved from https://www.mindtheproduct.com/5-product-management -hacks-for-product-leaders/

*multiply the effectiveness of effort—and then focuses and
concentrates action and resources on them.*[107]

Rumelt's words sum it up quite nicely: coming up with a strategy is
work, and someone (the talented leader!) has to wrap her head around
all the different aspects mentioned above. But this is unavoidable and
of central importance.

Goals

Goals allow everyone to measure progress toward executing the strategy—helping them know that the organization is moving in the right
direction. In a vision/strategy narrative, I personally believe that it's
enough to focus on the 1–3 most important things you want to keep
an eye on. Some organizations use a North Star to focus effort, while
others use objectives and key results (OKRs). Yet others have none of
this, so they need to develop a new set of goals from scratch.

If this is the case in your situation, I strongly suggest that you
consider using KPI trees.[108] They are a great tool for first capturing
the signals you are currently tracking, and then via the hierarchical
concept, fostering discussion about which KPIs everyone should be
looking at. (Be sure to check out my blog post on the topic of KPI
trees.) I also suggest you take a look at the HEART framework proposed
in 2010 by Kerry Rodden, Hilary Hutchinson, and Xin Fu at Google
Research.[109] (See Figure 15-2)

---

107 Richard Rumelt, *Good Strategy Bad Strategy: The Difference and Why It Matters,*
Currency (2011) p. 2
108 We briefly explore the concept in Chapter 16: Hypothesis-Driven Product
Development and Experiments
109 Kerry Rodden (December 2, 2015). How to choose the right UX metrics for your
product. Retrieved from https://library.gv.com/how-to-choose-the-right-ux
-metrics-for-your-product-5f46359ab5be#.9wv83yhj9

HEART	Goals	Signals	Metrics
Happiness			
Engagement			
Adoption			
Retention			
Task Success			

Figure 15-2: The HEART framework

Regardless of which approach you decide to take, try to pick something as specific, measurable, and understandable as possible that is also lined up against the hard problems described in your strategy.

Principles

Product principles are rule-like statements that help people decide what to do, for example: "If in doubt, do this instead of that." Here are some real-world examples:

- "Focus on the user and all else will follow." —Google

- "Job Seekers come first—Recruiters will follow." —Monster

- "Conversion trumps profitability optimization." —Klarna

Principles already exist in every organization, but they often need to be captured and written down. Here's a useful exercise for your product organization: Write down all the product decisions you need to make for two weeks (If your PMs are involved in crafting these principles, then ask them to do the same). Then review these decisions to see if they follow a common pattern.

The Process

Making vision, strategy, goals, and principles happen requires a well-defined process. I suggest the following four-step approach: create it, share it, live up to it, and refine it (illustrated in Figure 15-3). One thing before we start: I assume you are creating the narrative and your PMs are supporting the effort. If your PMs are responsible for coming up with these organizational elements, this still makes a valid checklist for you to coach them through the process.

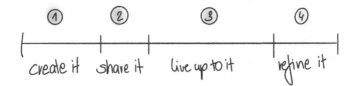

Figure 15-3: A four-step approach to making your vision, strategy, goals and principles happen

1. **Create it.** Creating your narrative—including parts for product vision, strategy, goals, and principles—requires looking to see what is going on around you: the current situation, the diagnosis, and the reality (**what is**). This includes:

- Customers, noncustomers (a.k.a. *humans*), behavior changes;

- Market, industry, competition;

- Trends, macrotrends; and

- Technology.

Envision a brighter future **(what if)** and understand the outcomes you are aiming for:

- Outcomes for the little company planet: Employees need salaries, stakeholders and shareholders have interests, and customers have needs.

- Outcomes for the rest of the planet: That's where the motivational part usually comes from.

Identify the 1–3 critical issues or hard problems you want and need to tackle. Then create a vision and strategy narrative based on the issues or problems you have identified:

- Write it down and carve your story line.[110]

- Make sure your strategy is the *how* to your vision and the *why* for your roadmaps

Make sure that the strategy part is considered very ambitious but feasible under favorable circumstances. You don't want to demotivate people at the beginning of the effort by giving them something that is unattainable. Think back to your current throughput: How many strategically relevant initiatives have seen the light of day and really had an impact on your users?

2. Share it. Sharing what you have created is usually not something people put much thought into, but they should. How do we share it? What are the next meetings we are going to have once we actually create it? How will the rollout happen? How can we make sure that people actually really start to use it in their day-to-day work? And how do we measure if it's actually speeding up our decision-making or accomplishing our other aims?

---

110 See Chapter 23: Product Evangelizing and Storytelling for more ideas.

Here are some suggestions for sharing what you have created:

- Review and test your storyline of why and how using the decision stack model.

- Start with a small audience, refine the story, and try it again to see if it works better.

- Make sure the story brings clarity in the end. As John Maeda puts it:

  Clarity = Transparency + Understanding[111]

  ○ Allow people time to digest it.
  ○ Think about how you could measure it if it sticks.

- Collect some examples of initiatives already going in the right direction, especially for the how/strategy part and for things that would not have made it or will not make it from now on. Invite the people from the initial testing round to come up with their own examples. This bottom-up contribution fosters alignment within the team later on and helps anticipate the questions people will for sure ask after the big announcement.

Finally, announce, explain, and repeat.

- Make a big splash with the announcement, at an all-hands meeting or similar venue.

- Tour the company and explain it to everyone in smaller groups.

- Repeat the core message. Whatever event it might be, start with a one-minute recap, for example: "Because we want

---

111 John Maeda (July 15, 2009). Leaders Should Strive for Clarity, Not Transparency. Retrieved from https://hbr.org/2009/07/leaders-should-strive-for-clar

to achieve this, we know we need to tackle 1, 2, and 3, and this is why we are discussing topic XYZ today."

3. **Live up to it.** You will, of course, need to make sure that you're actually living up to your strategy and your principles. Actions speak louder than words! Focus all your efforts and actions—and encourage your PMs to focus all *their* efforts and actions—toward it. Specifically,

- **Review staffing.** Do the number of people working on a topic reflect our strategy?

- **Ask PMs to review their objectives and goals.** Do they need a tweak?

- **Immediately stop doing things that are not in line with your strategy.** (Sometimes immediately is not possible...but you get the idea.)

- **Use it as a filter for your discoveries.** "Okay, so if this is our strategy, what assumptions are we making and how much risk is there of being wrong? How can we minimize the risk?"

- **Redo task boards or roadmaps or whatever you're using to visualize your now, next, and later.** Check to be sure these items reflect the strategy.

- **Inspire, guide, refocus.** Every meeting should start with at least one sentence on why we are here, referencing your current strategy. It will feel like massive overcommunicating, but that's what it needs! And if there are examples to share how other teams have embraced the strategy, make sure these are shared as well.

- **The golden apple.** There will always be golden apples—hard to resist distractions—that others roll into your path. So, everybody needs to know that the treasure at the end of the road will be much more rewarding than a few golden apples along the way. Tell your people not to focus on the golden apples.[112]

4. Refine it. Find your cadence for periodically reviewing these elements. Every organization is different, so the timing of this review may vary. It should definitely *not* be monthly—that's too frequent. And only once every three to five years is probably not frequent enough. The elements may need just a little adjustment, or the world may change in a big way, and they will require major change. Regardless of when someone says you should update your product vision, strategy, goals, and principles, if you think it's time to update them, then by all means do.

A Final Note

Creating these elements is hard work! And to make it clear once again, when creating your product vision, strategy, goals, and principles, you can't get it done by simply completing a fill-in-the-blank document. Nevertheless, I created the following templates (Figure 15-4) to help you capture the individual aspects you'll need to consider as you create these things. It goes without saying that you have to think about each of the individual aspects in detail.

---

112 Christina Wodtke, *Radical Focus: Achieving Your Most Important Goals with Objectives and Key Results*, Cucina Media (2016) p. 8

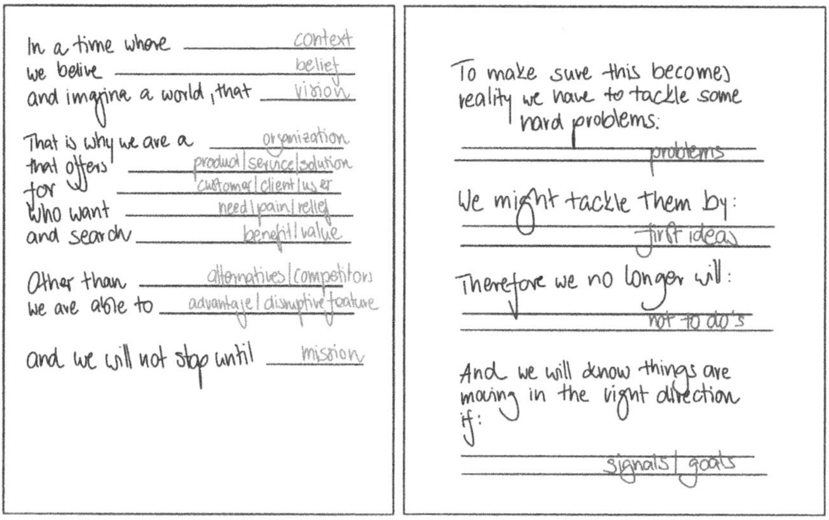

Figure 15-4: A simple framework for creating your product vision, strategy, goals, and principles

After you have created your narrative, ask your PMs or yourself the following questions:

- Does this help us make better decisions sooner?

- Does this help us focus on the critical business problems?

- Does this help us to explain our "not-to-do" list?

- Does this help everyone understand where we are headed?

- Does this give us a purpose and a meaning?

If you answered no to any of these questions, then you know you have more work to do.

Keep in mind that your product vision, strategy, goals, and principles don't have to be packaged in a shiny slide deck. In most cases, a 4-6-page narrative that addresses these elements is all you need. And it's not necessary to stick them to every wall in the office. As long as people understand and apply them in their day-to-day decision-making, that's good enough.

Remember: no matter how well you have presented them, these essential elements need constant repetition. People need to see that all your efforts and actions are aligned with your product vision, your strategy, your goals, and your principles. Ensure that they are.

Further Reading

- Marty Cagan on product strategy: https://www.strong productpeople.com/further-readings#chapter-15_1

- Podcast on product vision by Hope Gurion: https://www .strongproductpeople.com/further-readings#chapter-15_2

- A strong example for an inspiring KPI—Tristan Harris's TED talk and the couchsurfing example: https://www .strongproductpeople.com/further-readings#chapter-15_3 (Go to minute 8:30 if you just want to hear the example)

- An alternative approach to KPI trees by Jim Morris: Make data-driven decisions by turning your vision into a math equation: https://www.strongproductpeople.com /further-readings#chapter-15_4

- A great resource if you want to learn more about Strategy: https://www.strongproductpeople.com/further -readings#chapter-15_5

- Helpful framework for goal setting—Google's HEART framework:
  - https://www.strongproductpeople.com/further -readings#chapter-15_6
    Or a bit more visual—Kerry Rodden's Medium post:
  - https://www.strongproductpeople.com/further -readings#chapter-15_7

- On product principles:
  - Applying Product Principles to Guide Better Product Decisions – Nir Gazit https://www.strong productpeople.com/further-readings#chapter-15_8
  - How to Define Your Product Principles – ProductPlan https://www.strongproductpeople .com/further-readings#chapter-15_9
  - We Don't Sell Saddles Here – Stewart Butterfield https://www.strongproductpeople.com/further -readings#chapter-15_10

- Books:
  - *Good Strategy Bad Strategy* by Richard Rumelt
  - *The Art of Action* by Stephen Bungay
  - *The Art of War* by Sun Tzu
  - *INSPIRED* by Marty Cagan
  - *Turn the Ship Around!* by L David Marquet
  - *Product Leadership* by Richard Banfield, Martin Eriksson, and Nate Walkingshaw
  - *Drive* by Daniel Pink

CHAPTER 16

HYPOTHESIS-DRIVEN PRODUCT DEVELOPMENT AND EXPERIMENTS

- Understanding discovery as HoP

- Getting the discovery basics right

- Helping PMs understand core concepts

- Helping PMs refine their toolset

If you can't confidently state why people are going to use your product, who those individuals are, what makes your product stand out from the crowd, and why it's worthwhile for your business to develop and provide the product, then you are not in a position to build the actual solution.

—Roman Pichler[113]

I have a confession to make. Despite the title at the top of this page, this is primarily a chapter about product discovery. "So, Petra,"

---

113 Roman Pichler (January 9, 2018). Product Discovery Tips. Retrieved from https://www.romanpichler.com/blog/product-discovery-tips/

you might ask, "why is this chapter not called Product Discovery?" The reason why it's not is because the term *product discovery* is so widely used that everyone thinks they know what it's all about and that they're already doing a good job at it. Which might lead readers like you to skip right over this chapter.

I don't want you to be tempted to skip this chapter. Instead, I want you to read about some great concepts you can discuss with your product managers to get better at minimizing the risk of building the wrong thing in a really beautiful way.

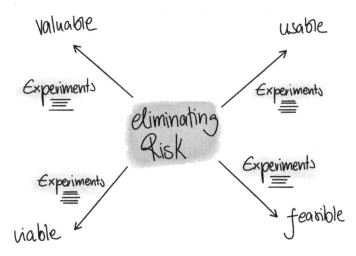

Figure 16-1: The four main risks you want to minimize: Building something that has no value, is hard to use, you are not able to build or ship it, or it doesn't work for the various aspects of your business.

I'm pretty sure you know a lot about product discovery and that your product team tries to put the user in the center of everything they do. Teams routinely conduct user interviews, usability tests, and A/B tests. These are things that most companies have adopted these days. But do all these things play well together in your own organization? Is it a well-choreographed dance where everybody knows why they are doing what they are doing, and when they need to do it? And what is your next goal for improving your discovery capabilities?

My goal in this chapter is to provide you with what you need to know to implement a state-of-the-art approach to discovery. First, I will be sure that you as head of product understand what product discovery is. Second, I will provide you with some basics you need to get right for this hypothesis-driven approach to product discovery to work. Third, I will explain what you need to know to help your product managers understand *some* of the core concepts of product discovery.[114] And finally, we will explore how you can help your product managers define or refine their own toolsets, depending on the extent of their experience and their career level—junior, senior, or somewhere in between.

Understanding Discovery as a Head of Product

As we consider the topic of hypothesis-driven product development or product discovery, it's first useful to note that it's difficult to showcase stellar company examples of this process. First, most companies shy away from sharing the results of their product discoveries. And second, it's superhard to follow the process: what companies had as a hypothesis, why they had this hypothesis, the assumptions behind it, and how they validated it. Without a great example, it's not easy to point you in the right direction.[115]

So, what to do?

As it turned out, the recent coronavirus (COVID-19) crisis provides us with a great example of how discovery has been done on a really global scale, and it's one that we can all resonate with. We all watched the news, checked the dashboards, and became hobby virologists. We've all seen how scientists are making hypotheses and experimenting the

---

114 I won't attempt to address all of the core concepts of product discovery in this chapter. If you need more depth on the topic, then there are many books on product discovery for you to explore.

115 Teresa Torres did a great job explaining what good product discovery looks like in her keynote at the Productized Conference 2016: https://www.youtube.com /watch?v=l7-5x0ra2tc

hell out of them in no time. Let's use this timely example to better understand the discovery process.

There are five key factors that make the coronavirus global pandemic a good example for real product discovery:

- **A real problem and a shared goal.** COVID-19 kills people and is spreading rapidly—let's minimize the number of deaths without also killing the economy.

- **A strategy.** This strategy will be used as a filter by everyone creating ideas and working on solutions. The first strategy for dealing with COVID-19 is "flatten the curve."

- **Cross-functional teams.** These teams—comprised of politicians, physicians, virologists, scientists, economists, psychologists, and others—are ready to figure things out.

- **Data the teams can work with.** This includes tracking of many data points without knowing in the beginning which will end up on public dashboards and which will be the main KPIs.[116]

- **A sense of urgency.** Everyone wants to run experiments quickly to learn how COVID-19 acts and is spread through the human population, which people are most vulnerable, possible cures and vaccines, and so forth to learn how to address the problem.

Let's consider each of these factors in turn.

---

116 See the Our World in Data site: https://ourworldindata.org/

A real problem and a shared goal

To address the coronavirus crisis, scientists—and to some extent, politicians—are taking a hypothesis-driven approach to try to solve the problem. And, as I'm sure you know, there are many different aspects to the problem. There is the actual virus itself—can it be killed, can a vaccine be developed, can it be contained or slowed in some way? Then there are the social aspects: How can people avoid being exposed to coronavirus in the first place? What should they do if they become ill? Or if a loved one becomes ill? There is the overburdened medical establishment to consider, and the impact on businesses and travel and so many other aspects of our lives.

In any case, these different people who are trying to resolve these issues and many others are making observations of the world around them, and they have assumptions. They then combine these observations and assumptions to create a rock-solid hypothesis, which they try to validate or invalidate. There is a real problem: COVID-19 kills people and it is spreading rapidly. And there is a shared goal—to minimize the number of deaths and the economic impact of this crisis. This is the balance that everyone is trying to find. It's not so much about too many people getting infected, it's more about finding ways to prevent people from being killed by the virus or suffering long-term from the destructive effect of COVID-19 on their bodies.

A strategy

You've got a real problem and a shared goal, so next there is a strategy for how everyone should look at this shared problem. The first strategy that emerged in response to the COVID-19 crisis was to "flatten the curve"—to reduce the rate at which new infections are emerging and deaths are increasing. Having a strategy like this helps you to think about which initiatives would be helpful for flattening the curve and should be put in place now, and which are maybe not so helpful and should be discarded. And why do we want to flatten the curve? Because we want to buy ourselves more time to figure things out, for example, to find a vaccine that will be effective in preventing further infections or to prepare the hospitals for a large influx of patients. The strategy is really useful as a filter. If an initiative is not flattening the curve, and it's not buying us more time, then it's probably not something we want to look into right now.

Cross-functional teams

The next step is to enlist the help of cross-functional teams all around the globe ready to figure things out. These teams consist of people of different kinds of expertise coming together to solve the problem. For example, there might be psychologists who know how to spread the news so that people don't panic. And there might also be politicians and physicians and virologists and others who work together to figure out what the best approach is and what are the best activities and steps to be taken.

Data the teams can work with

And then there is data—a lot of data. The team members, along with most of the people on this planet, can go online to look at it, work with it, and make their own assumptions based on it. If you are looking at dashboards and graphs, however, be aware of the story behind the data—you can never know all the mechanics that led to its creation. For example, German laboratories are not testing at full speed on weekends. So, it is expected to see in charts of new confirmed cases of COVID-19 in Germany that there is a dip in reported cases on Saturday and Sunday, and a rise Monday through Thursday.

If you look at the data for the number of people who have died due to COVID-19 in Europe in the early stage of the pandemic, you might ask the question: Why are more people dying in Spain and France than in Germany? To answer this question, we might make some assumptions:

- Germany is testing more and so people who are infected get their treatment earlier in the infection's course.

- Germany is testing more so the number of unknown cases is higher in Spain and France.

- The number of hospital beds, especially intensive care beds, has an impact on lethality of the virus.

- Social systems influence how the virus is spread, for example, government-mandated paid sick leave makes it easier to go in quarantine for two full weeks.

Are any of these assumptions true? No one knows for sure until they are tested with experiments.

A sense of urgency

Eventually, a sense of urgency develops—to deal with the problem, scientists and others must start their experiments, and they must start them *now*. One very large experiment that is being tried is the lockdown—legally mandating that people stay in their homes except for certain narrow exceptions such as going out to purchase groceries or to pick up medications at a pharmacy. In the case of this experiment, nobody really knows what the impact will be—there was no scientific research proving that lockdowns help. As an experiment, however, the risk was low, the probability high, and initial data was promising, so governments (some more quickly than others) asked us to #stayhome.

What we have observed through the COVID-19 global pandemic is a world in full-speed discovery. No one knew where this would all end, but there were things that could be done. Many initiatives were started in parallel: more hospital beds, more ventilators, more restrictive rules for social contact, more people working on testing, more people working on finding a vaccine, more companies allowing employees to work from home, more homeschooling, more food delivery, and so on.

And at the same time, everyone is formulating new assumptions. Toilet paper is sold out—either because people are hoarding it or because people are at home all the time and just need more of it! Discovery is a messy process. There are many initiatives happening in parallel all around the globe, and this is exactly how it is when you do product discovery in your company. Many teams are running many experiments in parallel, and it may look like total chaos from the outside. But as long as teams know what they they're doing, this is perfectly fine.

When it comes to experiments, there are always some easy-to-implement things you can do to gain knowledge, and some harder ones. It was kind of easy to require people to stay home. It sounds like a massive thing, but at first, it's as simple as a governmental organization simply telling people to just stay home. They issue an order, publicize it through news organizations—newspapers, television, radio, online—and explain to people why it's important that they stay home. They may later also implement fines and other incentives to keep people in their homes, but as a first attempt, telling them to do so might be enough. And there are other initiatives that are way harder to nail, for example, to discover a vaccine for the coronavirus. The same applies with experiments run by your product teams, and it is, therefore, important that every PM is empowered to find creative ways to validate their hypotheses.

There is no global product lead or project lead telling people what to do. It's either a game of high autonomy or high alignment. Everyone is aligned because of the problem, the shared goal, and the strategy. Coronavirus is a real threat to all of us. That's where the alignment comes from.

But there is also a lot of autonomy—*how* these cross-functional teams work together to figure things out. There was never more autonomy of teams forming and spending money on finding the next big vaccine than there is now. These teams are reallocating money, people, and other resources to the most important initiatives. Everyone is focused on learning as fast as possible and on really driving outcomes, which are important ingredients of great hypothesis-driven product discovery. It should be focused on learning as fast as you can, and the outcome should be as good as possible. To accomplish this, you use the best tools and the best frameworks you have available to you. And these are usually the ones that you already know. Scientists tend to use the exact same procedures that they have used for decades.

They used it on different viruses before this one because they are familiar with these ways of working. If you want to change tools and frameworks and methods now, then it's to ones that help you learn faster about what it is you want to look into. The focus is on learning and outcomes, and at the heart of all of this is a scientific approach known as the *hypothesis-driven* approach.

Ultimately, that's what discovery is all about: Coming up with assumptions and validating them to maximize value for our users/customers and impact for our company.

The Basics You Need to Get Right

If you want your product development teams to work in a hypothesis-driven way, you need to make sure that there is a shared goal and a strategy that can be used as a filter. You need to make sure you have the right people on board who like to work in your cross-functional teams. They need to get some time to really work on this stuff.

You need to make sure that your company values this culture of experimentation even if it's a messy process. And this is mainly your job as head of product too. So, really reflect—is this in place? And if some of these ingredients are missing, you should focus on getting them in place before you ask all your product managers to work in this hypothesis-driven world.

As our COVID-19 discovery example shows, you need some basics for your discovery process to be effective, and it's your job to be sure these things are in place. This doesn't necessarily mean that you have to do it yourself, but you do have to make sure *somebody* is doing it. In short, you need in place:

- A shared goal,
- A strategy,

- The right people, and

- A culture that allows experimentation and time to experiment.

Some Core Concepts of Product Discovery

Let's have a look into some of the core concepts of product discovery. I find these core concepts superhelpful when I'm coaching PMs. Most of them have done some discovery work already but have not thought that much about the process itself, or about how to get better product discovery. And, as you know, there is always room for improvement.

The hypothesis-driven approach

A hypothesis always starts with an observation and some data points. You next create assumptions and you then prioritize them because some assumptions can be more devastating to your company if they are not true. And then there are ones that, maybe it's annoying if they're not true, but it would not have that big of an impact on your organization. This risk assessment is one part of prioritization of your product discovery.

One thing that has a massive impact in most of the companies I see is to *really* work with your assumptions. Make them explicit. Write them down. Stick them on a wall. Prioritize them and then create proper hypothesis statements out of them and see what you can do to either validate or invalidate your hypotheses. This sounds like a massive process but that's not how it should be. Do it in small chunks! What are your current assumptions, which ones are the most promising ones, how will you get some data to see if you are right and then go build it if data says yes? If the data says no, then refine your hypothesis or move on to the next one.

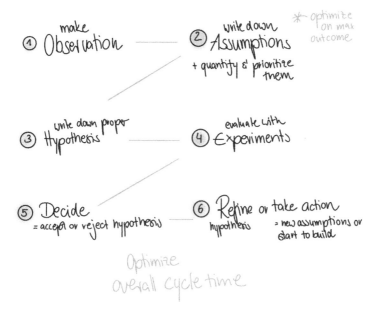

Figure 16-2: The hypothesis-driven approach and what to optimize for once it's in place

Prioritize assumptions

Laura Klein has created a framework I use a lot to discuss which assumptions are the most promising ones and which ones need a lot of experimentation, research, and learning before we know if it's a good idea and if we want to continue working on it.[117] Here are the four steps of the framework:

Step 1: Write down all your current assumptions.

Step 2: Cluster them in three categories.

- Problem assumptions (about the user). As a <u>lazy</u> parent, I need <u>monthly</u> diaper delivery to <u>spend less time</u> shopping.

---

117 Laura Klein, Identify and Validate Your Riskiest Assumptions, LSC14 https://www
    .youtube.com/watch?v=gbArObiU1Y0

- Solution (about how we are solving it). We assume a platform offering a diaper subscription and delivering the diapers to a user's doorstep will solve the problem.

- Implementation (ask: What do I have to do? Do I have to do it?). We can source diapers at a low cost. We can negotiate good shipping deals with a major carrier.

Step 3: Put them on a scale

- How devastating is it if the assumption is wrong? Or is it just annoying?

- How likely is it that you are spot on with your assumption? Or is there a lot of uncertainty and you know too little to say it is likely to be true?

Step 4: What to test? Use the graph in Figure 16-3 to decide which assumptions to test and which to discard.

- It's pretty obvious that you should invest more time and resources to learn more about the devastating assumptions you don't know a lot about (indicated by (1) in the graph below).

- And you should reflect on the uncertain/annoying ones as well: If they show promise for great potential, maybe just give it a go. If they don't have that much potential, then just kill them. And last but not least, reflect on the devastating but most likely to be true assumptions. Discuss how much risk you are willing to take—maybe it's better to be safe than sorry? In this case, you should do some experiments for the assumptions indicated by (2) in the following graph.

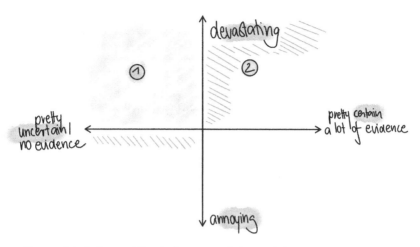

Figure 16-3: Laura Klein's framework for validating assumptions

Hopefully you are trashing some of your ideas. Others will need refinement while others really look promising and then you start to take action—you start the development phase.

Writing hypothesis statements

Now is the time to write some proper hypothesis statements. This will help your PMs and their teams agree on how to measure impact, when to stop research, and when to make a decision and go to the next step. In the same way that there are three kinds of assumptions (problem, solution, and implementation), there are also three kinds of hypothesis statements, focused on problem validation (valuable), solution validation (viable and usable), and implementation validation (feasible). Here is my template for each type:

We believe that **this problem/challenge** exists for this persona and solving it will result in... (customer behavior and company gain). We will know this to be true if...

We believe that **this solution** (to validated problem X persona Y is having) will generate value for persona Y. We will know this to be true if...

We believe **this implementation** of solution A for persona Y will deliver the value we want.

We will know this to be true if...

Getting the right idea versus getting the idea right.

Another mental model I really like when talking to my PMs about product discovery is IDEO's version of the double diamond, illustrated in Figure 16-4.[118]

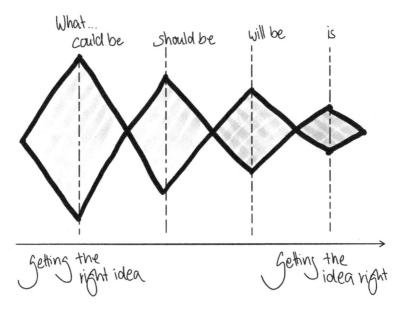

Figure 16-4: IDEO's version of the double-diamond mental model

This model helps to understand the difference between exploring the problem space (getting the right idea) and the solution space (getting the idea right) and it explains these two phases of diverging (going

---

118 Mike Peng (n.d.) To Unlock Innovation, Guide Your Team Through Creative Collaboration. Retrieved from https://www.ideou.com/blogs/inspiration/to -unlock-innovation-guide-your-team-through-creative-collaboration; There are others you can use as well, such as: Dan Nessler (2016) How to apply a design thinking, HCD, UX or any creative process from scratch. Retrieved from https:// medium.com/digital-experience-design/how-to-apply-a-design-thinking-hcd-ux -or-any-creative-process-from-scratch-b8786efbf812

broad) and converging (narrowing down). And the what could be, what should be, what will be is supernice to use in 1:1s. "Tell me where in your discovery process are you for idea XYZ?" This model illustrates early-stage discovery versus late-stage discovery and it also helps to explain the process to executives.

Don't base decisions on one single experiment/data point

A lot of companies I see tend to run just one A/B test, and then they will base their decision on this one A/B test. Or they run three user interviews, and then all the decisions for the next three months are based on these three interviews.[119] This is not the right way to go. I like how Henrik Kniberg once put it: You have to find some data that supports your decision, a bit of user feedback, and you have to listen to your gut feeling. If all three of these things say go, then just go ahead. If two say go, then it's a strong signal. And if only one supports your point of view, then do some more research.[120]

The gut feeling part is something I want to add a few more words to: It takes time to actually to build up this gut feeling in a PM or in a product development team. Every bit they learn about their customers, the company, and the world helps building this gut feel. And this is why you should *not* outsource your discovery work. If you do so, someone else—someone who might not even care at all about your product—is learning things you will need in the future.

Beware of the waterfall

Product discovery must be handled like modern product development. Development teams went from burning software on CD to releasing new stuff twice a year, once a month, once a week, daily, continuously. And this is how discovery should he handled: Use the

---

119 https://www.nngroup.com/articles/why-you-only-need-to-test-with-5-users/

120 James Gadsby Peet (October 25, 2019). Minimise the Gap Between Maker and User by Henrik Kniberg. Retrieved from https://www.mindtheproduct.com /minimise-the-gap-between-maker-and-user-by-henrik-kniberg/

rock, pebbles, sand time-management framework in Chapter 18: Time Management for Product People to create a superlightweight process for sand while you want to do more discovery work for the rocks and for the "dangerous" pebbles.[121] And have a lean process in place for your pebbles.

Slice the big discoveries so that you are constantly generating insights and can make your first decisions. Like with our coronavirus example, you can't wait until you see the whole picture to take action. You start working on the things you have enough evidence about—things you know are valuable, usable, feasible, and viable.

Or, as Marty Cagan says, it's a dual-track thing—discovery and delivery are always on, always making progress, always shipping, always learning.[122]

Outcome and learning faster

People should always focus on, are we learning fast enough in our discoveries or should we tweak our discovery toolset so that we learn faster? And are we optimizing for outcomes, that is, are we making sure that we are not discovering just for the sake of discovery? Ask your PMs in your 1:1s how they make sure that the next few discovery efforts are generating more outcome (for users and company) than the ones before. Ask: "Is there a way to make sure you are maximizing outcome in your discovery process?" And how are they making sure to learn faster?

Good answers include:

- We will be faster because our gut feeling is building with everything we learn.

---

121 This framework divides tasks by size: very large ones (rocks), smaller ones (pebbles), and very small ones (sand) and prescribes the order in which they should be approached

122 Marty Cagan (September 17, 2012). Dual-Track Agile. Retrieved from https://svpg.com/dual-track-agile/

- We will be faster because we have a proven process and tools and frameworks we know well.

- We will be faster because we are going to try a new framework that looks superpromising and will make us faster.

Helping Your PMs Refine Their Own Toolsets

There are many different approaches for doing product discovery, and some are naturally better than others. So, it's important for you as head of product to take time to help your PMs add the right tools to their toolset and learn how to use them appropriately and well. Here are some of the most important:

How to work with data

One particularly important tool for your PMs is how to work with data. I suggest introducing the North Star metric, the concept of KPI trees, and superimportant is desk research. In my experience, a lot of people are not doing desk research at all. But why not go and just see the data that is already out there and that is related to your topic?

One thing you can do as HoP is to find the *one* North Star metric the entire company can use to align all their efforts. And no, revenue is not it! It's a metric that reflects the point in time when you are actually delivering the promised value to your customers. Many good articles are written on how to find your company-wide North Star metric, so I leave it to you to dive a bit deeper on this.[123]

KPI trees are a powerful tool that brings about transparency, alignment, and focus. They aren't rocket science—they are simply a way to visualize the hierarchy of the things you are tracking and are optimizing for. And they can help you understand which of the things you are tracking and optimizing for a leading or lagging indicator. You put your North Star metric—your major KPI—on top of the tree.

---

123 See this chapter's Further Reading for some good places to start

Then you ask the question: "Which metric is directly influencing our North Star?" Write it down, then think about whether it is a proven connection and if it is really driving the North Star. If the answer is yes, then draw a solid line from the metric to the North Star. If the answer is no, then draw a dotted line. Continue in this way until all the things you are tracking are integrated into the tree. Here's an example:

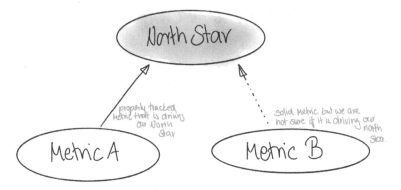

Figure 16-5: A supersimple KPI tree

I'm often asked by HoPs how they can help their PMs come up with new ideas and assumptions. How do they find these big problems that need to be solved, and how can they come up with innovative solutions to those problems? My short answer is always: "Tell them to do some desk research: find some statistics, studies, and so forth."

If they use some of their time to learn a thing or two about what competitors do, about current trends of the industry, about the big macrotrends, and if they generally know how to find data on specific user clusters (how many teachers, how many pensioners, etc.) they will be in a good position to get creative in the diverging phases of product discovery. They will see patterns and they will come up with new assumptions.

If someone on your team knows how to use data in a good way to tell stories, foster decisions, and come up with assumptions, ask them to educate the rest of your team.

Interview skills

Everyone on a product development team should know how to conduct an interview. No matter whether it's a stakeholder or user interview they are planning, there are many dos and don'ts. Fortunately, some very smart people have summarized these dos and don'ts in articles and books.[124] My short summary is this: Interviews are *the* greatest source of insights if done right. But if you don't know how to interview well, the insights from the interviews will make your team bark up the wrong tree!

Knowledge about humans

Let me briefly mention some concepts here that are helpful in the product development context.

If a team is in the "getting the right idea" phase of product discovery, the value pyramid can help them find a good problem to solve.[125] And it helps if they (or the PM and the designer at least) know a bit about what motivates people. This helps to answer: "But why would they?!" For example, you want to create another job board on your platform, but why would companies use it?

The answer to why someone would use your new product is that it provides value. According to the value pyramid, products and services deliver fundamental elements of value that address four kinds of needs: functional, emotional, life changing, and social impact. In general, the more elements provided to customers, the greater their loyalty and the higher the company's sustained revenue growth.

It helps to know the basics of behavioral economics[126] or how people form habits, and it helps to know basic concepts such as those in the

---

124 See this chapter's Further Reading for some selected articles and one book for your review
125 Eric Almquist, John Senior, and Nicholas Bloch, "The Elements of Value," Harvard Business Review (September 2016). Retrieved from https://hbr.org/2016/09/the -elements-of-value
126 (n.d.) Behavioral economics. Retrieved from https://en.wikipedia.org/wiki /Behavioral_economics

book *The Paradox of Choice* by Barry Schwartz, where he talks about the fact that the more options you have, the harder it is to decide and decide well. In addition, the more options you have, the less happy you will be, no matter what you decide on.[127] Understanding these ideas is helpful when the team starts to think about solutions (for example, how many navigation items, how many items are we showing on a product listings page, and so on). And throughout the discovery process, everybody involved should be aware of their biases.[128] You have to constantly work against them.

Knowledge about digital products and how to make money

Another important piece of knowledge is about different kinds of business models and what their main drivers are, including SaaS, e-commerce, advertising, platform subscriptions, and so on. All these models are fundamentally different.[129] And reflecting on what this means for your business can spark new ideas (problem space) and lead to innovative solutions (solution space). Maybe you could solve a bigger customer problem if you change your business model or if you decide to add another business to your existing one. Content providers often sell their content and sell advertising space to enterprises, just to mention one example.

It might sound shocking, but it's not uncommon that, when I draw this funnel in one of my first sessions with a product team, they (a) have never seen something like this (b) they have no clue where to get the data from to add numbers to each step of the funnel, and (c) when starting to collect these numbers, they figure out that nobody ever tried to get that much visibility. So please make sure your PMs know

127 Barry Schwartz, *The Paradox of Choice: Why More Is Less,* Ecco (2004)
128 Cognitive bias cheat sheet https://medium.com/better-humans/cognitive-bias-cheat-sheet-55a472476b18
129 See this chapter's Further Reading for some selected articles on online business models

what a funnel is and how to optimize its throughput or even how to apply growth-hacking methodologies.[130]

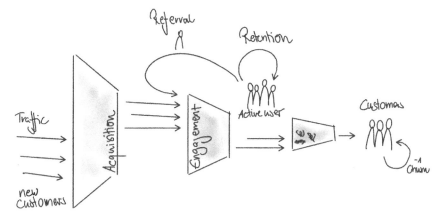

Figure 16-6: Using a funnel to visualize how new customers are acquired

Types of experiments and when to use which type

There are countless types of experiments that a PM can initiate. Some give you a hint that your hypothesis is correct (individual user interviews), while others provide strong evidence (fake door testing). Some are complicated to set up (really solid A/B tests), some simply take time to prepare (a usability test with a prototype), and some are set up in no time at all. Since there is a lot of good literature about this, I don't want to waste too many words on the topic. I recommend that you have your PMs read the following books (and if you haven't yet read them yourself, please be sure that you do):

- *Testing Business Ideas* by David Bland and Alex Osterwalder

- *The Lean Startup* by Eric Ries

- *Sprint* by Jake Knapp

---

130 Sean Ellis and Morgan Brown, *Hacking Growth: How Today's Fastest-Growing Companies Drive Breakout Success,* Currency (2017)

Encourage them to try some of the experiments described in these books. And make sure that your organization has a culture of learning and experimentation!

Ways to document and share insights and results

This is what most people are obsessed with: methodologies and frameworks.

And if your product team still argues about which ones are the best to get their work done, you need to make sure they understand the core concepts of discovery. It's never about the methodology. If story maps are a great tool for one of your PMs,[131] and all the others are using the jobs to be done (JTBD) framework,[132] that's fine. It's all about learning as fast as possible while getting the value to the customer, and to do this they have to share the insights of their product discovery work with many people.

So, no need for a one-size-fits-all solution. As long as they can show/talk about their customer segments—what they know about them, what their assumptions are (personas could be helpful), the problems these people might be or are having (some use story maps for that, others JTBD), and the potential solutions (that might be a video or a vision type)—then you are all good.

Ways to plan and navigate your discovery

Some of the frameworks I've already mentioned can help to navigate the discovery process as well. Story maps are often used to document what users need and—usually by color coding each individual story item—when the team will start to look into this a bit more.

Another great methodology to use is Teresa Torres's opportunity solutions trees—a visual representation of the overall goal, the opportunity hypothesis everyone has, the various potential solutions that

---

131 Jeff Patton with Peter Economy, *User Story Mapping,* O'Reilly Media (2014)
132 Anthony Ulwick, *Jobs to Be Done: Theory to Practice,* Idea Bite Press (2016)

are on the table, and the experiments a team wants to conduct to gain enough evidence to start or stop working on one of these opportunities. It's the perfect discovery roadmap, if you would like to put it that way.

And I always find it necessary to have some kind of a task board that shows the status and progress of all discovery efforts. But that's a topic we'll explore in detail in the next chapter.

Further Reading

- Hypothesis-driven product development
  - Sylvia Lai—5 steps to a hypothesis-driven design process https://www.strongproductpeople.com /further-readings#chapter-16_1
  - Falsification—Karl Popper https://www.strong productpeople.com/further-readings#chapter-16_2
  - Fearless Product Leadership podcast https://www .strongproductpeople.com/further-readings #chapter-16_3

- How to find your company-wide North Star metric
  - What is a North Star Metric by Ward van Gasteren https://www.strongproductpeople.com/further -readings#chapter-16_4
  - Every Product Needs a North Star Metric by Sandhya Hegde https://www.strongproductpeople .com/further-readings#chapter-16_5
  - What is a North Star metric? – Mixpanel https://www.strongproductpeople.com/further -readings#chapter-16_6

- Leading and lagging indicators
  - KPI Library: https://www.strongproductpeople .com/further-readings#chapter-16_7
  - The Business of IT Blog: https://www.strongproduct people.com/further-readings#chapter-16_8

- How to conduct an interview
  - 6 Tips for Better User Interviews – Veronica Cámara https://www.strongproductpeople.com/further-readings#chapter-16_9
  - Why Product Trios Should Interview Customers Together by Teresa Torres https://www.strongproductpeople.com/further-readings#chapter-16_10
  - Why You Are Asking the Wrong Customer Interview Questions by Teresa Torres https://www.strongproductpeople.com/further-readings#chapter-16_11
  - Conducting User Interviews: How to do it Right by Nick Babich https://www.strongproductpeople.com/further-readings#chapter-16_12

- Online business models
  - Harvard Business Review – Making Money With Digital Business Models https://www.strongproductpeople.com/further-readings#chapter-16_13
  - The 9 types of online business models by Boris Veldhuijzen van Zanten https://www.strongproductpeople.com/further-readings#chapter-16_14
  - The 11 Most Popular Online Business Models Today by Andrej Ilisin https://www.strongproductpeople.com/further-readings#chapter-16_15

- Books:
  - *The Lean Startup* by Eric Ries http://theleanstartup.com/
  - *Predictably Irrational* by Dan Ariely
  - *The Art of Thinking Clearly* by Rolf Dobelli

- ○ *Testing Business Ideas* by David Bland and Alex Osterwalder
- ○ *Interviewing Users* by Steve Portigal
- ○ *Trustworthy Online Controlled Experiments* by Ron Kohavi, Diane Tang, and Ya Xu
- ○ *Escaping the Build Trap* by Melissa Perri

CHAPTER 17

BALANCING PRODUCT DISCOVERY AND PRODUCT DELIVERY

- Get your day right

- Get your week right

- Get your month right

- Get your quarter right

- Product management task boards

In every product organization, you as HoP—along with your product managers—must constantly balance product discovery (what to build) and product delivery (build it). Do too much of the former, and you'll never get anything built. Do too much of the latter, and you'll fall victim to building the wrong products in a beautiful way.

Even the most senior PMs are in an ongoing struggle to balance the "forces of evil." First, they must prevent feature creep and constantly say no to things that don't move the needle on their goals/KPIs or that don't have a significant impact on the lives of their users. Second, they have to make sure they have enough time to do some deep thinking, which means not sitting in 15 meetings every day. And, finally, they have to be sure that they aren't feeding the beast, that is, that they aren't handing developers random tasks simply because they are waiting and the PM has run out of meaningful work in the backlog.

As HoP, you'll need to provide your junior/associate PMs with guidance to make sure they don't fall into one of these traps. But even your more experienced PMs may sometimes fail to get the mix of product discovery and product delivery right, so you'll need to keep an eye on everyone in your organization—not just the juniors.

Keep in mind that there's really no right or wrong here, so long as you're not operating at the extremes. It's all about getting the mix right, and that will depend on your organization, your people, and the products you are building. But keep this one thing in mind: making sure you are building the *right* things is far more important than just building things. Or, as our good friend Albert Einstein (every tech book needs a good Einstein quote, right?) reportedly said,

> *If I had an hour to solve a problem, I'd spend*
> *55 minutes thinking about the problem and*
> *5 minutes thinking about solutions.*[133]

I have found that a particularly effective way to check in with PMs is to ask them to reflect on how they are balancing discovery and delivery in their day, week, month, and quarter. Task boards are also an important tool for finding and maintaining this balance. In this chapter, I consider each of these approaches. Note that I will be using the PMwheel buckets from Chapter 4: Define Your Good (listed in Figure 17-1) to discuss the different PM activities.

133 Retrieved from https://www.goodreads.com/quotes/60780-if-i-had-an-hour-to-solve-a-problem-i-d

Figure 17-1: The PMwheel buckets

Get Your Day Right

For your PMs, getting your day right is the first and easiest part of balancing product discovery and product delivery. Ask your PMs to reflect on whether or not they have enough time to do deep thinking and learning, conduct user interviews, research data, develop new hypotheses, have brainstorming meetings with their team, and so on. These are all things related to PMwheel buckets 1, 2, 3, and 5, which usually require larger chunks of uninterrupted time.

Doing this right means not getting stuck in meetings all day long. As I show in Figure 17-2, the right balance is approximately 50 percent discovery and 50 percent delivery. It's not so important *what* exactly you are doing each day so long as you have set aside *maker time* that is used mainly for discovery-related tasks.[134]

---

134 See Chapter 18: Time Management for Product People for more on the manager and maker schedules

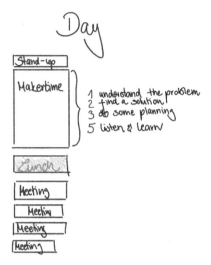

Figure 17-2: Getting your day right

Get Your Week Right

To determine whether or not your PMs are getting their week right, first ask them to review the previous six weeks on their calendar. Then consider the following guidelines with them:

- **Are they getting in touch with the customer every week?** If not, encourage your PMs to block out time in their schedules for this essential task or offer to help remove the obstacles that prevent them from doing so. I personally insist on one customer/user touchpoint each week. This can simply be a "listen-and-learn" activity such as reading some app-store reviews or a quick call to two or three of your loyal customers to ask them what they think about your latest release.

- **Are they looking at user data to refine existing assumptions or create new ones?** At least once a week, PMs should see how people are using the product.

By doing this, they can come up with new ideas/
assumptions to work on.

- **Are they looking at their success metrics and progress on their goals?** And at least once a week, every PM should also look at how they are performing against their current success metrics. How are your products performing? Are people using them like they are supposed to use them, and is everything going well on the revenue side of the business?

- **Are they spending time with their team?** How many hours a week is the PM sitting at her desk in the team space and available for questions asked by developers, designers, and other team members? And are they also engaging in other team-related activities, such as the occasional table tennis match or after-work get-together?

- **Are they reviewing and adjusting their short-term and midterm planning?** Every week, PMs should also check in on their short-term and midterm planning. How is the current iteration/sprint going? Will we ship what we hope to ship? How are our experiments going, what are the next most important experiments to conduct, and is there enough time to do them? If not, how will this affect my overall planning and roadmap, along with stakeholder and customer communication?

All this can be a challenge to balance. However, by using product management task boards (covered later in this chapter), PMs and their teams can be easily reminded of what they should do to get the week, month, and sometimes even the quarter right.

Get Your Month Right

To get the month right, there are a series of questions I personally like to ask my own PMs:

- Is there meaningful work on the development backlog? (Meaningful for the user, the company, and the team)

- Is there some improvement in the life of your user this month? If not, why not?

- What do PMs want to learn this month about their users or their team that they don't know now?

- Is there a way to improve their discovery work to learn faster and/or to improve the quality (the things that get coded have more potential than the month before) of the discovery?

- How many ideas can move to the ideas trash can this month? (I'll explain this in detail in the task boards section below)

- Are we accumulating tech debt for the sake of finishing new features earlier? If yes, how can we make sure we get back to a healthy balance?

Get Your Quarter Right

To ensure that product discovery and product delivery are balanced, it's also important for PMs to get their quarter right. I have found the following three exercises to be particularly helpful in doing this:

- **Draw the quarter.** Ask your PMs to reflect on how much time they want to devote to "understanding the problem" versus "getting it done (with their dev team)" versus any of the eight PMwheel buckets. Make sure these different areas are in some sort of balance. Figure 17-3 is an example of how you can draw the quarter using eight PMwheel buckets.

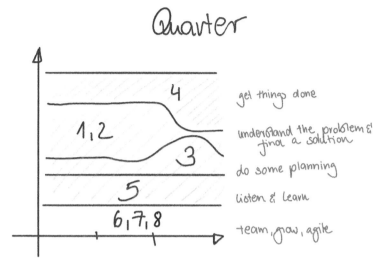

Figure 17-3: Draw the quarter using the eight PMwheel buckets. More "understand the problem" and "do some planning" at the end of the quarter to prepare for the next one.

- **Plan the quarter.** PMs engage in a variety of repetitive activities every quarter. Help your PMs remember to start them early enough and to set aside enough time for them. More specifically...
  - Check your product strategy—is it still on a solid foundation? Does it help your PMs decide what to do? If not, then plan to refine it.
  - Collect (if necessary) and review open ideas, then plan bigger opportunity assessments.
  - Set goals. If you are doing OKRs, review and set your objectives and agree on key results and metrics.
  - Beware the sand (we'll discuss the rock, pebbles, sand time-management framework in the next

chapter). Collect the little things—reserve time for them but don't really plan them. You'll end up doing other little things.

- ○ Make sure PMs ask their team whether or not the tech stack needs an update.

- ■ **Do a reality check.** Once there's a plan in place, ask your PMs to do a reality check. More specifically...
  - ○ Check staffing levels—what's the availability of the team? Do all calculations on person-days minus holidays, conferences, all-hands meetings, and other activities that take them away from the team. This is always an eye-opener for everyone involved in the planning process. Ask your PMs to check again if there is enough time for discovery-related tasks.
  - ○ Make assumptions on your throughput—how many large, medium, and small tasks can the team deliver?[135]
  - ○ Make sure your PMs won't keep getting too busy at the end—plans should be challenging but not overly ambitious. Constantly falling short does not feel good!

Product Management Task Boards

As I mentioned earlier in this chapter, project management task boards and the related standups can help PMs and their teams be reminded of what they should do to get the week, month, and their quarter right. A task board is simply a way to visually depict work at various stages of a process using cards to represent work items and columns to represent each stage of the process. Cards are moved from

---

135 This correlates with the rock, pebbles, sand framework that I explore in Chapter 18.

left to right on the board to show progress and help teams coordinate their work with one another, as shown in Figure 17-4.[136]

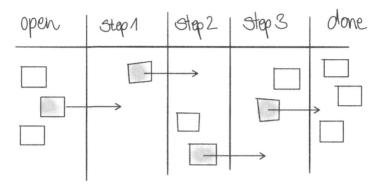

Figure 17-4: A simple task board

Task boards can be simple or complex. Simple boards have columns for open, in progress, and completed—or to-do, doing, and done. Complex boards start there but subdivide in-progress work into multiple columns so that work across an entire value stream can be more easily visualized. Each board usually also comes with its own standup meeting where team members update one another on progress—and obstacles that are blocking progress—and move the cards. These standup meetings are usually conducted weekly.

Depending on the size of the organization, it's useful to create task boards with different levels of detail and focus. These range from a high-level idea board, to an overall product board, down to a product discovery board, to a development team board. Let's consider each in turn.

Idea Board

An idea board visualizes the flow of an idea or assumption from the point that someone has it to the point when the idea becomes a

---

136 To learn more about task boards, I recommend reading some basic Agile, scrum, and Kanban literature.

qualified opportunity to the point where it is assigned to a PM or team for next steps. Figure 17-5 shows the flow of this board.

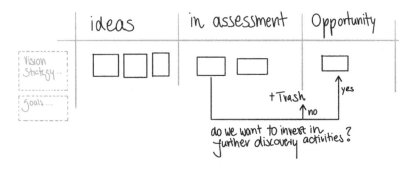

Figure 17-5: An idea board—do we see enough potential?

Product Overview Board

This board visualizes high-level product initiatives and their current status, and it is most helpful to you as HoP. The cards on this board make their way from being qualified opportunities, through product discovery, to the implementation phase (in delivery), on to the really important and often forgotten phase of validation and incremental improvements, and finally to the sunsetting phase—when obsolete features get first hidden, then buried, then developers delete their code. If an idea doesn't survive the discovery phase, it's moved directly into the trash can. Figure 17-6 shows the flow of this board.

Figure 17-6: A product overview board

Product Discovery Board

The product discovery board visualizes all the activities you need to do to create a valuable, usable, feasible, and viable product.[137] The board is owned by your PM and the related standup meeting usually involves all the people invested in this process—most often, the PM, the designer, and at least one engineer. (Some call this the "holy trio" or "product trio."[138]) But it can also include data analysts or interested stakeholders who just want to stay informed. Figure 17-7 shows the flow of this board.

Figure 17-7: A product discovery board

Product Delivery Board

This is *the* task board for the development team. It's usually owned by the team and most companies I see these days are pretty good at creating product delivery boards that really help them getting their work done. I have found it helpful if PMs insist on the validation column at the end of the process to make sure everyone is aware of the fact that "done and released" doesn't mean we are not touching this again. There is a lot of value in iterating on a feature based on the learnings you are making once something is released and used by your users!

And there is also a lot of value in getting rid of things that just don't take off as expected. That's what the trash can is for. But please— if things are routinely ending up in this trash can, then refine your

---

137 Chapter 16: Hypothesis-Driven Product Development and Experiments explores the details of this process.

138 Teresa Torres (March 11, 2020). Why Product Trios Should Interview Customers Together. Retrieved from https://www.producttalk.org/2020/03/interview -customers-together/

discovery process and make sure this happens less often. Writing code to implement something that doesn't work in the end is the most expensive mistake a company can make! Figure 17-8 shows the flow of this board.

Figure 17-8: A product delivery board

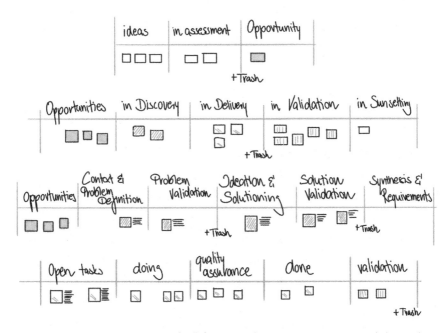

Figure 17-9: A summary of all four product management task boards

How Boards Help Keep the Balance

Keeping the balance between product discovery and product delivery always requires you to make sure you know *what* to balance. And this is only possible if there is some kind of a written/visible representation of the activities you need to balance. Task boards help to do exactly that. They are a visual representation of your workflows and of all the tasks assigned to each of the steps of the flow.

If, for example, one of your PMs is doing a lot of "solution hypothesis" work but forgets to understand and validate the underlying problems, a task board can remind them of these essential steps. It's a friendly reminder of what the PM and her team have agreed on as their ideal workflow to balance things.

In addition, the rhythm of adding, moving, and finishing work items to the board helps everybody balance their own workload and more readily see hiccups in the process. Are tasks stuck in one of the columns for a long time? Why is this? Is the board starting to get empty and there are few open tasks? Then it's probably time to find new work, opportunities, experiments, and backlog items.

Both things—a workflow that is focused on balancing forces, and the fact that the board visualizes shortcomings of this workflow—help PMs and teams to keep the balance without thinking about it every minute of their day. This is a liberating structure.

Further Reading

- Jeff Patton's take on finding the right balance—
  Balancing Continuous Discovery and Delivery
  https://www.strongproductpeople.com/further
  -readings#chapter-17_1

- How Much Time Should You Spend in Product
  Discovery? by Teresa Torres https://www.strong
  productpeople.com/further-readings#chapter-17_2

- Fix Delivery to Make Time for Discovery by Teresa
  Torres https://www.strongproductpeople.com/further
  -readings#chapter-17_3

- Product Discovery in the Multitrack of Madness by Lucio Santana https://www.strongproductpeople.com/further -readings#chapter-17_4

CHAPTER 18

TIME MANAGEMENT FOR PRODUCT PEOPLE

- The paradox of time

- Time management frameworks

- Lead by example

When, in the beginning, God created the heavens and the earth, she decided that there should be a certain number of hours in each day on this planet, and a certain number of days in the year. As we all know, there are just 24 hours in a day.

For busy product managers, this is a problem. In fact, it is perhaps the biggest, most fundamental problem of all. Why? Because not only are these talented individuals managing their own time, but also they are often responsible for managing the time of their team in one way or another. And if someone can't manage her own time, how can she be good at managing the time of others? That's why it's particularly important that product managers be aware of time management tools and methodologies, and that they use them.

But product people also struggle with time management for one more important reason: they are deeply empathic creatures. If the hiring has been done right in your organization, your product managers will often struggle with time management because they want to help their colleagues, teams, executives, users, customers, and of course the company they're working for. You can imagine how difficult it is for product managers to keep up with their own work—user research, internal product evangelizing, answering developer questions ("Checkboxes or radio buttons here—what do you think?), long-term strategy work, and much more—while they're helping out everyone else.

Time management is something that can be learned, and the skills themselves are not all that difficult to apply. The only things you need are some discipline, an understanding of the paradox of time, and a framework to help decide where your time should be spent. While we can't directly impact the discipline your PMs bring to their job—that is up to them to supply—in the sections that follow, we'll explore the paradox of time and a couple of powerful time management frameworks.

Before we dive in, however, I must add this disclaimer: *There's a natural limit to good time management.* If the workload is too much, or if the goals or direction are unclear, then even the best product people will be unable to stay on top of their to-do list. It's just not possible. And this applies to your people as much as it applies to you personally. If you're leading product managers, please take a minute or two to reflect on whether or not the workload your people face is reasonable, and if you are setting them up for success—or failure.

With that disclaimer behind us, let's take a closer look at the nature of time itself.

The Paradoxes of Time

For most of us, there always seem like there are too many things to get done in the fixed amount of time that we have available to us to do them. We all have the same 24 hours in a day, the same seven days a week. But why do some people seem to get so much more done than others? Well, there are these little things called the *paradoxes of time*.

The paradoxes of time express themselves in many different ways. You may, for example, be familiar with what is known as **Parkinson's** law, which was originally articulated by Cyril Parkinson in an article published in *The Economist* in 1955:

Work expands so as to fill the time available for its completion.[139]

In the real world, this means that when you give someone a week to do a task, it's going to take a week before it is done—no matter how many hours it actually takes to complete it. So, for example, if the task takes just eight hours to complete, people will tend to prioritize other things—putting off the task that is due in a week until it is actually due. Research supports Parkinson's law. When subjects in an experiment were "accidentally" given additional time to complete a task that should have taken just five minutes to do, they took longer to complete it.[140] Which brings us to the **Stock-Sanford corollary** to Parkinson's law:

If you wait until the last minute, it only takes a minute to do.[141]

To help your people understand how to overcome the effects of Parkinson's law and the Stock-Sanford corollary—and this is something you should be recommending to your PMs as well—introduce them to the power of timeboxing. *Timeboxing* is when you allocate a fixed, maximum amount of time—say, four hours—for a particular activity in advance of doing it, and then completing the activity within that specific amount of time. This block of time is known as a *timebox.*

---

139 C. Northcote Parkinson (November 19, 1955). Parkinson's Law. Retrieved from https://www.economist.com/news/1955/11/19/parkinsons-law

140 Elliot Aronson, David Landy (July 1967). Further steps beyond Parkinson's Law: A replication and extension of excess time effect. Retrieved from https://www.sciencedirect.com/science/article/abs/pii/0022103167900297

141 Hemant More (March 27, 2019). The Parkinson's Law. Retrieved from https://the factfactor.com/life_skill/life_changing_principles/parkinsons-law/764/

Another paradox of time is the **Pareto principle**—named after the nineteenth-century Italian economist Vilfredo Pareto—which states that 80 percent of consequences come from just 20 percent of causes.[142] This principle, also known as the *80/20 rule*, can be applied to work and the time it takes to complete it. More specifically, 80 percent of the work you do takes 20 percent of your time, while 20 percent of the work you do takes 80 percent of your time. The trick is to avoid getting trapped by that time-eating 20 percent of your work.

To help your people overcome the effects of the Pareto principle, provide them with examples and discuss strategies for identifying the last 20 percent that takes up 80 percent of their time. Remind them of a task or a project they just finished. Then you could say, for example, "You finished that many things in the first eight sprints (80 percent), and then there were just a few smaller things that you finished in the last two (20 percent). Those last few things didn't add that much customer value. So, maybe you could have released the app without doing those last two sprints."

Now, let's talk about the concept of flow. When you're immersed in a task that has your full focus and attention, you may feel like time stretches—moving much more slowly as you become more engaged in your task and your productivity increases. This paradox of time is known as **flow**. And while flow is a fabulous thing when you attain it, if you're interrupted—by a coworker, a text message, a frantic call from home—you may have a difficult time getting back into it. Some people find that they can return to flow quickly after an interruption while others are not able to.

To help your people get the most from flow, introduce the concept to them then ask them to list moments in their work and life when they have experienced it. How did they achieve it? How did they stay in it? What made them lose it? Provide them with strategies for ensuring

---

142 Vilfredo Pareto, *Cours D'Economie Politique,* F. Rouge (1897). Retrieved from https://books.google.com/books?id=fd1MAQAAMAAJ&pg=PP9#v=onepage &q&f=false

they aren't unnecessarily interrupted, such as turning off their email and text messaging, and muting Slack for two hours in the morning, or by finding an empty meeting room to work uninterrupted. And if they are interrupted from their flow state, you can help them discover and adopt strategies to get back into flow. Music can be conducive to flow as can creating a comfortable environment to work in.

One more paradox of time is what is known as **the time fallacy**, which is when you think that others have more time than you do, they are more effective as a result, and that you can compensate for this simply by working extra hours. And while you may, indeed, get some small additional amount of work done by working extra hours, this comes at a cost—sometimes severe. These extra hours can have a negative effect on your personal and family life, and it can also negatively impact the mental health of your product managers as they desperately try to keep up while feeling increasingly overwhelmed.

To help your people overcome the effects of the time fallacy, point out to your people what it is and how it can have a negative impact on their lives—both at work and at home. Reassure them that everyone has the same 24 hours in a day, no more no less, and that it's much better to learn how to use those 24 hours more effectively than to sleep fewer hours or to neglect their physical or mental health.

Frameworks

In this section, we'll review a few time-management frameworks that I have found to be particularly effective. Ultimately, the best time-management framework is the one that works best for you and the ones that work best for your people. Experiment. Try different frameworks. Shake things up. In that way you'll find the one that works best.

Learning to Say No

The first of these frameworks is very simple and quite easy to use when applied. However, it's the application that can be difficult for many product people. Product people are used to getting requests for all sorts of things from every direction—bosses, colleagues, users, customers, and more. And, of course, since we product people are naturally biased to want to solve problems and help others, our natural response is to say yes.

From a time-management perspective, this is in many cases a big mistake.

Product people need to learn to say no to the flood of requests they receive from others more often than they say yes. And saying no gets easier if they can confidently state what the team is currently looking into/working on and why this is important. You need to be able to give some context to take people's requests down.[143]

Better Meetings

In my own personal experience, I have found that meetings done well save everyone a lot of time. So, talking about meeting culture with your product managers is time well spent. Make sure they always pick attendees consciously and only call a meeting if it is really necessary. And, of course, meetings should always have an agenda, and someone needs to volunteer up front to organize the meeting.[144] One thing I find supereffective is to talk about different types of meetings.

In my world, there are only three types of meetings. The first type is the **update meeting** where someone is giving me an update on something or I am updating someone. An update meeting can be a standup, a 1:1, or a more formal meeting such as a quarterly update.

The second type is the **brainstorming meeting** where we actually get creative—coming up with new ideas for products, features, or approaches to creating them. These usually require more time than an

---

143 See Chapter 21: Planning and Prioritization
144 Amazon takes this to the next level. They start meetings with reading time, specifically, a six-page, evidence-based narrative memo prepared by an individual or team to explain in detail what the meeting is about and the issues to be addressed. PowerPoints are banned. More details here: https://www.linkedin.com/pulse/beauty-amazons-6-pager-brad-porter/

update meeting, which is often fairly quick. And we'll usually get a meeting room where everyone can work together on the task at hand.

The third type is the **decision meeting**. In the product world, these meetings usually take 15 minutes or so—not too long. I make a point to talk with everyone who is going to be in the meeting beforehand, so they know exactly what we are going to discuss and make a decision about.

Try to hold all update meetings as standups and try not to mix meeting types. If you need to mix meeting types, say in a 1:1, then clearly separate the blocks and make sure everyone knows that the meeting mode has changed.

Encourage your PMs to use these three buckets (update, brainstorm, decision) and encourage them to explain this to meeting attendees as well. Usually everyone loves this approach because it tells them what is expected from their side as well: Should they mainly just download the update, should they actively participate and get creative, or should they actually decide something?

The Manager and the Maker Schedules

The typical product person works for eight hours straight, packed with meeting after meeting—even regularly attending brown-bag lunch meetings. This is (finally!) then followed by two hours of spec writing or setting up the next customer survey.

But this is *not* how stellar product people work. You need to take the time necessary to engage in uninterrupted, deep thinking, and this is not possible when meetings continue to disrupt your day and drag you out of your flow. So, let's see what we can do about that.

If you're a head of product or product manager, chances are you have to work on two schedules while most other people in your company have to work on just one schedule.

In an essay, tech investor Paul Graham suggested that people who *make* things operate on a schedule that is significantly different than people who *manage* things. According to Graham, managers' days are "cut into one-hour intervals. You can block off several hours for a single task if you need to, but by default, you change what you are doing every hour."[145] If you are a manager and your day is packed with meetings, that's fine because your role is to get updates and make—or foster—decisions. Meetings are a good format for doing this. And if you need an hour to read or review something in detail, that will fit your schedule well too.

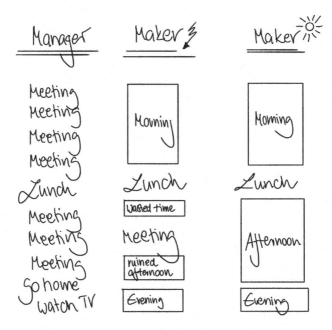

Figure 18-1: The manager and maker schedules—and the one meeting that can ruin a maker's afternoon

However, makers "generally prefer to use time in units of half a day at least. You can't write or program well in units of an hour. That's barely enough time to get started."[146] Developers need to get

145 Paul Graham (July 2009). Maker's Schedule, Manager's Schedule. Retrieved from http://www.paulgraham.com/makersschedule.html
146 Paul Graham (July 2009). Maker's Schedule, Manager's Schedule. Retrieved from http://www.paulgraham.com/makersschedule.html

their heads around complex problems, and they need long periods of uninterrupted time where they can get their work done. Meetings disrupt makers' flow—making them unproductive until they are able to get back to their last thought.

Managers often don't understand why developers are so allergic to meetings. However, if you consider Graham's manager and maker schedules, you can see that the reason is because meetings prevent makers from doing their work, while meetings *are* the work of managers.

Product managers actually need to do both—they need to maintain manager *and* maker schedules. Meetings are their work, and ironically, meetings prevent them from doing their work. It's your job to help your product managers find the right balance. The rule of thumb I use for most product managers is this: four hours of uninterrupted work, four hours for meetings, and lunch in between. But as I said, everybody needs to find her own balance here.

The Eisenhower Matrix

The Eisenhower matrix is a simple 2 × 2 matrix as shown in Figure 18-2.[147] You can use the Eisenhower matrix to easily decide what needs to be done sooner, and what needs to be done later—or even never. The vertical axis of the matrix represents the importance of the task, while the horizontal axis represents the task's urgency. This framework can easily be discussed with a product manager in your next 1:1 and it is especially helpful if they have never thought about delegation at all. In addition, it helps them to explain why they are saying no to some things.

---

147 The origin of the Eisenhower matrix is attributed to an excerpt from an address given by Dwight D. Eisenhower in 1954 on the campus of Northwestern University in Evanston, Illinois. It was there that he said, "I have two kinds of problems, the urgent and the important. The urgent are not important, and the important are never urgent."

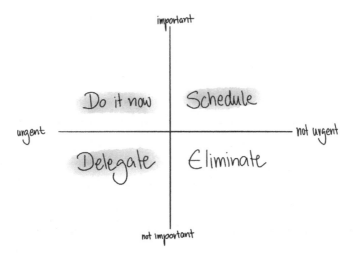

Figure 18-2: The Eisenhower matrix

The matrix has four quadrants:

- Upper left: Important *and* urgent–do it now!

- Upper right: Important, but not as urgent–get it on your schedule to do later.

- Lower left: Urgent, but not as important–delegate the task.

- Lower right: Not urgent *and* not important–just don't do it!

Here are some tips to keep in mind for using the Eisenhower matrix as a time-management tool:

- Putting things on a to-do list frees your mind. But always question what is worth doing first.

- Find your delegation pool–there are always people you can ask for help.

- Try limiting yourself to no more than eight tasks per quadrant. Before you add another one, complete the most important task first. Remember: It's not about collecting tasks—it's about *completing* them!

- Don't let others distract you. Don't let others define your priorities for you. Plan in the morning, then work on your stuff. And, in the end, enjoy the feeling of completion.

- Finally, try not to procrastinate that much. Not even by overmanaging your to-dos.

Rock, Pebbles, Sand

The rock, pebbles, sand time-management framework provides a very visible way to see how stacking up your tasks determines whether or not you'll be able to complete them on a timely basis.[148] You can either explain this to your PMs by drawing it, or you could just do it in a team offsite. It's a fun little experiment and it helps people understand why it's important to plan large amounts of work early on.

Figure 18-3: The rock, pebbles, sand exercise

---

148 This story appears in many forms, some even incorporating a fourth element of water. However, its original source is unknown.

As you can see in the illustration, you've got a variety of tasks: very large ones (rocks), smaller ones (pebbles), and very small ones (sand). If you put all your sand into a container first, then your pebbles, then the rocks—your large, most important tasks—won't fit.

However, if you put in the rocks first, then shake the pebbles so they fill the gaps in the rocks—and add the sand at the very end to fill the even smaller gaps—then everything will fit into the container.

The lesson is this: If a task comes up, think about its size. You need to figure out in advance how many rocks and pebbles you can work on in parallel. Make a point to limit your work in progress.

Lead by Example

Ultimately, as head of product, it's up to you to set the example for your people to follow. Step back for a minute and look at yourself in the mirror. What do you see? Are you modeling the behavior you want your people to engage in?

Here are some tips for leading by example:

- Don't be their biggest disturbance! Instead of bombarding your people with questions every time one pops into your head, save them up and wait for your next regular 1:1 or after a meeting you both attended.

- Respect office hours, lunch breaks, and vacations. We all need to get away from our work for a period of time to recharge our batteries. Don't send or schedule chat, text, or Slack messages during these times.

- Always tell your people when you need something from them. This can be a precise "tomorrow at 3:00 p.m." or a less exact "I expect to see something from you by the end of the week." This is especially key for junior/ associate product managers because it will help them understand how big the task is.

And here are some general tips that any product person can and should apply. Encourage your PMs to:

■ Eliminate meeting double bookings! In some companies, PMs have all their meetings in series, and rather ad-hoc ones show up in parallel—all fighting for the PM's attention. Ask your PMs to find their own way of prioritizing meetings and get rid of them once a week or don't accept them at all!

■ Respect Maslow! Make sure you have enough time to take care of your basic needs: sleep, food, water, bathroom time, exercise, relaxation.

■ Allocate time in your calendar for the important things! One example is the 50:50 split between product discovery and product delivery I advocate for in Chapter 17: Balancing Product Discovery and Product Delivery.

What You as a Manager Can Do If Someone Asks for Help in Time Management

■ Help them to see clearer, help them to understand why they think this is an issue.

■ Help them to understand if they think this might "just" be a temporary thing (perhaps someone on the team is out sick and they've stepped up).

■ Ask them if they are up for a calendar checkup with you and help them to prioritize their tasks.

■ Ask them to get specific feedback from peers on their time-management capabilities.

■ Ask them to rephrase the issue and help them from there.

What You as a Manager Can Do If You See Someone Struggling with Time Management

- Make sure goals and directions are clear.

- Make sure the workload they are facing is appropriate.

- Help them to understand the paradox of time.

- Help them to understand time-management frameworks.

Further Reading

- HBR: Meetings article collection: https://www.strong productpeople.com/further-readings#chapter-18_1

- When An Employee Says "I'm Too Busy"—Jaimy Ford: https://www.strongproductpeople.com/further -readings#chapter-18_2

- Getting things done methodology: https://www.strong productpeople.com/further-readings#chapter-18_3

- Books:
  - *Creating Effective Teams* by Susan A. Wheelan (An alternative, more research-based model on team-development stages.)

CHAPTER 19

WORKING WITH THE CROSS-FUNCTIONAL PRODUCT DEVELOPMENT TEAM

- All about teams

- Help your PMs learn more about teamwork

- Help your PMs remove obstacles

As a head of product, you know that much of the work in your organization gets done in teams. You probably also know that the best teams are cross-functional, that is, teams that draw people in different roles from across the organization.

This leads us to a very important question: How can you create cross-functional teams that are more efficient, more effective, and more enjoyable—even *fun*—to be a part of?

You can do this by helping your PMs learn more about teamwork while resisting the urge to personally interfere with or "touch" the teams. In addition, you should remove the obstacles that your PMs are flagging at the same time as you are fostering an agile mindset throughout your entire company. Let's take a deeper look at teams and teamwork.

The Nature of Teams

There's a reason why teams have the potential to be so efficient and effective—when done right, their very nature multiplies the value they create for organizations, customers, and other stakeholders. But first, what exactly is a team?

In their book, *The Wisdom of Teams*, authors Jon Katzenbach and Douglas Smith present the following definition of exactly what it is that "distinguishes a team from a mere group of people with a common assignment":

> *A team is a small number of people with complementary skills who are committed to a common purpose, performance goals, and approach for which they hold themselves mutually accountable.*[149]

A *cross-functional* team has members from many different functional areas in an organization. They have shared goals and commitments, and they generally self-manage. Consider the example of product development teams, most of which are cross-functional. They are often comprised of developers, designers, quality assurance folks, product managers, and analysts. Sometimes, they also include members from marketing, business development, and other company departments.

Just putting together a group of people—even a group of very talented people—and calling it a team does not guarantee its success. Fortunately, there are some things that you as HoP can do to create an environment that sets up your teams for success. Here are a few of the most powerful:

---

149 Jon Katzenbach and Douglas Smith, *The Wisdom of Teams: Creating the High-Performance Organization,* Harvard Business Review Press (2015) p. 41

- **Empower the team.**[150] Team up with your fellow leads (engineering lead, design lead, etc.) and make sure that the team has the necessary mix of skills, that team members really can make decisions because they have end-to-end responsibility to create a product that delivers value—both to users and to the company— and that team goals are in line with other teams and company goals.

- **Create the smallest possible "maker-to-user" gap.**[151] Ensure that your PMs (and ideally the whole team!) are directly exposed to users. This could be as simple as granting them some budget to create more usability testing, or encouraging them to do more user interviews, or assigning a user research person to the team for some time to get them in the groove of talking to users on their own.

- **Help your organization adopt an agile mindset.** Equip your PMs to foster the agile mindset throughout the organization—not just in product—to prevent the team from constantly being asked to justify their way of working.[152]

Once you have prepared the ground for your teams' success, your role becomes one of coaching your product managers—not micromanaging or "tweaking" the team. In other words, you should not touch the team. When you manipulate or interfere with this fragile team chemistry, you'll inevitably do more harm than good. Let me explain why:

---

150 Marty Cagan and Chris Jones, *Empowered: Ordinary People, Extraordinary Products*, Wiley (2020)

151 Henrik Kniberg on how this can be done: https://www.mindtheproduct.com /minimise-the-gap-between-maker-and-user-by-henrik-kniberg/

152 Please see Chapter 25: The Product Organization's Location in the Company's Org Chart for more details.

In 1965, psychologist Bruce Tuckman suggested that every group or team goes through four specific stages of development:

- **Forming.** This is where everyone understands that they are now part of a team.

- **Storming.** It is during this stage that the first problems arise and the team needs to find its own way to solve them. Team norms and rules become clear to everyone and team culture develops.

- **Norming.** In this stage, team members start to build trust and find their role in the team.

- **Performing.** In this final stage, team members really trust one another.[153]

Tuckman found that team chemistry is fragile—even small changes to a team's setup requires them to go through the four stages all over again. This is, of course, both superinefficient and difficult for the members of the team. Put your focus on coaching PMs in how to better run their teams. Let them find their way!

Help Your PMs Learn More About Teamwork

As HoP, you are in a unique position to help your PMs understand how teams are working, how team spirit can be created and lifted, and what their role is as lateral leaders.[154] They have to keep an eye on the teams' output—and therefore its performance—while they have no formal authority. So, your job is to help them understand the actions they can take to influence the output in the best way they can.

---

153 Bruce Tuckman (1965). Developmental sequence in small groups. *Psychological Bulletin,* 63(6), 384–399. Retrieved from https://doi.org/10.1037/h0022100
154 Tim Herbig, *Lateral Leadership: A Practical Guide for Agile Product Managers,* Sense & Respond Press (2018). Retrieved from https://www.senseandrespondpress.com/lateral-leadership

The most important thing a PM can do is to make sure that the team understands the challenge/mission they are up for. A team needs a shared goal and it's the PM's responsibility to develop this goal and to rally everyone behind it. PMs need to have a vision for their product, and they have to share it with the team on a regular basis. They have to make sure everyone understands what value they want to deliver to the customers and what the company needs to achieve to make the efforts worthwhile.

Once this is done, the next thing for PMs to consider is the team's ways of working. If there is an Agile coach somewhere in the organization, then that's when they come into the picture. If not, it's a good idea to help the team define its own team values. And the session to do this could look like this:

- Write down five characteristics of the worst colleague you could ever imagine.

- Collect the characteristics then dot vote on them (which ones are the worst—the ones driving everyone nuts!).

- Pick the top 10 and ask the team to come up with the contrary positive characteristics.

- Let the team discuss which ones of the 10 characteristics are most important for them.

- Rephrase them as values: We value this [the behavior] because [reason].

- Put them on the wall if you want to, but more important, use them in discussions and in your retrospectives.

Another workshop your PMs might want to run is a workshop on Agile basics. Review the Agile Manifesto, Agile principles and values, and discuss what this means for the team.

A more operational thing might be to create a "definition of done" or a "definition of ready." When is a feature well-enough defined so that the development team can start working on it, and when is a feature really completed? Is it when it's tested, it's working, it's deployed, it's live, or when users can actually use it? All these discussions really help team members get to know one another and make the process of creating a product even smoother.

It can be helpful to explain the Tuckman stages to your PMs so they better understand the dynamics of their teams.[155] In addition, I think it is often helpful to get someone who is closer to the team, called an Agile coach in some companies. This person doesn't work on the product itself, but he or she helps the teams with processes, rituals, meeting moderation and facilitation, and similar kinds of things. An Agile coach brings a different point of view into the team.

Your PMs will inevitably encounter difficulties with their teams. In his popular book, *The Five Dysfunctions of a Team*, author Patrick Lencioni suggests that problems in teams can often be the result of these five dysfunctions:

- **Absence of trust.** An unwillingness to be vulnerable. Team members who are not genuinely open with one another about their mistakes and weaknesses make it impossible to build a foundation of trust.

- **Fear of conflict.** Teams that lack trust are incapable of engaging in unfiltered and passionate debate of ideas. They instead engage in veiled discussions and guarded comments.

- **Lack of commitment.** Without having their opinions aired in the course of passionate and open debate, team

---

155 (n.d.) Tuckman's Team Development Model. Retrieved from https://www.salvation army.org.au/scribe/sites/2020/files/Resources/Transitions/HANDOUT_-_Tuckmans _Team_Development_Model.pdf

members rarely buy in and commit to decisions, though they feign agreement during meetings.

- **Avoidance of accountability.** Without committing to a clear plan of action, even the most focused and driven people often hesitate to call their peers on action and behaviors that seem counterproductive to the good of the team.

- **Inattention to results.** When team members put their individual needs (ego, career, recognition) or even the needs of their divisions above the collective goals of the team.[156]

In my own experience, by turning each of these five team dysfunctions into a positive, you can see what kinds of behavior the members of truly cohesive teams engage in:

- They trust one another.

- They engage in unfiltered conflict around ideas.

- They commit to decisions and plans of action.

- They hold one another accountable for delivering against those plans.

- They focus on the achievement of collective results.[157]

I have found it is a tremendous help to PMs when they know about these factors. They enable PMs to describe the things they are observing while working with the team in a better way. And this ultimately helps that they are taking things like trust, often considered to be one

---

156 Patrick Lencioni, *The Five Dysfunctions of a Team: A Leadership Fable,* Jossey-Bass (2002) pp. 188–189

157 Patrick Lencioni, *The Five Dysfunctions of a Team: A Leadership Fable,* Jossey-Bass (2002) pp. 189–190

of the soft factors, seriously while working with their team. For more details on how to tackle the five dysfunctions, I recommend that you read Lencioni's book.

So, if you made sure your PM has created and communicated her compelling product vision and the related goals, the team has talked about its ways of working and rituals—and they are reflecting on how things are going—and the PM is aware of possible difficulties a team can encounter and how to solve them, then you did your fair share of coaching.

Help Your PMs Remove Obstacles

Every team will encounter obstacles on the path to success. As head of product, you should first and foremost encourage the team to remove these obstacles on their own. But offer help if it is something they cannot influence. In this case, you can do a lot to help your PMs identify and neutralize these obstacles or remove them altogether. Here are some of the most common obstacles your teams are likely to encounter:

The team is slow or not delivering at all. When this is the case, the reason is most often an issue with team alignment or autonomy.

- **Not enough alignment.** There are no shared goals; no clear targets; or the product vision is missing, it needs to be repeated, or it is not motivating the team. Work with your PM on all of this along with their storytelling capabilities (for example, ask them to write the press statement for their next big release and share it with the team).[158] Suggest that they use the UBAD model—Janet Fraser's model for measuring buy-in, shared at the 2018

---

158 Midvision Admin (May 25, 2015). Amazon's Secret to Customer Focused Features: Write the Press Release First. Retrieved from https://www.midvision.com /amazons-secret-to-customer-focused-features-write-the-press-release-first/

Mind the Product conference in London.[159] The model has four levels, and you need every level—in order, from bottom to top—in order to achieve buy-in. Here are the four levels:

- ○ **Decision.** Are they making decisions in support of it (the overall goal or vision)?
- ○ **Advocacy.** Have you seen them speaking accurately, effectively, and supportively about it?
- ○ **Belief.** Do they believe in it?
- ○ **Understanding.** Do they understand it?

- ■ **Not enough autonomy.** It's possible that a team is not cross-functional enough. Are the right people with the right skills involved? Is the PM encouraging the team to make decisions on their own—relying on their expertise—so they can really feel this autonomy? (It's not a good sign if all decision-making is blocked when the PM is out of the room.) Is the team just lacking some budget so they can improve their ways of working? (This can go from buying new hardware for the devs to speeding up their work to investing some money to buy a certain study that helps their current research work.) You as HoP can help your PM with all of these issues. Talk with your peers in IT and Design (most likely the Head of IT and the head of Design) if there are issues of team staffing. Make sure the organization grants the team enough autonomy to actually make decisions and help them get some budget allocated to the teams and that they are really allowed to spend it on whatever they think will help them deliver great products faster.

---

159 James Gadsby Peet (January 18, 2019). Uncovering the Truth by Janice Fraser. Retrieved from https://www.mindtheproduct.com/uncovering-the-truth-by -janice-fraser/

Another possible reason for a team that is delivering slow or not at all is that the PM is not encouraging team members to bring their own tasks—leading to the buildup of a huge pile of legacy. There are usually a lot of business ideas in an organization, and PMs have lots of ideas for features that should be in the next big release or what should be finished until the end of next week. But there are always technical things that the developers know they need to do at some point—maybe they're not urgent for right now, and they pile up. These can slow the team down. Encourage your PMs to really listen to their teams when they point out that something needs to be fixed now to avoid a future slowdown.

The team disagrees with prioritization. Check product vision and storytelling. Ask yourself: Are the members of the team involved enough in discovery to understand the user needs? Check to see how the product manager shares information with the team.

There are conflicts between team members. Help your PM solve this by using Lencioni's five team dysfunctions or encourage them to get more involved of their team's retrospective by organizing or moderating it. The Retromat (https://retromat.org/) is a good source of inspiration or the Team Radar described below could help here as well. If conflicts are more serious, then enlist the help of an Agile coach or one of the line managers.

Team Radar (see Figure 19-1) allows the team to discuss how they think they are doing in eight different team characteristics, including such things as customer centricity, courage, communication, and trust. They have to agree on a score which is added to the spider web graph and will, therefore, share their thoughts about each of the buckets. In the end, the team can define action items for some of the weaker points.[160]

---

160 If you would like to learn more about Team Radar, please see a 2019 blog post I wrote: The Secret Weapon of Retrospectives—the Team Radar: https://www.mindtheproduct.com/the-secret-weapon-of-retrospectives-the-team-radar/

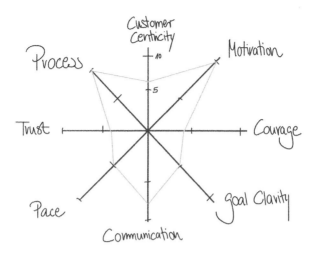

Figure 19-1: Team Radar example

You've got an unsuccessful product. This clearly is an obstacle an HoP can't fix quickly. It may occur when not enough discovery has been done, the wrong experiments were tried, or the team was not involved. Creativity and innovation may be missing, and the PM may not be paying attention to detail or the focus is on outputs instead of outcomes. Check all of these points with your PM.

The PM is a bottleneck. If the product managers aren't spending enough time with their teams, they can become bottlenecks to progress. When this is the case, talk to your PM, help them to see the issue, and encourage them to review their time allocation. Maybe it makes sense to delegate some of their tasks to their team? (Which might be a good idea anyway speaking about team autonomy!)

Again, you have the ability—in fact, the duty—to remove obstacles that get in the way of team success. Not touching the team but helping to clear the path. Encourage your PMs to solve any problems they have with the team first. However, understand that some impediments will need your personal attention. Take them seriously.

Consistently work to foster the agile mindset throughout the organization. If the company understands the benefits of agile ways of working, the work of your cross-functional teams will be made easier because their way of working won't be questioned as often.

Finally, observe your PMs—are they good lateral leaders? Make sure you have the right people in the right seats. Maybe your PMs are not as good as you think they are—do they have the trust of their team, or have they for some reason lost it? Or maybe some members of the team aren't as good as everyone thinks. Take time to check in with the heads of the tribes/departments of all the other team members—usually the head of IT, but perhaps the head of design—to get their feedback and insights.

Happy teams believe that the team itself is great and the mission they are dedicated to is worth it. Team members need to see that the effort they personally put into an adventure—building great products for users who will get value from them—adds up to something bigger. As HoP, you can help them do this.

Further Reading

- Measuring team buy-in: https://www.strongproduct people.com/further-readings#chapter-19_1

- Henrik Kniberg on how to create the smallest possible "maker-to-user" gap: https://www.strongproductpeople .com/further-readings#chapter-19_2

- Team Radar https://www.strongproductpeople.com /further-readings#chapter-19_3

- Retromat: https://www.strongproductpeople.com /further-readings#chapter-19_4

- Agile values: https://www.strongproductpeople.com /further-readings#chapter-19_5

- Tuckman stages: https://www.strongproductpeople.com /further-readings#chapter-19_6

- Interesting Twitter thread on decision-making: https://www.strongproductpeople.com/further-readings #chapter-19_7

- Cross-functional teams:
  - Collaborating effectively in cross-functional product team settings by Nima Torabi https://www.strongproductpeople.com/further-readings #chapter-19_8
  - Empowered Product Teams by Marty Cagan https://www.strongproductpeople.com/further-readings #chapter-19_9

- Books:
  - *The Five Dysfunctions of a Team* by Patrick Lencioni

CHAPTER 20

COMMUNICATING DIRECTLY AND OPENLY

- Communication basics

- Common communication problems and solutions

- How to make your communication clearer

Without a doubt, communication is one of the most important skills any manager needs to have in today's workplace. Almost everything you do calls for good communication, and good communication offers a variety of benefits to the managers that practice it, along with their organizations and customers. Not only does good communication help to improve relationships, teamwork, productivity, and performance, but also it fosters an open and creative environment and better enables employees to solve problems effectively. And with more employees working from home than ever before, communication is the vital link that keeps them closely linked with their managers, coworkers, and the organization as a whole.

There are also proven financial benefits to good communication. According to a Towers Watson study on effective communication and ROI, companies that have highly effective internal communication strategies are 3.5 times more likely to outperform their industry peers significantly than organizations that do not have effective internal communications.[161]

However, open communication is much easier said than done. While many companies (and the managers who work for them) say that open communication is one of their core values, the reality is often quite different. If you ask the people deep down in the organization what they think about the communication that's going on, they often have a very different story to tell. Instead of clarity, they lack clear guidance from their managers, they are missing the big picture, they haven't been told why the current initiative is so important, the so-called "open-door" policy their managers promote is mostly broken (leaders' doors are open, but they are difficult to get time with), and conflicts are not handled well.

So, what can you do to improve communication in your organization? First, you need to make it clear that good communication is *everyone's* job—not just *your* job. Second, you should lead by example to make this company value a *living* value. Listen more than you talk, be transparent and honest, and keep an open mind. Finally, as HoP, you need to make sure that your organization is a safe space to communicate openly and honestly. There must be psychological safety and trust.

Unfortunately, I routinely find that few organizations invest much time and money in training their people in how to be better communicators. I'll hear, "What's that?" or "Where would we get such a training?" The simple truth is that no one is born being an amazing communicator, and we can all benefit from training in the basics of communication. Let's explore some of these basics.

Communication Basics

Communication theorist Harold Lasswell developed a model of communication (commonly known as Lasswell's communication model)

---

161 John French (March 10, 2014). Towers Watson research study on effective communication and ROI. Retrieved from https://www.bizcommunity.com /Article/196/500/110632.html

that explains the communication process.[162] I modified Lasswell's model just a bit to make sure it still fits our 21st-century workplace. Here's my take:

Who communicates **what** via **which channel** to **whom** with what **reason** and **effect?**

As you can see, all the **bolded** parts of this model reveal key aspects of the communication process. The model tells us who is communicating with whom; what, how, and why they are communicating; and what the ultimate effect of the communication is. Let's work through some of the parts of Lasswell's model.

Why we communicate: 9+1 reasons

The motivations for communicating might seem on the surface to be quite simple and straightforward, so much so that I think we tend to take communication for granted. In a business context, we communicate to...

- Form and maintain relationships;
- Give, receive, and exchange information;
- Persuade and influence;
- Alleviate anxiety and distress;
- Regulate power;
- Provide intellectual and emotional stimulation;
- Express emotions and explain our thoughts and opinions;
- Brainstorm and problem solve; and

162 Wikipedia (n.d.). Lasswell's model of communication. Retrieved from https://en.wikipedia.org/wiki/Lasswell%27s_model_of_communication

- Seek alignment on a certain topic or to agree on a shared goal.

Most of these nine reasons why we communicate all boil down to one thing (and this is the +1): expressing wants and needs.

How, when, and to whom we communicate

The how, when, and to whom we communicate is defined by the reason why we are communicating. Each of these is a critical choice to be made by the communicator because it's not communication unless the transmission is understood.

As Figure 20-1 shows, the *how* of communication (channels) can be:

- Spoken,

- Written,

- Drawn, or

- A combination.

The *when* of communication normally occurs in two different ways:

- Synchronously—in real time, for example, the discussion during a 1:1

- Asynchronously—at some later time, for example, a video recording of your product strategy presentation available for viewing on the company wiki

And the *to whom* is typically:

- 1:1 (one human being to another human being),

- One to a few, or

- One to many.

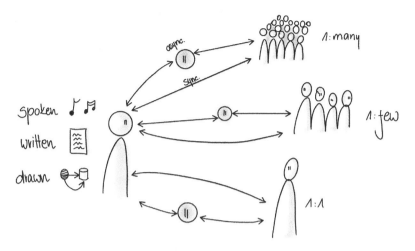

Figure 20-1: The how, when, and to whom of communication

So, what is the best way to decide exactly how you will communicate your information and messages to others? Before you initiate any communication, I suggest that you first ask yourself, "What am I trying to accomplish?" Conversely, if someone else initiates the communication, ask yourself, "Why is the conversation taking place?" If the answer isn't immediately obvious, then I suggest you guide the conversation to the *why* before you proceed any further. Understanding the why allows you to avoid side issues and ratholes that might otherwise obscure what you and the other parties are trying to accomplish.

- Spoken words are powerful because we receive more than just the verbal message. We also get a lot of information from the *way* someone says something: their emotional expression, tone of voice, facial expression, and more.

- Written messages have the advantage that you can reflect on what you want to write, either before or while you are writing it. And written documents have less chance of being misread. It's more likely that everybody will get the same message from a written document than from a speech or chat.

■ Drawn information (drawings, illustrations, cartoons, etc.) are more easily remembered by the brain than written documents.

■ Synchronous communication has one main disadvantage: the people involved have to stop whatever they are doing to join a meeting/call together. So, you should always ask yourself if it's necessary to communicate in real time.

■ Asynchronous communication has the advantage that everyone involved can consume the info and respond to it whenever it fits their schedule. But it's nearly impossible to have a meaningful, problem-solving discussion or a creative, brainstorming type of conversation when communication is asynchronous.[163]

I have personally found the matrix in Figure 20-2 to be very helpful for deciding how you are going to communicate. As you can see, the matrix accounts for all the different communication parameters in the bullet points above and it helps to be aware of the different types of communication you can choose in different situations. And it's perfect for a 1:1 session with a PM you want to coach or communicate with.

---

163 https://arc.dev/blog/asynchronous-communication-synchronous-communication
    -remote-teams-801g1dr4pt

Figure 20-2: Communication decision matrix

Let's consider a couple of examples. The first example (Figure 20-3) is for a new strategy all-hands meeting. In this case, you want to persuade and influence, give information, and seek alignment on a particular topic or agree on a shared goal.

Based on the matrix, you decide to have a real-time (synchronous) all-hands presentation to a large group of people using a combination of spoken, written, and drawn communications along with real-time spoken follow-ups with small groups of people to get feedback and hear ideas. In addition, you decide to create a written wiki page and post a recording of the all-hands on the company Slack channel—both asynchronous.

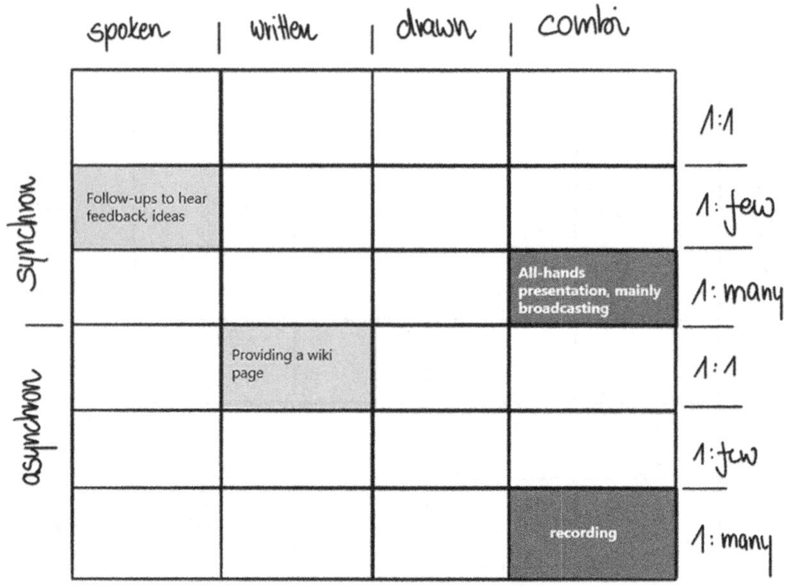

	spoken	written	drawn	combi	
synchron					1:1
	Follow-ups to hear feedback, ideas				1: few
				All-hands presentation, mainly broadcasting	1: many
asynchron		Providing a wiki page			1:1
					1: few
				recording	1: many

Figure 20-3: Decision matrix for new strategy all-hands meeting

The second example (Figure 20-4) is sharing that a team member has decided to join another team. In this case, you want to give information, alleviate stress and anxiety, express emotions and explain your thoughts and opinions, brainstorm and problem solve, regulate power, and form and maintain relationships.

Based on the matrix, you decide to make a real-time (synchronous) spoken announcement to a small group of people in the standup. In addition, you decide to create a written company announcement and follow up in writing on the company Slack channel—both asynchronous.

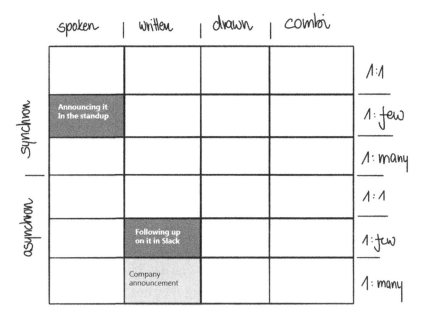

Figure 20-4: Decision matrix for sharing that a team member has decided to join another team

Keep in mind as you fill out the decision matrix that there is no right or wrong. The important thing is to think about the perfect mix of communication options.

Common Communication Problems—and Solutions

I routinely encounter similar communication problems in product companies, and these problems have a negative effect on their effectiveness.

More specifically, I often find that communication is never one way, but it is often perceived that way. So, an HoP will present the latest strategy, then expect people to embrace and execute it. In this case, alignment is missing and buy-in is not there.

In addition, many organizations do not allow sufficient time for personal, nontargeted communication. That is, time for informal chitchat (not gossip!) is missing.

Finally, I find that overcommunication is underrated by everyone in the product organization. Overcommunication needs to happen more, not less. Former Ford CEO Alan Mulally is widely credited with turning around an organization that was in deep trouble. Mulally communicated the company's plan often, and in a variety of different ways—in every executive team meeting, having special wallet cards printed and given to every Ford employee, talking about it to the press, and much more. According to Bryce Hoffman, a reporter at the time for the *Detroit News*, "After six months, those of us who followed the company had gotten sick of hearing about them."[164] Mulally overcommunicated the plan, but *everyone* knew what it was.

Please make sure your communication isn't just one way—that you always encourage feedback—and that you are spending time casually talking with your people, just enjoying the time. And, if the big goal has not yet been reached, don't stop talking about the plan until it has. Mention it one more time, and once more after that. And please consider using the following Effective Communications Checklist as you decide on the best approach to communicating. This will help you make your communication more effective while avoiding common problems:

What

- Is your message accurate and complete?

- Is your message well structured?

- Is your message necessary? (Don't contribute to the noise!)

- Is your message clear and concise?

---

164 Sean Conner (May 16, 2018). Say it 7 Times: The Art of Overcommunication. Retrieved from https://medium.com/unexpected-leadership/say-it-7-times-the-art-of-overcommunication-5d019b2c33d4

How

- Are you using the appropriate method for communication? (synchronous/asynchronous, the right tool, in person, call, mail, chat, etc.)

- Is your attitude positive? Are your body language and tone of voice positive?

- Are you engaged in active listening? (paraphrasing, summarizing the outcome of the exchange, asking questions, etc.)

- Are you open-minded, considering another perspective?

- Are you engaged, fully present, not withdrawn, not multitasking?

- Are you assertive but not aggressive?

- Can you remember to not make it personal?

Why

- Are you clear on what are you trying to accomplish? (see reasons for communication)

- Do you have the end result in mind?

Who

- Are you communicating with the right person/people?

- Are you including all the right people?

- Are you including *only* the right people?

When

- Is your communication timely? (lack of delays)

■ Is it a good time for the party you are communicating with?

■ Is the duration of the discussion/length of email/etc. tailored to the importance of the situation?

Where

■ Are you communicating in a place appropriate for the message and subject matter? (security, privacy considerations, etc.)

How to Communicate More Clearly

We all, of course, want to communicate more clearly. I find that putting some effort into preparing for your communication can pay large dividends in its effectiveness. The process I recommend has five steps: collect, structure, write the narrative, share early and iterate, and draw to simplify.

Step 1: Collect. Write something down in 15 minutes—what are your main points? Then think about other perspectives, collect data, and read what others think about the topic.

Step 2: Structure. Try to find patterns in the information. Create a mind map/hierarchy and find your main message.

Step 3: Write the narrative. Write coherently and simply—no jargon, no acronyms, no corporate speak. Get rid of filler words and apply the "by monkeys" test.[165] Stop after 1 hour.[166]

Step 4: Share early and iterate. Share your document and get feedback. Ask if the message is clear, if the next best action is clear, and if the structure and wording are good. Iterate on your narrative and anticipate the questions your audience might ask. Read it out loud.

---

165 The "by monkeys" test is a way to avoid using passive voice in your written communications. If you add "by monkeys" to the end of your sentence and it still makes sense, the sentence is likely written in passive voice. For example, "This issue will be fixed in the next iteration...by monkeys." Passive.

166 See the One Page/One Hour Pledge: https://www.onepageonehour.com

Step 5: Draw to simplify. Find one illustration that summarizes what you want to communicate. The rule is this: If you can draw it on a sheet of paper, you got your message straight. Now, do a final check: "Can I say this even more simply?"

Here are a couple extra bits of advice that can specifically help you with your spoken communication:

First, if you are a fast-paced speaker like I am, slow it down. It will help a lot if you know your main message and then pick fewer words and talk more slowly. This helps the recipients of your communication process all the things you are saying.

Second, I find it very helpful to master the "art of the pause." This means that after you say something to someone, you step back for a bit to allow the other person to respond. You don't just keep on talking. Communication is a two-way street, and you want to encourage and provide opportunities for the recipients of your communication to engage with you in it.

Remember: Communication is only effective if your recipients get the message and understand it. Communication is an art and a science. With a little effort, you can master this vital management skill.

Further Reading

- Communication:
  - The importance of being clear—Lindsey Jayne: https://www.strongproductpeople.com/further -readings#chapter-20_1
  - How to improve your writing skills: https://www .strongproductpeople.com/further-readings #chapter-20_2
  - Share early, share often—Matt LeMay, One Page /One Hour: https://www.strongproductpeople.com /further-readings#chapter-20_3

- How ego stages influence communication: https://www.strongproductpeople.com/further-readings#chapter-20_4

- Psychological safety:
    - Rework with google: https://www.strongproductpeople.com/further-readings#chapter-20_5
    - High-Performing Teams Need Psychological Safety. Here's How to Create It by Laura Delizonna: https://www.strongproductpeople.com/further-readings#chapter-20_6

- Filler words in English:
    - https://www.strongproductpeople.com/further-readings#chapter-20_7
    - https://www.strongproductpeople.com/further-readings#chapter-20_8

- Books:
    - *The Communication Book* by Mikael Krogerus and Roman Tschäppeler
    - *Communication Skills Training* by Ian Tuhovsky
    - *Say What You Mean* by Oren Jay Sofer and Joseph Goldstein

CHAPTER 21

PLANNING AND PRIORITIZATION

- Taking a closer look at planning and prioritization

- Coaching prioritization

- An approach to planning and prioritization

Planning and prioritization are *big* topics—big enough to fill a book or two all by themselves. So, instead of trying to cram all there is to know about planning and prioritization into one (humongous) chapter, I have decided to put the focus on *coaching* these two typical PM activities.

So, how do prioritization and planning become a coaching topic? Three things usually occur to bring this about. In the first case, a PM actively approaches you as a head of product, asking you for help with prioritization or planning because she is not happy with her capabilities in these areas. In the second case, you as head of product disagree with your PM's approach to prioritization and planning and you come to the conclusion that he needs a bit of help and guidance in these areas. In the third and most likely case, stakeholders—the dev team, marketing, sales, customers, or others—are complaining about the product manager's prioritization choices and want you to take action.

In each of these cases, you'll need to react. If people are complaining, make sure you follow my advice in Chapter 28: Handling Conflict. They should first talk to the PM on their own, and if nothing changes then it's up to you to deal with it. You then need to coach your PM in how to do planning and prioritization better and more effectively.

Once you realize that a PM needs coaching in planning and prioritization, then you'll need to identify the underlying issue. For example, it's possible that your PM has sufficient skills in planning and prioritization but is just really bad at explaining his process and criteria to stakeholders and to his development team. Or it might be that the PM simply doesn't have the skills she needs to do planning and prioritization well. (This is *super*bad—if this is the case in your organization, then be sure to invest a decent amount of time helping your PM with this!) Finally, it could be that the organization is stuck in a top-down, waterfall world and hasn't yet adopted state-of-the-art planning and prioritization techniques. This situation is going to be beyond the capability of your PMs to fix and you'll need to address it yourself.[167]

A Closer Look at Planning and Prioritization

While planning and prioritization are related, they are distinctly different activities. *Planning* is the creation of a list of future actions—commonly in chronological order—that seem necessary to achieve a goal. If, for example, your goal is to create a new product, then the plan will contain the various steps that are required to get you from where you are today, to your ultimate goal sometime out in the future.

Prioritization, on the other hand, is a conscious choice in which considered alternatives are ranked against deliberately chosen criteria. And the deliberately chosen criteria that someone uses to rank their priorities are particularly important. Are people using such things as business value or team dependencies to develop their priorities, or just

---

167 I address this topic in Chapter 27: Foster the Agile Mindset.

gut feelings? As head of product, you can help your PMs figure out what criteria matter in their particular context.

The goal should always be for prioritization to be the much bigger task, and if done right, planning is rather easy. So, I almost always advise product people to focus more on getting their priorities straight. Don't get me wrong: sometimes it is necessary to finish something by a specific date. For example, you might have a trade fair scheduled for two months from now, and your product needs to be finished in time for your marketing team to sell it. However, my general advice is you should always avoid deadlines if they're not really, really necessary because people still tend to see them as a promise.

Sometimes a projection of work on a timeline helps a team to understand the upcoming tasks better. So, that's when I think timelines and maybe even something that looks a bit like a waterfall workplan is okay if it's more for the development team. Let's say they are in a meeting and wondering, "He's on holiday these dates and she's on holiday those dates, how can we make this all happen?" Then it's sometimes necessary to draw something like the next 8 weeks or the next 12 weeks to see how things are falling into place.

Encourage your people to create a plan, but then make sure that either they don't show it to anyone outside of the team, or that the organization really gets why they are doing this. It's not that they're promising something will be finished at that point in time because that would be a prediction of the future, which nobody is actually good at.

If planning is the problem, then advise your product people to read a bit more on Agile planning basics. I always like to explain to my people the time, scope, quality, and investment (staffing) rectangle.[168] For example, let's say you need some scope delivered with a hard deadline in eight weeks using your given team. This will most likely be a fail (not happening at all), or the quality of what gets delivered will not be as good as what you are normally shipping. But if quality

---

168 It used to be called the "triple constraint triangle" but was updated some years back: https://www.smartsheet.com/triple-constraint-triangle-theory

and scope can be variables, you can still deliver something valuable with your given team for the upcoming trade fair.

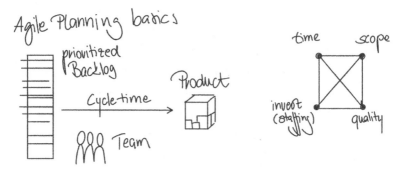

Figure 21-1: Revisiting Agile planning basics

So, make sure your PMs understand these dependencies and that they can explain them to their stakeholders Then I always advise my coachees to do really detailed calculations of team availability. Consider, for example, that each member of a team of six people takes four days' vacation each quarter. That's a total of 24 days each quarter you've got to work around, and if you're constantly planning without taking this into account, then your plans will always be off.

Coaching Prioritization

As we'll see later in this chapter, I have spelled out a specific approach for you to present to your PMs to better prioritize their work. However, as you coach them through the process of prioritizing their work, I suggest you ask them to keep the following general outline in mind:

1. **Set your priorities.** What's most important to get done right away, and what can wait until later? Encourage your PMs to reflect on the criteria they are using for prioritization, and to come up with their deliberately chosen criteria. Help them understand that there is no such thing as two #1 priority tasks—it's just not possible. There can, however, be

something like a Discovery Now/Next/Later backlog and a Delivery Now/Next/Later backlog to keep the big picture visible to everyone. But if your PM likes to have various backlogs, make sure each one of them is prioritized and up to date, and make sure the team knows what they are currently focusing on!

2. **Explain and (sometimes) defend your priorities.** Instead of just dropping your list of priorities with no explanation, it's always better to explain what your priorities are and why you chose them. Make sure your PMs understand that people may challenge their choices and that this is actually something they should embrace. Things will get better if more, clever people are involved.

3. **Stick to your priorities.** Unfortunately, after setting their priorities, product people often get distracted by what Christina Wodtke calls "golden apples" in her book, *Radical Focus*. Golden apples are things that seem to be more promising than the ones already sitting on your backlogs. Help your PMs assess these golden apples quickly to see if they're worth the distraction. If yes, then it's fair to react and change priorities.

4. **Adjust your priorities as necessary.** While it's important to stick to your priorities as indicated in the previous step, it's also important to realize that the world is always changing. This means that you should constantly review your priorities to ensure that they are still relevant, but if you do change them, find the best times to do that. For example, your development team is usually superhappy at the end of a sprint, and people won't care much if things are rearranged. But if you do it while you're in the middle of a sprint, that is going to be very annoying.

The Truths About Prioritization

There are some fundamental truths about prioritization, and they can create problems for even the most well-prepared and experienced PMs and their product organizations. Let's explore some of these truths:

Truth: There will *always* be more work than there is capacity to do it. No matter how large your development team may be, it will never be large enough to handle *everything*. This is what drives the need to prioritize. You'll never be in a situation where you've totally run out of work to do or ideas to look into.

Truth: At any given point in time, there can be one #1 priority. So, although you may have one #1 priority for discovery and one #1 priority for delivery, if these two top priorities involve the same people, then your PM will need to decide which one is actually the #1 priority.

Truth: You need to have vision and strategy in place. Why? Because those are the filters you usually use to prioritize things. If your idea or task doesn't fit your company's vision or product strategy, then you should ditch it.

Truth: You need to find a way to kill ideas that aren't winners early. A winner is an idea that has survived the necessary rounds of experimentation and become an opportunity.[169] *That's* what should go on your development backlog—if you focus on that, the point in time when you need to prioritize things is mostly in the discovery phase. Align your discovery and delivery trash cans—they will help you say no.

Truth: You need to use a prioritization approach that works for *you*. There are plenty of ways to prioritize your work, so the very best prioritization approach is the one that works for you and that you will consistently use. (My current favorite is Gabrielle Bufrem's framework.

---

169 For more on this topic, please see Chapter 16: Hypothesis-Driven Product Development and Experiments, and Chapter 17: Balancing Product Discovery and Product Delivery

You'll find a link to this and other approaches in the Further Reading section at the end of this chapter.)

Truth: There will always be "unforeseens" (bugs, support, ad hoc, tech stack, operations) and the "always on" to deal with.

An Approach to Planning and Prioritization

There are many different approaches your PMs can take to plan and prioritize their work. In the final section of this chapter, I'll show you an approach that has worked well for me and for the people I have worked with and coached over the years.

Step 1: Analyze your throughput. Have a look at what you have achieved the last two quarters. For example, if you now want to plan the next quarter, apply the rock, pebbles, sand model.[170] How many large, medium, and small items were you able to achieve during the last two quarters? The answer to this question will provide you with a pretty solid planning base for the next quarter.

Step 2: Collect all the items. Pile up everything everyone wants to see in your software: Talk with your users/customers and the relevant stakeholders (including your dev team) to get their thoughts. Check what is currently in your discovery and delivery backlogs (leftovers). Think about what you would love to do based on your well-educated gut feeling, your goals, and the outcomes you want to achieve. What does this product need to be? What would you be excited to test and build? Do a cross-check—have you thought about new opportunities, innovation, developing current opportunities, organizational improvements (e.g., easier life for your customer care team), and tech and org debt?

---

170 I detail this model in Chapter 17: Balancing Product Discovery and Product Delivery

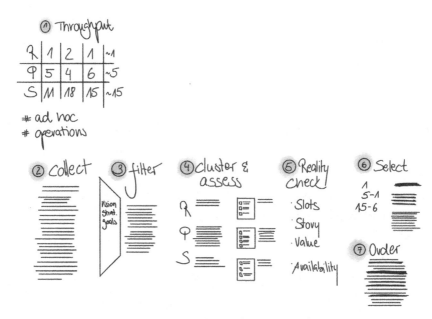

Figure 21-2: An approach to planning and prioritization

Step 3: Filter. Check to see if what you want to do fits the organization's vision and strategy as well as the current or next quarter's goals and objectives. This will result in your first round of nos. See the breakout opportunity assessment at the end of this list of steps for help with this.

Step 4: Cluster and assess. What survives Step 3 needs to be clustered and assessed because now you are using your list of criteria (for example, customer impact, business impact, cost of doing nothing, dependencies on other teams or parties, etc.) and you're prioritizing it and even killing some of the ideas. Cluster the ideas using the rock, pebbles, sand model. When you apply your assessments, this will result in your second round of nos.

Step 5: Do a reality check. Let's say you've decided you can do two rocks and five pebbles, then it doesn't make any sense to investigate 10 rocks since you will only have time to do 2. Do a reality check against the slots you have available, the story you're telling, the value for users, and availability of the team to work on it. This will result in your third round of nos.

Step 6: Select. Make your final selection.

Step 7: Put your list of priorities in order. Have just one list to make sure there is only one #1 priority for the team.

Note: It's important that everyone know that "no" means "later" or "next" for some things and "never" for others. Make transparent which no you are giving each idea/initiative/feature.

An Opportunity Assessment to Help with Step 3: Filter

Here are the questions I like to ask if someone comes up with an idea to see if it's worth investing some additional discovery time for it. If the answers to all those questions are promising, I call it an opportunity and I'm happy to add it to the discovery backlogs. If it's hard to answer these questions, you know it's not the right time to prioritize this idea.

- What are the underlying assumptions of this idea and have we understood the underlying customer problem?[171]

- Are you currently in the right position to validate these assumptions and what would it roughly take to validate them? (Massive experimentation or just a little bit more desk research?)

- How dangerous are the underlying assumptions? (Would it be devastating if we think we are right, then we build the thing and learn we were not right?)

- Is there any business potential and how big might it be? (If not, this idea should be killed now!)

---

171 See Chapter 16: Hypothesis-Driven Product Development and Experiments

- Can we think about a possible solution to this customer problem and an implementation for the solution, and do we think the effort-to-impact ratio is promising?

- What is the opportunity cost of doing nothing?

- Can we generate incremental value?

- Can we partner to reduce cost or maximize impact?

Ultimately, your PMs should aim for:

- Being able to explain their current priorities on each level (discovery, delivery, validation);

- Having tactics on how to get there (making sure they know what to prioritize, making sure they have their criteria, making sure they do a reality check);

- Being able to explain how they got there (decision log);

- Being able to explain what the priority is (now, next, later); and

- Being able to explain why something is not a priority (not fitting our strategy, not helping our current goal/ objective, has turned out not to be as promising as we thought (not delivering enough value to the user, too expensive to build).

Further Reading

- Great podcast episode on the art of saying no with Gabrielle Bufrem: https://www.strongproductpeople.com /further-readings#chapter-21_1

- Gabrielle Bufrem's assessment: https://www.strong productpeople.com/further-readings#chapter-21_2

- A framework to help assess the pile: https://www.strong
  productpeople.com/further-readings#chapter-21_3

- Nancy Duarte: The Secret Structure of Great Talks:
  https://www.strongproductpeople.com/further-readings
  #chapter-21_4

- Prioritization Quadrant: Collect and cluster work items
  and ideas for mature products:
  - Barry Overeem: https://www.strongproductpeople
    .com/further-readings#chapter-21_5
  - https://www.strongproductpeople.com/further
    -readings#chapter-21_6

CHAPTER 22

INCREMENTS AND ITERATIONS

- Why increments and iterations?

- Helping your people sort things out

- Telling the story

Increments and iterations are pretty basic topics, and as a head of product, I'm certain you are quite familiar with them. However, I have found that juniors tend to struggle with these concepts, so you will need to be able to explain and coach them. In this chapter, I recap all the important things to keep in mind while explaining these topics.

If you release early and often[172] (and we'll talk about why you should later in this chapter), then of course not everything is going to be perfect–the releases are going to require rework. This is what we mean by *iteration*–it's focusing on a specific portion of your product and improving it. However, in addition to iterating on *existing* functionality, it is also necessary to provide *new* functionality to provide customers with value and then generate capital from it. We do this by

---

172 One of the earliest references to this term originated in Jim McCarthy's book,
    Dynamics of Software Development: https://www.amazon.com/dp/1556158238

adding value in meaningful *increments*—"minireleases" that get you closer to your ultimate product.

So, how can you help your PMs better visualize and understand the concepts of increments and iterations? I have found that the drawing in Figure 22-1 will help. You can explain these ideas while drawing them.

In the top drawing—*increments*—we're adding new functionality, piece by piece, by delivering new increments (numbered 1, 2, 3, etc.). I also like to illustrate increments with circles as shown, where each increment creates a new, larger circle of functionality (labeled A, B, C, etc.) In the bottom drawing—*iteration*—we're improving existing functionality, indicated with a progression of numbering (1 to 1.1, 4 to 4.1, etc.)

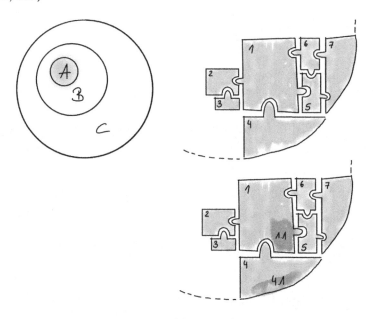

Figure 22-1: Increment (adding) and iteration (improving)

You may also use the term *zero to one phase* (also known as *phase zero*) for the time *before* your product is on the market. This is particularly common with startups or for larger companies that are opening up completely new business areas. This is a challenging phase for organizations—you must think a lot about the right size for each of your increments, and the right number of iterations—but it also offers the opportunity for creative solutions.

Why Increments and Iterations?

So, why do we ship software in increments, and why do we then iterate on the things we have shipped? Please explain to your PMs that increments and iterations can help them prioritize and make decisions. There are three main reasons for this.

1. **We want to ship as early as possible to start learning.** Learnings increase tremendously the moment we begin to receive user feedback and when we start observing user behavior. This is, of course, only possible if what we are shipping has a certain size, because if you can't do something useful with it, then you cannot observe user behavior, right? We're trying to answer questions such as: Are users buying the thing? And, if they are buying it, are they also using it? Or do they buy and then forget it because it's not so attractive to them? What can we do to improve the product and make it more attractive to users—and more likely to be used and provide value?

2. **We want to help our developers keep things easy.** If you're developing a big piece of software over months and months and months, it gets supercomplicated. It's, therefore, much better to enable the dev team to release as often as possible—even continuously,[173] if that's feasible. Then you'll have fewer merge conflicts in your code base, it will be easier for your quality assurance to test, and they will find fewer unintended side effects in your software.

3. **We want to have business impact as early as possible.** The point of building products is to eventually sell them and make some money. While you'll never get a lot of money from your first iteration—that should not be the goal—you do want to see if users will actually pay for it. Can you find some early adopters who will pay for a small, first

---

173 Jez Humble (n.d.). Continuous Delivery. Retrieved from https://continuous delivery.com/

version of your product? If so, this has the added benefit of shortening your time to market.

In summary, you want to have something small, simple, and shippable that generates value for the user, creates some learnings for your team, and that has a business impact.

Figure 22-2: A small, simple, shippable product that generates value, learnings, and business impact

The something small, simple, and shippable that generates value for the user, creates some learnings for your team, and has a business impact is often called an *MVP*—a term that actually causes a lot of confusion in product organizations. The acronym MVP has been defined to stand for everything from *minimum viable product* to *minimum valuable product, minimum viable prototype, minimum viable platform,* and more. Suffice it to say that there are a lot of definitions and a lot of arguments in our industry about what MVP stands for. I suggest you take a moment to consider exactly what MVP means to *you*.

We're all familiar with how Lean Startup's Eric Ries defines MVP: *minimum viable product*. According to Ries, MVP is the version of a new product that allows a team to collect the maximum amount of validated learning about customers with the least amount of effort. For most product organizations, this is good enough.

Instead of MVP, however, Henrik Kniberg suggests a different approach that tracks delivery in small steps using the terms *earliest testable product, earliest usable product,* and *earliest lovable product.*[174] I like this idea because the first round can be a superbasic prototype to test some ideas and assumptions, the second round can be a real software product delivering basic functionality, and the third round can be a well-rounded product that people fall in love with.

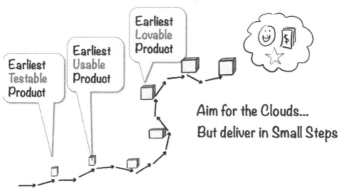

Figure 22-3: Henrik Kniberg's approach to MVP

If, for example, you like the idea of releasing prototypes that people can really use and touch, then maybe *minimum valuable prototype* is a good term for you. Or perhaps you resonate with Henrik Kniberg's idea and would like to give your basic prototype the name *earliest testable product.* Whatever you decide, I suggest you find the definition that fits your organization best, explain it to your people, then use it.

Help Your PMs Sort It Out

Now that you have explained the concepts of increments and iter-ations to your people, you may find that they're still superlost with all of this. In this case, what I usually do is first of all help them to

174 Henrik Kniberg (January 25, 2016). Making sense of MVP (Minimum Viable Product)—and why I prefer Earliest Testable/Usable/Lovable. Retrieved from https://blog.crisp.se/2016/01/25/henrikkniberg/making-sense-of-mvp

understand the user flow in the software and to increment their planning. I'll ask: Is this first/early product really generating value for users? Can you really use it and test it? Our focus should be on getting to the point in time when the user is actually able to experience the value we have promised to give them.

Consider the example of a job board. On each side of the board—the HR manager looking to hire, and the job seeker looking for a job—there is a progression of functionality and value:

- The HR manager can create a job posting vs. the HR manager gets applications vs. the HR manager finds the perfect candidate

- The job seeker can find a job vs. the job seeker can apply for a job vs. the job seeker lands her dream job

Help your people find their starting point, which might simply be to create a job or two and show them in a list. The next step might be to add the ability to do a search for jobs. Then keep adding more functionality until the product enables users to gain full value from the product—when HR managers are able to find the perfect candidates, and job seekers are able to land their dream jobs.

Getting to this point involves two competing rules: the *art of omission* (what can we leave out?) and the *art of completeness* (what needs to be put in?). You need to have both. The product needs to look as complete and helpful and valuable as possible to the user, but you should leave out all the things that are not 100 percent necessary for your first learnings. This is superimportant.

The art of omission

- What are our nonnegotiables? (e.g., we need to make them pay, so we must add enough value to the first version of the product to make this work)

- Do we need (to develop) this now? Will this add to our learning, to our user value? (e.g., HR people love stats, but is this something we need to add to our first version?)

- Do we need to create it, show it, update it, delete it? (Create a job posting but not updating it → delete and recreate. Perhaps not comfortable but may be acceptable for a short period of time.)

- Do we need to automate the function or is this something a human being can do manually in the beginning? Should consider getting the process right before automating it. (Invoices could initially be created and sent by an army of interns)

- But can it be ugly/rough? (Backend admin, tracking data, etc.)

- But does it scale? Does it need to *now?*

The art of completeness

- Can the user reach his goal? (Posting a job vs. getting applications)

- Customer support must be possible

- Learning must be possible (Tracking implemented)

- Are we tackling the biggest/most complex/riskiest problems/questions first?

After your zero-to-one increments session with your junior/associate PM for a job board product, your whiteboard might look something like this:

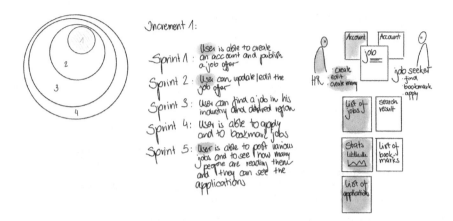

Figure 22-4: Visualizing increments for a job board product

One side note on the sprint allocation: Of course, this is something the PM has to work on with their team. But it sometimes helps to create a first draft to get everybody on the same sheet of paper.

When it comes to visualizing increments and iterations, there are a variety of different approaches. You can draw it using the onion or the pyramid—where each layer shows where the product is growing—or you can show flow.

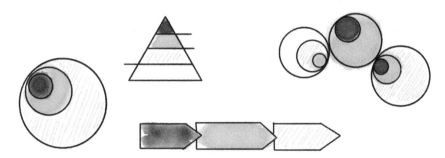

Figure 22-5: Drawing increments and iterations

Alternatively, you can use color-coded story maps (popularized by Jeff Patton)[175] as shown in Figure 22-6. The color-coded cards or

---

175 Jeff Patton (n.d.) User Story Mapping. Retrieved from https://www.jpatton associates.com/user-story-mapping/

Post-it notes stuck to a wall can also show your people where the product is growing.

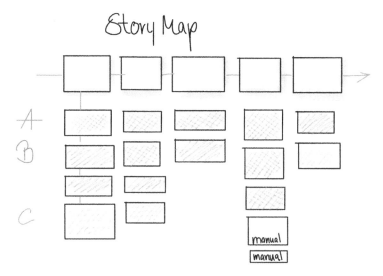

Figure 22-6: A story map indicating the next three product iterations

There is a common progression of iterations. The first iteration—1.1— is focused on fixing bugs and code hiccups, then later iterations focus on optimizing for performance. We ask whether or not the functionality is actually delivering as much business value as it could, and whether or not it is scaling in technical performance. To answer these questions, we look at user feedback and usage data—such things as happiness, engagement, adoption, and more.[176] We might remove functionality that didn't deliver as much value as we hoped for, and later, do some facelifts of functionality we kept. Finally, the last iteration is sunsetting—the product has done its work, but people are no longer using it. The final iterations may be to hide the product, bury it, and then kill it.

176 Marc Abraham/MAA1 (March 6, 2019). My product management toolkit (36): Google's HEART framework. Retrieved from: https://medium.com/@maa1/my -product-management-toolkit-36-googles-heart-framework-cdcdd49f4e53

Telling the Story

Once your PMs have decided on the path they are going to take to maximize the value their product offers, they need to tell the story that goes along with it to the product development team, stakeholders, and upper management. But chances are your junior/associate PMs are going to need help putting together a compelling story—especially if this is their first time. Help them put this story together and rehearse it—don't leave them all alone on this.

The good news is the next chapter—Chapter 23—is devoted to product evangelizing and storytelling.

CHAPTER 23

PRODUCT EVANGELIZING AND STORYTELLING

- We're wired for storytelling
- Telling a good story
- Making your stories sticky

While we are not exactly born telling stories (because we can't speak from the beginning!), each one of us has the ability to tell stories from a very early age—it's built into our DNA. We perfect our storytelling skills throughout our childhood because we learn early on that a good story helps us to get what we want. And it's not only the active storytelling: We love to listen to stories from a very early age because they captivate us, entertain us, and help us to gain new insights.

The best stories have a biological impact on us, triggering the release of hormones that act on us in very powerful ways:

- *Oxytocin,* which causes us to build trust, generosity, and a personal connection

- *Endorphins,* which can make someone laugh or help them deal with fear, pain, or uncertainty

- *Dopamine,* which leads to a desire to know what happens next when you tell a story with peaks and troughs that lead to cliffhangers[177]

As Carl Alviani points out in a post, "We think in stories, remember in stories, and turn just about everything we experience into a story..."[178] This ability to use stories to convince others to work with us to solve problems—particularly as a group—has given our species, *Homo sapiens*, a unique evolutionary advantage that has enabled us to collectively survive and thrive on this planet. Thousands of years ago, it was working together cooperatively to hunt down dinner. Today, it's working together to resolve the COVID-19 pandemic.

Figure 23-1: A dinnertime story thousands of years ago

---

177 David JP Phillips (March 16, 2017). The magical science of storytelling. Retrieved from https://youtu.be/Nj-hdQMa3uA

178 Carl Alviani (October 11, 2018). The Science Behind Storytelling. Retrieved from https://medium.com/the-protagonist/the-science-behind-storytelling-51169758b22c

What Stories Do

As you have probably experienced throughout your career, it takes a story to unite a group of people—from a small product development team to an entire company. Stories are the tool that enables one person to get others excited about using their skills and know-how to solve a hard problem. A story that does exactly that has a number of key elements:

- It paints a picture of a desirable future.
- It makes it clear why you should become part of this future.
- It acknowledges the current situation while describing the potential difficulties that may arise and why it's worth overcoming them.
- It suggests a common goal with just enough information to make next steps clear for listeners.

Companies with iconic brands are masters at telling stories. Even their shortest slogans (often, just a few words) can evoke images in the minds of customers that encourage their minds to wander to a better future. Think of Nike's "Just do it," or Apple's "Think different," or BMW's "The ultimate driving machine." And they have great personalities who tell these stories to the world, and also within their own organizations.

In my own experience, I have seen many products that never saw the light of day because the product manager was unable to tell a good story about it. As a result, the product team was uninspired and divided, and internal stakeholders were not convinced to support the effort. Let me tell you my own storytelling story.

I was once PM on a product team and I consistently nailed backlog management and prioritization, held well-prepared team rituals, and got things done. Our team's output was great, but the stuff we released wasn't making a big difference—it didn't change the lives of our users. We had already conducted quite a few product discovery initiatives (though we would understand our users much better as time went on) and we kept adding features, but I was frustrated because I didn't know what we could do to build products that actually made a difference.

My product coach at the time—Marty Cagan—had a suggestion: that I become better at product evangelizing. (He, in fact, told me that my product evangelization skills were nonexistent.) I was doing all the product discovery work with my designer and one engineer, and I just wasn't able to adequately explain what we had learned to the rest of the team and to the company. Important information was lost, sparks did not fly, and the team was neither inspired nor motivated by what we told them about our learnings.

Marty recommended that I read Guy Kawasaki's book, *Selling the Dream*, and I did exactly that.[179] After reading the book, I realized the critical importance of storytelling. Developing this skill changed the rest of my career as a product manager. I started telling stories that united my product development team, convinced stakeholders, helped marketing sell the product, and most important, I figured out what really mattered to our users by putting them at the center of the stories.

Ultimately, stories are a perfect design tool and good ones are essential for product evangelists. Everyone has the ability to create one, they're easy to iterate on, and they help you gain more clarity. In addition, if you're focused on a structure, there's less fluff. A lot of business presentations are filled with business buzzwords and jargon that actually mean nothing—empty words. People become numb to these empty words and they stop hearing them. In addition to making sure that your stories aren't filled with buzzwords and jargon, it's important that they have structure. Let's explore some helpful structures for your stories.

---

179 Guy Kawasaki, *Selling the Dream*, Harper Business (1992)

Telling a Good Story

A good story has a well-defined structure that makes it easy for people to understand and navigate. One of the most well-known story structures is "the hero's journey," which was elucidated by professor of literature Joseph Campbell. The hero's journey starts in the ordinary world with a call to adventure—which could be in the form of a big dream or desirable future—and progresses through a succession of challenges, tests, and trials before reaching the ultimate destination where the hero has achieved her goal and is transformed, sharing what she has learned with others.[180]

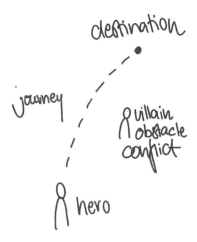

Figure 23-2: The hero's journey

In much the same way, we are called to adventure by the promise of a new product, or an improvement to an existing product. To achieve our goal, we have to inspire and align our team; sell a vision for a product or a service or an idea we have; ask senior management for more budget, time, or people for our product or team; get others to buy into our strategy; help others make tough tradeoff decisions; explain the value of our product to noncustomers; present our next-steps roadmap;

---

180 Ephrat Livni (October 26, 2018). This classic formula can show you how to live more heroically. Retrieved from https://qz.com/1436608/this-classic-formula-can-show-you-how-to-live-more-heroically/

recognize people; build and create personal brands; and more. The idea is to *inspire* our team, stakeholders and management, and users—not to *convince* them.

All this is made much easier by telling stories—*compelling* stories.

When your PMs create the compelling stories they will use to inspire their teams, stakeholders, and others, they should be sure to hit the following points:

- Paint a desirable future/big dream.

- Explain why someone should be a part of the story.
   - It's good for you
   - It's good for us
   - It's good for all

- Assess the anticipated difficulties and why it's worth the effort.
   - See their world
   - Appreciate them as human beings
   - Communicate understanding

- Present the shared goal.

- Create a sense of urgency and present information that enables action.

To overcome the paralyzing fear of the blank page, I like to start PMs with the following short task (which, in time, can become a complete story). PMs simply fill in the blanks with their own situation, providing them with the basic elements they need to create a compelling story:

We want to _____

In order to _____

Because if we don't, _____

Making Your Message Stick

Now that you have your story, how do you ensure that it will stick?

Humans are clearly inspired and motivated by the written or spoken word—most of us have been inspired to action by a CEO or manager who painted a compelling vision of the future. But we are also inspired and motivated by drawings and illustrations. It's a case where a picture really is worth a thousand words. And, of course, you need the story itself.

I always tell my product people that you need all three of these (written, spoken, illustrated) working together in unison.

When it comes to the narrative, I encourage product people to first decide if they want to put their team or the user in the center of the story. I then coach them to prepare their story in three different lengths: short, medium, and long.

Short is equivalent to an elevator pitch—no more than approximately 150 words or about 75 seconds. (Research indicates that, when you tell a short, informative story to an executive online, their attention span maxes out at 75 seconds.[181])

Medium is longer—about 900 words or 6 minutes. When you're at this length, think in terms of presenting three "acts"—like the acts of a play—of 300 words each. You'll tell people what you are going to tell them, then you'll tell them, and finally you'll tell them what you have told them. Jeff Bezos is famous for requiring his executives to write narratively structured six-page memos for presentations at Amazon. According to Bezos, "We silently read one at the beginning of each meeting in a kind of 'study hall.'"[182]

Long is for when short or medium just won't allow you to tell your story in a compelling way. Again, think in terms of acts—in this case, three acts of about 800 words each for a total of approximately 18

181 Jeremy Connell-Waite (October 22, 2019). The 72 Rules of Commercial Storytelling. Retrieved from https://www.linkedin.com/pulse/72-rules-commercial-storytelling-jeremy-waite/

182 Jeff Bezos (April 18, 2018). 2017 Letter to Shareholders. Retrieved from https://blog.aboutamazon.com/company-news/2017-letter-to-shareholders/

spoken minutes. It's no coincidence that TED talks have an 18-minute limit. Says TED curator Chris Anderson, "It [18 minutes] is long enough to be serious and short enough to hold people's attention...By forcing speakers who are used to going on for 45 minutes to bring it down to 18, you get them to really think about what they want to say."[183]

And, as you've no doubt noticed throughout the pages of this book, I am a big fan of drawings, illustrations, pictures, and other visual elements that help tell a story. When you decide what kinds of visual elements to use, think about ones that will actually emphasize whatever it is that you're going to say. You can, in fact, use drawings of exactly what you want to tell your audience—the messages you want them to receive.

Here are some suggestions for things to do—and *not* do as you craft your stories.

Dos...

- Light up their brains.
  - Use words that provoke emotions
  - Use words that trigger their senses, including smell, touch, vision, sound, and even taste
  - Make them laugh

- Make the story you're sharing relevant, important, and true.[184]

- Show your curiosity and passion and be vulnerable while telling your story.

---

183 Carmine Gallo (March 13, 2014). The Science Behind TED's 18-Minute Rule. Retrieved from https://www.linkedin.com/pulse/20140313205730-5711504 -the-science-behind-ted-s-18-minute-rule/
184 David Axelrod and Karl Rove (n.d.). The Campaign Message. Retrieved from https://www.masterclass.com/classes/david-axelrod-and-karl-rove -teach-campaign-strategy-and-messaging/chapters/the-campaign-message#

- Focus on speaking to the hearts and minds of your audience/readers and not so much on convincing them of something (your worldview, to follow your advice, to buy your product, etc.).

Don'ts…

- Don't use words that are used very often in your context or environment, such as "A rough day"–people will tune them out.[185]

- Avoid using buzzwords, tool names, and abbreviations.

- Beware of manipulation–storytelling can be misused, especially in a time where people look less at data and science and have a tendency to believe whatever fake news they are presented with so long as it is compelling.

Remember…

Anyone can create and tell a story, but someone (this means *you* as HoP) needs to tell and show PMs that this is an important skill to have. Point out how successful companies like Nike, Apple–and your own–use stories to build their brands. While creating and writing down a story is a lot of work, if you do it right, you'll be able to use the same story more months or even years.

If your PMs want to create *great* stories, then they should:

- Think about the audience and what they want to achieve;

- Use a proven storytelling structure to ensure nothing is missing (e.g., the hero, the journey, the destination);

---

185 Annie Murphy Paul (March 17, 2012). Your Brain on Fiction. Retrieved from https://www.nytimes.com/2012/03/18/opinion/sunday/the-neuroscience-of-your -brain-on-fiction.html

- Make sure there are a variety of ways to tell this *one* story: short, medium, and long, as well as written, spoken, and illustrated; and

- Make it *their* story. PMs should be able to tell the story without lengthy preparation because it's *so good* that it's impossible to forget anything about it!

And, finally, in the words of Ben Horowitz, "You can have a great product, but a compelling story puts the company in motion." What's *your* story?

Some Great Talks to Watch...

- Here's a perfect example of how powerful it is to use words that light up other people's brains. This talk has a good explanation of how you can figure things out by writing them down and how to start with your story: Sarah Kay: If I should have a daughter: https://www.ted .com/talks/sarah_kay_if_i_should_have_a_daughter

- Do you think storytelling based on a lot of data is boring? Not if you are listening to Hans Rosling: https:// www.ted.com/talks/hans_rosling_let_my_dataset _change_your_mindset

- Matthew McConaughey winning Best Actor at the Oscars. Pay attention to the simple, powerful structure: Something to look up, something to look forward, something to chase: https://www.youtube.com /watch?v=wD2cVhC-63I&t=127s

- One of the best product demos ever: Steve Jobs iPhone 2007 Presentation: https://www.youtube.com /watch?v=vN4U5FqrOdQ

- Complex topic explained well: Al Gore: The Case for Optimism on Climate Change: https://www.youtube.com /watch?v=u7E1v24Dllk

- Not possible to not listen to him! We need to talk about an injustice: Bryan Stevenson: https://www.youtube .com/watch?v=8cKfCmSqZ5s&tt=1270s

- A great speaker telling stories that matter to you: Simon Sinek on why good leaders make you feel safe: https:// www.ted.com/talks/simon_sinek_why_good_leaders _make_you_feel_safe

Further Reading

- How Stories Change the Brain: https://www.strong productpeople.com/further-readings#chapter-23_1

- Strategic Storytelling Is Product Management: https://www.strongproductpeople.com/further -readings#chapter-23_2

- My product management toolkit: Storytelling: https://www.strongproductpeople.com/further -readings#chapter-23_3

- Why We Need Storytellers at the Heart of Product Development: https://www.strongproductpeople.com /further-readings#chapter-23_4

- Storytelling for Product Managers: https://www.strong productpeople.com/further-readings#chapter-23_5

- 72 Rules of Commercial Storytelling: https://www.strong productpeople.com/further-readings#chapter-23_6

- Nancy Duarte: The Secret Structure of Great Talks:
  https://www.strongproductpeople.com/further
  -readings#chapter-23_7

CHAPTER 24

KEEP THE SENIOR PMS ENGAGED

- Mastery, autonomy, and purpose
- Two career paths
- Something new every year

When you've just hired a new junior/associate product manager, you know that you'll need to spend a lot of time with them, including onboarding them properly, introducing them to their coworkers, helping them learn the ropes of your organization, getting them started working with customers and products—the things we explored in Part IV. Junior/associate PMs take a lot of time.

However, what about your senior PMs? They already know all there is to know about the people with whom they work, about your customers, about your products. They're, in fact, so independent that you may think you can just forget about them.

That would be a big mistake.

I've learned through the course of many coaching sessions that being a senior PM can be both incredibly boring and remarkably stressful—all at the same time. There's something in many companies that I call the Individual Contributor Progress Vacuum. Here's how it works:

Junior/associate PMs know that they have many things to learn—they experience shortcomings in their knowledge and experience every day. So, they are laser-focused on closing their gaps and becoming competent PMs.

Senior PMs, however, have a choice to make when they reach that level of competence and expertise. The usual move is to move on to *people management*, where they are responsible not just for building products, but also for leading teams that build products—ultimately transitioning into HoP jobs and beyond.

Figure 24-1: Division of product vs. management work for different levels of PMs

The problem is that many senior PMs don't want to move on to people-management jobs—they would prefer to keep building products. As a result, in many organizations, they get stuck doing the same things—over and over again—and they get bored as a result. Many of these senior PMs see the writing on the wall, and they reluctantly move into management because that's the only way their careers can continue to progress. And if they don't, they feel like their careers have reached the point of stagnation. If their company can't solve this problem, then the senior PMs become increasingly frustrated and they inevitably start looking for positions in other companies.

That's a knowledge drain you can and should prevent! But how?

Mastery, Autonomy, and Purpose

In his book, *Drive*, Daniel Pink examines three elements of true motivation: mastery (the desire to continually improve at something that matters to us), autonomy (the desire to direct our lives), and purpose (the desire to do things in service of something larger than ourselves).[186] According to Pink, it's these three things that motivate people—not promises of carrots or threats of sticks.

Think about mastery, autonomy, and purpose as you work with your senior PMs. How can you help your senior PMs achieve these three things, and what can you do to help them visualize their progress? This can be as simple as saying to your senior PM: "I wanted you to know that I noticed you have improved in creating a compelling vision for our new product," or "I see that you are mastering this roadmapping effort—that's fantastic!"

There are four other words that I find to be superhelpful in reflecting on an organization's senior PMs:

- Appreciation
- Recognition
- Empowerment
- Inspiration

Are your senior PMs feeling these things from you and your organization? Do they feel appreciated, recognized, empowered, and inspired? If not, what are you and your organization doing to change this situation? Consider the answers to these questions—how did you do?

- Is the company valuing individual contributions?
- Are there rituals in place to celebrate PMs' achievements?

---

186 Daniel Pink, *Drive: The Surprising Truth About What Motivates Us*, Riverhead Books (2009)

- Do you provide opportunities for senior PMs to mentor junior/associate PMs?

- Is there a career path for individual contributors?

A Career Path for the Individual Contributor

When senior PMs reach full competence—where they have the skills needed to get the job done—they need to decide in what direction to take their careers. There are four ways for PMs to continue their personal growth and grow their careers:

- They can start to manage a bigger, more important/ successful product.

- They can start to manage several products.

- They can manage a product that is too big to be handled by one team.

- They can manage other PMs.

While the third item on this list can be partially a management role, the last one is clearly on the people-management path, and, therefore, not for everyone.

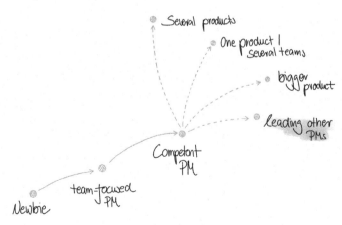

Figure 24-2: Typical PM career progression

Balance Your Tree

Every product organization needs to draw a clear line between the career paths of those PMs who want to remain individual contributors and those who want to get into people management. As your PMs rise up the organization—moving from junior/associate PMs to senior PMs over the course of their careers—they will all reach a point where they have to decide which path to take. Here are typical career progressions for PMs who decide to take the people-management path and those who decide to take the individual-contributor path:

Big Corporate—Management Career Path

1. Chief Product Officer
2. SVP, Product Management
3. VP, Product Management
4. Director, Product Management
5. Group Product Manager
6. Senior Product Manager
7. Product Manager
8. Junior Product Manager / Associate Product Manager

Big Corporate—Individual Contributor Career Path

1. Distinguished Fellow PM
2. Principal Product Manager
3. Group Product Manager
4. Senior Product Manager
5. Product Manager
6. Junior Product Manager / Associate Product Manager

I personally like the idea of having a Group Product Manager position in each of these career paths—it's here that a PM needs to make the decision whether to stick with being an individual contributor or make the move to becoming a people manager. The Group PM is a hybrid role, where the Senior Product Manager is still hands-on with a product and also has some line-management responsibility for more junior product managers. (If your organization is small, then this can be part of the role of your senior PMs, which is why it's important to define this!)

If you're working in a midsized company, then here's a typical PM career progression, from senior to junior:

Midsized Company

1. Head of Product
2. Team Lead Product or Principle Product Manager
3. Senior Product Manager
4. Product Manager
5. Junior/Associate Product Manager

Something New Every Year

I believe two of the biggest problems we continually run into with senior PMs is that they get bored and they feel that they're not being sufficiently recognized for their good work. This is something that you as HoP have the power to resolve—well before your senior PMs lose motivation and begin looking for other opportunities with different employers.

My suggestion is to plan one big change for each of your senior PMs every year. Not only will this shake things up—turning boredom into excitement—but also if you pick a big change that fits their situation and achievements well, it will make your senior PMs feel seen, recognized, and valued. They'll have a story to tell.

Here are some ideas for keeping your senior PMs interested in their jobs and work:

- Ask them to help you build the better shipyard by inviting them to work with you to shape and refine the product-development process (if this is needed).[187]

- Get them involved in onboarding new PMs, specifically, the process, content, and actually doing a fair share of it (but not all of it—this is still your responsibility).

- Involve them in giving back to the product community (talks, blog posts, meetups, and so on), which usually helps your employer branding as well.

- If your organization is fairly large, you may already have communities of excellence—small groups of people who share their know-how regarding a certain topic, such as rapid growth or growth hacking. Put your senior PM into the position of leading/orchestrating such a group.

- Ask them to create guidelines that help all the teams, such as Product Principles and Design System work.

- Offer them a new title, a new product, a new shipyard, more money, etc.

It's not easy keeping senior PMs interested and engaged in their jobs. Take the time to work with them to create opportunities that not only tap their considerable experience and expertise, but that also create true value for your organization and your customers. When you do this, your senior PMs will feel appreciated and valued, and they'll be that much more likely to want to stay right where they are—on your product team.

---

187 In Chapter 1: Your Role in This Game, we introduced the idea of shipyard as a metaphor for the product-development process of a company.

PART V

CREATE THE RIGHT ENVIRONMENT— BUILD A GREAT CULTURE

Of course, you and your team work in an organizational environment that is comprised of many other functions besides product development, including such things as sales, marketing, finance, operations, and much more. It's up to you as head of product to create the kind of environment within this given setup that will enable your people to give the best of themselves every day of the week. In this final part of the book, we'll consider the product organization's location in the company organization chart, how to make change happen from within, how to foster the agile mindset, and dealing with conflict.

As Melissa Perri says, "I tell every leader that says 'no let's just focus on fixing the teams' this: they're going to get really good at their jobs and realize they can't do them here because you didn't take the time to build the space for them to succeed. Then they're going to leave."[188]

Build a space for your product people to succeed.

---

188 https://twitter.com/lissijean/status/1188439570955853824

CHAPTER 25

THE PRODUCT ORGANIZATION'S LOCATION IN THE COMPANY'S ORG CHART

- Striking a balance

- Healthy friction is a must

- When the organization structure prevents balance

As I'm sure you know, the product manager is in a unique position—sitting in the center of tech, business, and the user. PMs are committed to delivering a product that is usable, feasible, valuable, and viable—all at the same time.

It is superhard (or perhaps even impossible) to treat each one of these dimensions with the same love and to keep the necessary balance if your product team reports to the CTO or the CMO of the company. Why? Because they will naturally be biased in that org's direction. In fact, if your product team is embedded in the tech or business areas, that might be the reason why your products are not as successful as you want them to be. This is because the PM's decisions are not as nuanced and balanced as they should be, or your PMs are trying to find the necessary balance but the endless discussions they find themselves in as a result frustrate them.

Don't get me wrong—there is value in tension, but this tension can't come fully into play if the players aren't on eye level. It's key that product has the same say in the organization as does engineering and marketing.

Product Managers Must Strike a Balance

Product managers are under pressure to constantly try to satisfy every possible interest in your company while at the same time working to build an innovative, usable, value-adding, and technically good product for your users. That means, PMs are constantly performing a balancing act. When one voice is louder than the rest—say, when your product organization reports to the CMO—then it's harder for PMs to find the balance.

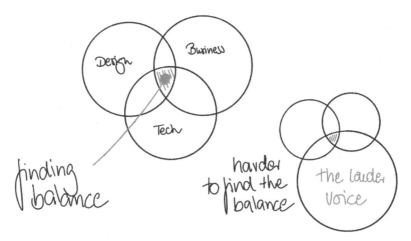

Figure 25-1: The PM's job: to find balance

So, why am I devoting an entire chapter to telling where in the org chart the product organization should be located? Because it plays a key role in the ultimate success of your products. I myself have worked as a PM for quite some time and have done my service in a variety of different structures. From this experience, and with the experience of seven years of consulting, I can say that there are organizational structures in which a product manager has major problems in achieving this important balance.

Let's consider the case of a product department located in the marketing area and reporting to the CMO. Since your boss is the CMO, you will naturally be included to support the goals of the marketing department, which tend to be focused on the sales of existing products. Marketing success will, therefore, take priority over technical issues, simply because of the distance to technology. This is clearly also the case with topics such as consistent user experience and information architecture, which tend to run counter to the goals of the marketing department.

Similarly, if your product department is located in the development/engineering area—and you report to the CTO—introspection will tend to predominate. Instead of taking time to better understand basic customer problems in detail before starting to find solutions, questions such as: "How do we have to build this product?" or "What would the best solutions look like and how can we implement them?" will tend to dominate. And topics like: "How can we tweak the business model to support user needs better while earning even more money for the organization?" or "How do we make sure our go-to-market strategy for the product is rock solid?" are not so much the focus.

Another difficult situation is when the development team is a part of the product area. This is a more common situation than you might think, and I encounter it often—particularly in companies that don't want to hire their own developers and instead work with an agency or a few freelance developers. In this situation, PMs directly steer the entire development team and the emphasis is on delivering functionality to customers quickly—even when this functionality does not scale sufficiently, is not easy to maintain, or is difficult to expand later.

Healthy Friction Is a Must, But Only at Eye Level

There will always be friction between the three different areas—business, tech, and product—and this is a normal, even an important thing. This friction forces the PM to listen to each of these areas carefully to understand how to support their needs while he is listening to the users to create a product that is upgrading their lives. When PMs are able to successfully find and maintain this balance between these areas, then this friction is what I call a *healthy friction*. This can only occur, however, when the product management team is on an equal footing with the business and tech teams and have a say on the same level.

Figure 25-2 illustrates the structure I have seen work successfully in many organizations. (This is a supersimplified, hierarchical example—companies usually live in a matrix organizational form and PMs, of course, should work colocated in their cross-functional team! So, the figure is focused solely on the department part of your matrix.) As you will see, the product organization is on eye level with development, marketing, and other key departments. In addition, design and user research are part of the product organization, but at eye level with the product management team.

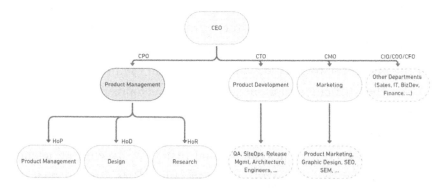

Figure 25-2: Best practice: putting the product organization on eye level with development and marketing

In this organizational structure, while PMs will have to justify their decisions conclusively and show to what extent they have tried to protect all interests, they are never accountable to one department more than the other. And a CPO or HoP can discuss things with his management colleagues on an equal footing and explain the balance decisions of his PMs.

What If the Organizational Structure Gets in the Way of Balance?

So, what can you do if your product department is not located at eye level with the tech and business departments? In this situation, you will need to use your powers of persuasion.[189] The key is to move from a rigid, hierarchical structure to one that is organic, responsive, and agile. Ultimately, a reorganization may be in order.

How can you decide if you need to reorganize? Consider the answers to these questions:

- Is it possible to make decisions quickly within the structure, that is, when a question arises do you always have to run it up the entire reporting chain?

- Is it possible for PMs to strike a balance and make decisions without being constantly overruled?

- Are roles and responsibilities clearly described and are they clear to the employees?

- Does the current structure help us to exchange know-how so that people with similar roles and responsibilities can learn from one another?

- Are the goals and topics of your own working group sufficiently focused?

---

189 I first suggest you refer to Chapter 19: Working with the Cross-Functional Product Development Team and Chapter 27: Foster the Agile Mindset.

- Is it possible for managers to take time in this structure for the personal development of their employees? And do they have the right skillset/background to do so?

- Does this structure enable you to achieve maximum autonomy with maximum alignment?

The more no answers you have, the greater the need to revise your organizational structure. McKinsey published the following nine golden rules for making a reorganization more successful. The more rules you follow, the greater the chances of success.

Rule 1. Focus first on the longer-term strategic aspirations—dwelling only on pain points typically creates new ones.

Rule 2. Take time to develop an accurate, verifiable picture of today's structures, processes, and people.

Rule 3. Select the right blueprint carefully by creating multiple options and testing them under scenarios.

Rule 4. Go beyond lines and boxes; consider all three elements of organizational design (structures, processes, and people).

Rule 5. Fill well-defined roles in an orderly, transparent way.

Rule 6. Identify and actively change the necessary mindsets. Do not assume that people will automatically fall in line.

Rule 7. Use metrics to measure short- and long-term results.

Rule 8. Make sure business leaders communicate, and create a powerful redesign narrative to inspire and mobilize the company.

Rule 9. Monitor and mitigate transitional risks, such as interruptions to business continuity, loss of talent, and customer-care lapses.[190]

If an organizational structure is found that meets these basic conditions and in which product managers are able to create the necessary balance and make the necessary decisions under healthy friction with

---

190 Scott Keller and Mary Meaney (February 2018). Reorganizing to capture maximum value quickly. Retrieved from https://www.mckinsey.com/business-functions/organization/our-insights/reorganizing-to-capture-maximum-value-quickly

all internal stakeholders, which will then also endure, then a company is optimally positioned. As an HoP, one should, therefore, address this topic in order to avoid unnecessary friction or half-baked products.

If it is not possible to change the organizational structure, however, then it is all the more essential to provide the best possible working environment with detailed role descriptions and a clear definition of responsibilities as well as the right attitude of everyone (build bridges and break silos!) to ensure the best possible working environment and the least possible shear forces.

Further Reading

- Basics about organization structures: 9 Types of Organizational Structure Every Company Should Consider: https://www.strongproductpeople.com /further-readings#chapter-25_1

- On reorganizations: Reorganizing to capture maximum value quickly: https://www.strongproductpeople.com /further-readings#chapter-25_2

- Books:
  - *ReOrg: How to Get It Right* by Stephen Heidari-Robinson and Suzanne Heywood

CHAPTER 26

CHANGE FROM WITHIN

- Encouraging new ways of working

- Fostering bottom-up change

- Some common bottom-up change initiatives

Most product and development teams are constantly improving their ways of working to deliver better products faster—it's an integral part of their DNA. They naturally try many new things all the time, and as a result, develop very strong opinions about their ways of working. Consider the example of development teams, which were the first ones in most organizations to embrace and use agile ways of working. They first used agile techniques to orchestrate their own work, had success with that way of working, and then they influenced those around them—product people, designers, QA people, and so on. Eventually, they all caught the agile bug.

In most organizations, the agile bug continues to spread until everyone has adopted at least some agile ways of working. However, lasting organizational change like this has rarely been mandated from the top down. Instead, it started as a grassroots movement somewhere deep within the organization—from the bottom up. In this chapter, we'll consider what it takes to make lasting change from within the organization.

Encourage New Ways of Working

As an HoP, it's in your interest—and in the interest of your organization and users—to foster the spirit of discovering new ways of working in your PMs. There are two main reasons for doing this. First, discovering new ways of working can help the organization become more efficient—improving performance. What made us successful yesterday is unlikely to continue to make us successful tomorrow. We must constantly try new ways of working to stay a step ahead. Second, it can prevent the frustration among your product managers and developers that occurs when only one or a small number of teams are successfully using a new approach and the rest of the organization is working in a completely different way.

Consider the example of OKR: objectives and key results. From what I see, product teams are often the first people in an organization to fall in love with this methodology because of the clarity and positive impact it brings. Inevitably, however, they experience limitations in the method because not everyone in the organization is using it. When OKR is not widely adopted throughout the organization, the framework cannot reach its full potential. And when it doesn't reach its full potential, many teams end up dropping OKR because they become frustrated and tired of the friction created with the rest of the organization that's not using it.

Fortunately, as HoP, you can help with this. You can be the one who tells them that this is the problem and then help them to foster lasting, bottom-up change.

Foster Bottom-Up Change

Now that I've said that you as head of product can help your PMs foster lasting, bottom-up change, how exactly can you go about doing that? Here are six approaches I have found in my own personal experience that can go a long way to help:

1. Start small and make sure it works. In many cases, one of your teams will independently start working in a new way. This is a good thing, but you'll want to make sure the team is actually achieving something positive with this new approach before it is adopted more widely. If so, then offer the team your help (expertise, coaching, budget, etc.) to help ensure they get the results they're aiming for (faster cycle times, more clarity, more transparency, etc.).

2. Create a success story. Once the team has successfully adopted a new way of working, make sure there is a success story to tell and something to show to people that are interested. Make sure the team can explain how this has been achieved in an appealing way—they're the ones who should be telling the story. Shine the spotlight on your team, not on yourself!

3. Find the ally. Fostering bottom-up change requires finding allies in the organization who will support the change—growing and perpetuating it. There are three ways how this usually happens. First, some other team or department reaches out because they heard about the success and they want to benefit from the learnings. Second, members of the initial team are excited about their initiative and they reach out to other teams on their own. Finally, you might see the benefit of what the team is doing new and you reach out to other teams to encourage them to give it a try. Be sure there is an "easy next" (for example, introducing task boards and standups to the internal IT/desktop support team) and a "surprising next" (for example, introducing these tools to the HR department, which in most orgs is usually open to change).

4. Ask them to share their success story. As other teams adopt the new way of working and find success using it, encourage them to also tell their success stories throughout the organization.

5. Start to convince the org. At some point, you'll need to get the support of upper management to decide if this is something they want to support growing bottom up, if they want to invest in it and tell everyone top down that this is the new normal, or kill it (which might cause some people to leave the company—not the best option).

6. Help everyone succeed. Once upper management agrees to support this new way of working, it's important that you come up with a (superlightweight) rollout plan and then help everyone succeed as they implement it.

Some Common Bottom-Up Change Initiatives

There are a number of change initiatives that product management and product development teams often gravitate toward. Keep an eye on your teams to see if they adopt these initiatives, then decide if they merit your support to spread throughout the organization. Here are some common examples:

- Hypothesis-driven experimentation and decision-making[191]

- The use of KPIs to make data-informed decisions

- The adoption of OKRs to gain clarity on current objectives and the key results that will help them reach these objectives

- The adoption of "show, don't tell" as their mantra
  A team creates a working prototype (in contrast to a comprehensive specification) to make sure they can get feedback on their work as early as possible. Other teams can do this too!

- (More) agile ways of working. Not everybody understands the basics, and this still causes friction in many companies. So, keep it on your radar.

---

191 Described in Chapter 16: Hypothesis-Driven Product Development and Experiments.

When I think about how we can foster bottom-up change in our organizations, I am reminded of the words of Götz Werner, founder of dm-drogerie markt, Germany's largest retailer in terms of revenues (more than $12 billion).[192] He once said, in German, *"Führen heißt nicht, Druck aufbauen, sondern einen Sog erzeugen."*[193] In English, this translates roughly to: "Leading does not mean building pressure, but creating a pull." In other words, the best leaders don't push their people to do things—they provide the conditions that draw employees into the work they are responsible for of their own accord, fully engaged and inspired to give the very best of themselves every day.

This is the kind of environment that you as head of product should strive to create to produce the best outcomes for your organization—and your customers.

Further Reading

- Explaining bottom-up organizational Change: https://www.strongproductpeople.com/further-readings#chapter-26_1

- Top-down or bottom-up approaches to successful change: https://www.strongproductpeople.com/further-readings#chapter-26_2

- Books:
    - *Switch* by Chip Heath and Dan Heath
    - *7 Rules for Positive, Productive Change* by Esther Derby

---

192 https://www.esmmagazine.com/retail/dm-drogerie-markt-ceo-looks-position-business-future-81964
193 Petra Blum, *Mitarbeiter motivieren und Kunden begeistern: Ein Blick hinter die Kulissen erfolgreicher Unternehmen,* Haufe-Lexware (2014)

CHAPTER 27

FOSTER THE AGILE MINDSET

- Understanding the agile mindset

- Using the Agile Manifesto and Agile principles

- Helping the entire organization adopt the agile mindset

We live and work in a world that is constantly changing–some say faster than ever before. While it's difficult to quantify the rate of change we're experiencing today, it's clear that we are doing business in a VUCA environment that is volatile, uncertain, complex, and ambiguous.[194] The companies that are best able to deal with a VUCA world are those that have the ability to adapt quickly.

They have an agile mindset.

I'm sure that, as an HoP, you are very familiar with Agile principles. However, I summarize the basics here so you'll have everything you need in your pocket as you advocate for Agile in your organization.

---

194 Wikipedia (n.d.). Volatility, uncertainty, complexity and ambiguity. Retrieved from https://en.wikipedia.org/wiki/Volatility,_uncertainty,_complexity_and _ambiguity

The Agile Mindset

To survive and thrive in a VUCA world, companies must be structured in a way that enables them to deal with a constant stream of new influences, changing requirements, and unclear future goals. So, what is it that makes an organization agile—that creates an agile mindset? Here are four common characteristics:

- Forward thinking in alternative, well-thought-out plans for the future

- Constant exchange with the environment through heterogeneous networks

- Lean structure and process organization, an agile understanding of leadership

- Draws on internal, different, experienced-based strengths[195]

In my experience, there are three types of organizations today. The first type has not started its agile transformation. In my opinion, these organizations are fated to die sooner or later because other organizations do adapt and, therefore, have a competitive advantage. The second type has agile development teams and agile product delivery, but other parts of the organization have not adopted an agile approach. (If your company is this second type, you'll find this chapter to be particularly useful.) The third type is the organization that is truly agile—an agile organization.

Different company departments have found different ways of adapting to a world that is volatile, uncertain, complex, and ambiguous. For development teams, the agile approach to software development

---

195 Wouter Aghina, Karin Ahlbäck, Aaron De Smet, Gerald Lackey, Michael Lurie, Monica Murarka, and Christopher Handscomb (January 2018). The five trademarks of agile organizations. Retrieved from https://www.mckinsey.com/business -functions/organization/our-insights/the-five-trademarks-of-agile-organizations

was the answer to these challenges. This includes Scrum and extreme programming (XP), which have been around since the 1990s. Another well-known model is Toyota's Kanban scheduling system for just-in-time (JIT) and lean manufacturing, developed by industrial engineer Taiichi Ohno.[196]

The Agile Way of Working

Agile was codified in 2001 by a group of 17 software development "organizational anarchists" who created and signed a document commonly known as the *Agile Manifesto*. According to the manifesto, while there is value in the items on the right side of the below list, the items on the left side are valued more:

- Individuals and interactions over processes and tools

- Working software over comprehensive documentation

- Customer collaboration over contract negotiation

- Responding to change over following a plan[197]

The agile values derived from this include such things as commitment, focus, openness, respect, courage, simplicity, communication, and feedback. When an organization is not committed to these values, then like a candle that goes out because of a lack of oxygen, the agile mindset will be smothered.

As an HoP, you know the value of having an agile mindset in your product organization. But, unfortunately, not all companies have fully adopted this mindset.

196 Y. Sugimori, K. Kusunoki, F. Cho, and S. Uchikawa (1977). Toyota production system and Kanban system Materialization of just-in-time and respect-for-human system. *International Journal of Production Research*, 15:6, 553-564. Retrieved from https://www.tandfonline.com/doi/abs/10.1080/00207547708943149
197 *Manifesto for Agile Software Development* (2001). Retrieved from https:// agilemanifesto.org/

Most companies have adopted just some of the agile ways of working, and it's that *some* that is the problem. These days I see so many companies that are what I call "kind of" agile. They have started their agile journey somewhere in Engineering: One team starts to use Scrum as a delivery framework—they are introducing Scrum Rituals, Artefacts, and Roles and they start to work in a colocated, cross-functional setup. The agile virus usually spreads until all product development teams are working in this way: They constantly improve their way of working, they make their progress as transparent as possible, and they respond to change quickly.

But somehow, the virus doesn't spread beyond the product development organization. People are still living in a siloed, hierarchical organization where command and control or micromanagement are the dominant management styles.

Working in a partially agile organization sucks for product managers and other product people. Specifically, it sucks because they will invariably have to do a lot of translation efforts. So, if their development team is working in agile, but the rest of the organization is not, then roadmaps and similar things need to exist in two versions—one for the agile development team and one for departments outside of this world.

And once product managers experience the benefits of an agile way of working, they naturally want to see them used across the entire organization. When they aren't, this causes a lot of frustration for these PMs. They need to explain agile basics over and over again and they have to protect or even defend their way of working against the surrounding organization. This requires a lot of effort and it is a source of constant energy drain.

So, it makes perfect sense for you as an HoP to foster the agile mindset and to help the entire company—not just the product organization—become more agile every day. But, how to do this? I suggest the following three steps:

The first step is to assess the status quo, and there are two ways to approach this. One way is to conduct a full organizational assessment.

The Prosci Agility Attributes Assessment—illustrated in Figure 27-1—is one such formal assessment.[198]

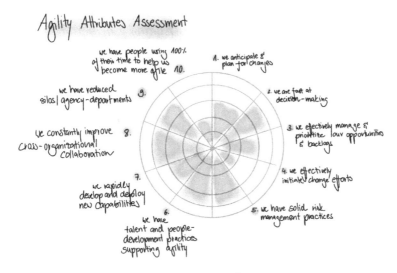

Figure 27-1: Prosci Agility Attributes Assessment

Another way to assess whether or not an organization is truly agile is simply to observe how your people react under pressure. Are they exhibiting agile reflexes? Are they naturally gravitating to sharing insights, to thinking of alternatives, to adapting to changes fast? Are they reacting as a team, leveraging the strength of every team member? If they are, then you have your answer.

The second step is to define your story to tell. As a head of product, what is the story you're telling other departments that are not agile, or even the management team? How will they picture a truly agile organization? My favorite metaphor is moving from the company as a *machine* to the company as an *organism*—a living creature that can react to changes in the outside world and the environment. According to a McKinsey report, the advantages of making this move are compelling:

---

198 Figure 27-1 is based on the article: Stop Confusing agile with Agile. Retrieved from https://www.prosci.com/resources/articles/stop-confusing-agile-with-agile

When pressure is applied, the agile organization reacts by being more than just robust; performance actually improves as more pressure is exerted. Research shows that agile organizations have a 70 percent chance of being in the top quartile of organizational health, the best indicator of long-term performance. Moreover, such companies simultaneously achieve greater customer centricity, faster time to market, higher revenue growth, lower costs, and a more engaged workforce.[199]

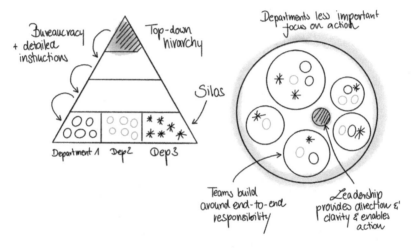

Figure 27-2: From machine to organism

The third step is for you to decide where to invest your time. You usually can't work on all these dimensions in parallel when it comes to helping the organization develop an agile mindset. There are three primary areas to consider:

---

199 Wouter Aghina, Karin Ahlbäck, Aaron De Smet, Gerald Lackey, Michael Lurie, Monica Murarka, and Christopher Handscomb (January 2018). The five trademarks of agile organizations. Retrieved from https://www.mckinsey.com/business -functions/organization/our-insights/the-five-trademarks-of-agile-organizations

- **Mindset:** Are people already living the agile values of openness and feedback? How can you help them to be more open and to give more helpful feedback?

- **Structures and processes:** Review your investment decisions and prioritization and how the organization is measuring performance. Do these already reflect the agile mindset? Have you implemented colocation, cross-functional teams, and collaboration across departments?

- **Methods and tools:** Do people know the basics of existing agile frameworks, collaboration tools such as chats or wikis, and do they know why working in increments is so important?

Where to Get Started

As you can see, there are many moving parts when it comes to fostering an agile mindset in an organization—especially a large organization or enterprise. So, where to start? In my experience, heads of product should consider focusing on the following:

- **Agile basics.** Make sure that everyone knows about Agile principles,[200] values, and the Agile Manifesto and how these agile basics apply to the work they do.

- **Agile decision-making.** There is more to making good decisions than simply asking the team what they think, counting votes, and going with the majority. You should know agile decision-making strategies (majority, discourse, consent, consensus, veto, and so forth) and be prepared to explain them to other teams and management.

---

200 The Agile principles were enumerated by the same group of software developers who created the *Agile Manifesto*. You will find the complete list here: https://agilemanifesto.org/principles.html

- **Retros.** Retros are a good starting point for every team that wants to start their agile journey. Help them to pause to reflect and think about what should be done differently in the next iteration to be more successful. This can be applied to every team—even if they are not using sprints, they can still have a monthly retro.

- **Task boards and standups.** These are helpful artefacts that every team can start using right away. I helped several HR departments create their task board and they were consistently a big success. Does everyone know the tasks they are currently responsible for and what the status is for each of these tasks? Help them to see the benefits of it: more transparency, more control over their own workflow, and the possibility to optimize their throughput.

- **Team dynamics and motivation.** Everyone should be familiar with some basic principles of team dynamics and motivation, including Tuckman's stages of group development,[201] the Five Dysfunctions of a Team,[202] Theory X/Theory Y,[203] and so forth.

To help the entire organization adopt some of the agile basics, help management understand the advantages of an agile mindset and make sure your PMs are leading by example and are multipliers for agile ways of working in the organization. If you do so, you will help teams feel less friction in their daily work and you will see a much more resilient company—thriving in a VUCA world!

---

201 Covered in Chapter 19: Working with the Cross-Functional Product
     Development Team
202 Covered in Chapter 19: Working with the Cross-Functional Product
     Development Team
203 Covered in Chapter 9: Motivation Do's and Don'ts

Further Reading

- In this keynote speech at MTP Engage, Jeff Patton deconstructs Agile methodologies from a product manager's point of view and explains why we often struggle with the PO definition in today's product organizations: https://www.strongproductpeople.com/further-readings#chapter-27_1

- From Agile Delivery to an Agile Organization (paper published by Management Solutions): https://www.strongproductpeople.com/further-readings#chapter-27_2

- 33 structures to help agile teams overcome major challenges together: https://www.strongproductpeople.com/further-readings#chapter-27_3

- Books:
  - *Agile: The Insights You Need from Harvard Business Review* by Harvard Business Review, Darrell Rigby, Jeff Sutherland, Peter Cappelli, Phil Simon, et al.

CHAPTER 28

HANDLING CONFLICT

- The nature of conflict

- Understand and minimize the reasons for conflict

- Resolving conflicts in the workplace

The simple truth is that managing a product means managing frustrations. You are constantly in the position of saying no to your team, your stakeholders, and your users—all so you can focus your energy and the energy of your team on the few things that you say yes to. As a result, the probability is quite high that there will be people outside of your product organization who feel that they are being neglected and that their needs are not being heard, acted on, or met.

Long story short, product organizations are conflict magnets.

Surprisingly, however, when I ask my own clients about conflict in their work environment, at least 50 percent will tell me that there is none. This is, of course, just not possible. When we take a closer look inside the organization, we'll invariably discover that there are just as many conflicts occurring there as any other organization anywhere else in the world.

Someone gets frustrated because a team member always shows up late to the standup. A PM hasn't made role expectations clear, so employees argue over who should be responsible for writing the backlog item. One of your PMs interrupts and talks over other PMs in meetings, making them visibly angry in the process.

Please keep in mind that, when I talk about conflict in a product organization, I'm not talking about the healthy kind of friction or tension that arises when smart people debate complex ideas or concepts. That kind of debate helps your people create better products that will deliver increased value to users.[204] The kind of conflict I address in this chapter is much more serious and can be quite destructive—leading to broken trust, broken relationships, broken teams, and ultimately, broken products.

However, some organizations and the people in them are well-suited to dealing with conflict—it's not a big deal for them. I have found that, when this is the case, there are usually several things these organizations all share in common:

- Their **employees are empowered and encouraged to resolve conflicts** that arise in their direct environment on their own. At the same time, they are encouraged to escalate as early as possible if they can't figure things out on their own.[205]

- Their **employees know how to personally deal with their first reaction/emotions** when they find themselves is a confrontational situation. And they know how to overcome this first rush of hormones to figure out what the real problem is.

---

204 I briefly address this kind of debate in Chapter 10: Building Individual and Team Alignment
205 See my discussion of XING's Clarification Manifesto in Chapter 10: Building Individual and Team Alignment

- Everyone makes sure that, not only does the current conflict get resolved, **the system gets an update so that this ideally never happens again** (Example: HoPs can make sure to talk with other department heads to resolve conflicting goals of two teams, fighting for resources, and so on)

How can you apply the lessons of these companies and others like them to manage and perhaps even avoid the damaging effects of conflict in your organization? This can be accomplished by first understanding the nature of conflict, then minimizing the reasons for conflict, and finally, training everyone in conflict management.

The Nature of Conflict

As I explained earlier, conflict is a natural thing in any organization—when you have two or more people working together, then the stage is set for conflict. It's important to keep in mind that in most conflicts, neither person is right or wrong. Instead, different perceptions (such as when one or both parties perceive a threat to their well-being or "survival," whether real or not) collide to create disagreement and conflict.

As an HoP, there are three main ways to address conflict. You can...

- Ignore it and hope it goes away;

- Handle it poorly; or

- Handle it well.

Of course, ignoring conflict and hoping it goes away is rarely the right approach—conflicts usually tend to fester when they're ignored. Because conflicts are often the result of perceived threats, they tend to stick around until we face and resolve them. Clear and open communication is the cornerstone to successful conflict resolution.

When you deal with a conflict and resolve it, the outcome can be very positive—for you, the other parties, your team, and the organization as a whole. When you deal with conflicts openly and transparently, you will...

- Gain the cooperation of team members;

- Improve performance and productivity;

- Reduce stress and preserve integrity;

- Solve problems as quickly as possible;

- Improve relationships and teamwork;

- Enhance creativity; and

- Increase staff morale.

Understand and Minimize the Reasons for Conflict

Before you can minimize conflict, you'll need to understand the reasons that drive it. In the three lists that follow, I have assigned some of the most common drivers of workplace conflict to specific categories covered in this book.

The first group of conflicts is the result of your organization's systems and processes. These can often be avoided by learning from each conflict, solving them on a bigger scale, and setting up systems the right way.[206]

- Competing goals

- Limited resources without clear allocation

- Competitiveness, toxic work environment, unhealthy workplace competition

---

206 See Chapter 5: Being a Great Boss and Chapter 25: The Product Organization's Location in the Company's Org Chart

The second group of conflicts will occur less often when everyone cares more about communication and alignment.[207]

- Different context, knowledge, information
- Unclear job expectations
- Different opinions and perspectives
- Different work styles

The third group of conflicts mainly relates to hiring.[208] If you hire the right people, you have made sure their personal values are not in conflict with the culture and values of your organization. And if you check for conflict-solving and communication capabilities during the interview process, you'll know they can handle any misalignments.

- Different values
- Toxic behaviors
- Poor work habits/slackers

To minimize these drivers of workplace conflict, always try to get rid of the underlying reason for a conflict: Hire smart, create the right setup, and truly care about alignment. Ultimately, you'll need to make sure everyone feels safe (psychological safety) and is equipped with the communication skills and conflict-handling competencies they'll need to resolve conflicts in the workplace.

Proven Approaches to Resolving Conflicts

So, now that we know some of the many reasons for workplace conflicts, what can we do to resolve or even prevent them? As you work

207 See Chapter 10: Building Individual and Team Alignment
208 See Chapter 13: Interviewing, Assessing, and Hiring Candidates

with your PMs to resolve conflict, it's important to consider the following:

- **We respond to conflicts based on our perceptions of the situation,** not necessarily to an objective review of the facts. Our perceptions are influenced by our life experiences, culture, values, and beliefs.

- **Conflicts trigger strong emotions.** If you aren't comfortable with your emotions or able to manage them in times of stress, you won't be able to resolve conflict successfully.

Ultimately, your ability—and the ability of your PMs—to resolve conflict depends on your ability to:

- **Manage stress quickly while remaining alert and calm.** By staying calm, you can accurately read and interpret verbal and nonverbal communication.

- **Control your emotions and behavior.** When you're in control of your emotions, you can communicate your needs without threatening, intimidating, or punishing others.

- **Pay attention to the feelings being expressed** as well as the spoken words of others.

- **Be aware of and respect differences.** By avoiding disrespectful words and actions, you can almost always resolve a problem faster.

A two-step strategy for conflict resolution

I have personally found that the following two-step strategy is a very effective one for resolving conflicts in product organizations.

I along with my coachees have used it to great effect over the years, and it will hopefully help you coach your PMs.

Step 1: Don't make it worse!

When a conflict erupts, your goal must be to remain calm, to name and acknowledge the conflict, and to signal a willingness to talk. However, instead of discussing the topic immediately, it's better to prepare for a timely follow-up meeting to discuss the issue, clarify whether or not to involve other people (for mediation purposes, or because they are also affected), and consider where you can best exchange ideas in peace.

As a PM, you might say, "Let's meet in 10 minutes in meeting room A with our Agile coach." Or you might say, "I understand your displeasure very well and I would like to talk to you about it, but I would like to involve the whole team. Would it be okay with you if we discuss this in our next retrospective?" Your goal is to let the "boom" moment pass.

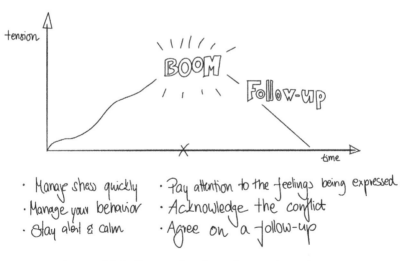

Figure 28-1: The cycle of conflict and resolution, and six things to remember

Step 2: Have a follow-up meeting

After you identify a conflict and call it out, your next step is to have a follow-up meeting with the parties involved. Here are some specific things to do during the course of the meeting:

1. Acknowledge the conflict—this builds common ground. "We agree to disagree."

2. Listen to the other person(s).

3. Acknowledge similarities.

4. Admit mistakes.

5. Focus on the present—it's not important to figure out who is right and who is wrong. It's important to ask, "Where do we go from here?"

6. Stick to the issue and focus on behavior, not personality.

7. Be willing to forgive and know when to let something go.

8. If necessary, use a mediator.

If you or someone in your organization takes on the role of mediator in resolving a conflict, here are some specific things a mediator should do during the follow-up meeting:

1. Acknowledge that a difficult situation exists.

2. Don't let the parties play the blame game. "You never..." "Every time I _____ you do _____."

3. Let individuals express their feelings. (Consider cultural differences but avoid stereotypes.)

4. Allow time to reflect/pause/check for understanding.

5. Define the problem.

6. Make sure they acknowledge their similarities.

7. Determine underlying needs.

8. Find common areas of agreement, no matter how small.

9. Find solutions to satisfy needs.

10. Determine what follow-up you will take to monitor actions. Consider the bigger picture to give it a positive spin: "By taking these steps, something like this will never happen again."

11. Determine what you'll do if the conflict goes unresolved.

Marshall Rosenberg's nonviolent communication framework

Another good approach to resolving conflict is one developed by Marshall Rosenberg, which he dubbed *nonviolent communication*.[209] I can see the question mark over your head right now—"Violence? Not in *our* company!" And that's the point—to resolve conflict without resorting to yelling and screaming. Instead, according to Rosenberg, we should express ourselves in a way that inspires empathy in others, and then listen empathically to them.

Figure 28-2 details Marshall Rosenberg's approach to conflict resolution. Consider the example of two PMs in conflict. Whenever one of the PMs makes a presentation, the other constantly checks their mobile phone for text messages—causing the presenting PM to get upset.

Encourage the first PM to address this conflict nonviolently. They might say, for example: "When I make a presentation, I notice that you're always checking your phone for messages. This makes it difficult for me to focus on giving my presentation because I'm getting distracted wondering why you are doing this. Is my presentation too boring? Would you rather be somewhere else? The end result is your behavior makes me feel upset. I need to focus on communicating my messages clearly, so please refrain from checking your phone all the time when I'm making presentations."

I highly recommend you give Rosenberg's approach a try. You might even consider running small workshops in your organization and schedule everyone to attend.

---

209 https://youtu.be/DgaeHeIL39Y

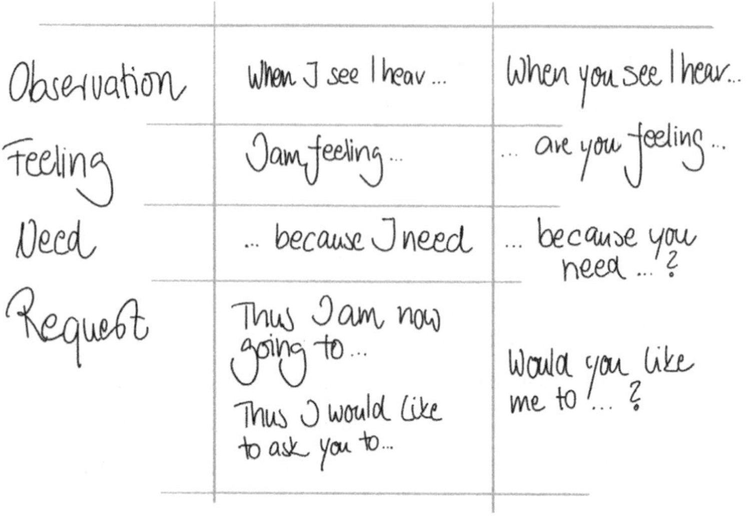

Observation	When J see I hear …	When you see I hear…
Feeling	J am feeling …	… are you feeling …
Need	… because J need	… because you need … ?
Request	Thus J am now going to … / Thus J would like to ask you to…	Would you like me to !… ?

Figure 28-2: Nonviolent communication

Regardless of which approach you take to helping your PMs (and everyone else in the organization) handle conflict, it's important that you take time to do it. Here are some tips for doing just that:

- Dedicate some of your time to improve your company conflict culture.

- Lead by example—your people need to see how management deals with conflicts.

- Create a conflict vocabulary and communication training.

- If you need a mediator to help, enlist your Agile coaches or HR colleagues.

Expressing Feelings

It helps to remind people of the many different words we use to express our emotions, feelings, and needs. Here are lists of words expressing feelings that I edited from the Center for Nonviolent Communication website:[210]

Feelings when your needs are satisfied

ENGAGED	EXCITED	CONFIDENT	INSPIRED
absorbed	amazed	empowered	amazed
alert	animated	open	awed
curious	ardent	proud	wonder
engrossed	aroused	safe	
enchanted	astonished	secure	
entranced	dazzled		
fascinated	eager		
interested	energetic		
intrigued	enthusiastic		
involved	giddy		
spellbound	invigorated		
stimulated	lively		
	passionate		
	surprised		
	vibrant		

210 (c) 2005 by Center for Nonviolent Communication Website: www.cnvc.org Email: cnvc@cnvc.org Phone: +1.505-244-4041

Feelings when your needs are not satisfied

AFRAID	ANGRY	SAD
apprehensive	enraged	depressed
dread	furious	dejected
foreboding	incensed	despair
frightened	indignant	despondent
mistrustful	irate	disappointed
panicked	livid	discouraged
petrified	outraged	disheartened
scared	resentful	forlorn
		gloomy
		heavyhearted
		hopeless
		melancholy
		unhappy
		wretched

Ultimately, leading a product organization is all about *people*, and it's all about how you as an HoP answer and respond to their emotions and needs. And what a great topic this is to close the book. Succeeding as a leader in a product organization requires being deeply *human*, and it requires that you have a real desire to help others become the very best version of themselves.

Strong product people help others develop and build their strengths, they create a psychologically safe workplace, they challenge their people to have greater impact on customers and on the world around them, and they shine a bright light on the path ahead—leading the way.

And when they do, *everyone* wins.

Further Reading

- Nonviolent Communication and Self Awareness (Maria Engels): https://www.strongproductpeople.com/further -readings#chapter-28_1

- Nonviolent Communication—a Brief Introduction (Marshall Rosenberg): https://www.strongproductpeople .com/further-readings#chapter-28_2

- How to Mend a Work Relationship: https://www.strong productpeople.com/further-readings#chapter-28_3

- How to Quickly (and Effectively) Repair Damaged Relationships in the Workplace: https://www.strong productpeople.com/further-readings#chapter-28_4

- The Real Cost of Workplace Conflict:
  - The Real Cost of Workplace Conflict by Jennifer Lawler https://www.strongproductpeople.com /further-readings#chapter-28_5
  - Conflict Resolution Skills via helpguide.org https://www.strongproductpeople.com/further -readings#chapter-28_6

A FINAL NOTE

The process of writing a book includes a step that is called *peer review*. In my case, 38 people have read parts of the manuscript, and 22 fellow product folks read and commented on the full body of work. And, besides the many small things they have brought to my attention (stuff we would call *usability issues* in a tech product), almost all of them said, "This book is intense, dense, packed with advice—maybe a bit too much, maybe a bit over the top."

But when I asked deeper: "Is there a specific chapter where you think the framework or canvas is unnecessary or not useful?" The answer was always: "Frankly...no. All of them are relevant to me. In fact, now that you are asking, maybe you can talk more about psychological safety, morals and ethics in product development, and add a bunch more stories and examples about how to craft a vision and strategy."

So, totally mixed signals.

Should I radically shorten the book, ditching some key concepts? Or should I add even more stories, even more topics? The thing is, my goal was not to write a product compendium. I wanted to write a book about people development with some advice on how to coach people on specific, product-related topics.

But what I realized from the feedback is that, once product leaders start reading this book, they realize just how intense their job actually is.

So, I am going to assume that this is exactly what you are currently feeling. There are so many things you have to take care of when you lead a product organization.

- You have to form your product team and hire the right people.

- You have to make sure the product development org is delivering successful products—products that solve an actual user problem and, therefore, generate so much value for the user that they are happy to pay you for it.

- You have to make sure every person on your team is continuously learning and getting closer to mastery so that the work they do gets better over time, and they stay happy and motivated.

- You have to influence the whole organization to make sure product development teams can operate in the best possible environment.

In short: You have to take care of the people, the product, and the processes. Those are a lot of responsibilities. And this is why the job feels so intense, and why this book feels intense as well.

But I hope that this book (in all its intensity) will make your life as the leader of a product organization a bit easier. That you will use this book as a guide, a companion, your trusted source of advice whenever advice is what you need. At least the people-development-related topics should be well covered.

So, let me leave you with a reminder of the key takeaways—a handy list to recap what I talked about through the last 300+ pages:

- Please write down your definition of what you think a strong and competent product manager is and what it takes to be a Good PM in your current organization right now (Use the PMwheel to get started and then customize it to your own needs).

- Use this definition for hiring, onboarding, feedback, and personal-development conversations.

- Think about your vision for each of your PMs. What can they ultimately achieve in their careers? How can you help them get closer to this?

- Always know what "the next bigger challenge" is you would assign to each of your PMs to make sure they keep learning.

- Get in a coaching mindset and help your PMs understand what you think makes a Good PM. Help them identify their gaps to see what they should get better at, and—maybe my most important tip—help them understand what better really looks like.

I know all of this is hard work and it takes time. But it is time well spent. Numerous studies show that people tend to stay longer with a company if they have the chance to work on meaningful things in an environment that values continuous learning and personal development.

Please make some time in your busy schedule and give people development a higher priority.

And, one last thing: I know leading a product organization can be a very lonely profession. If this is the case for you (and I know it often was for me), make sure to reach out to your fellow product leaders. There are an increasing number of events, meetups, Slack groups, and more solely created for product leaders.

If you want to learn more about these product leader resources, feel free to get in touch with me or follow #strongproductpeople on Twitter or Instagram to see who your peers are.

I hope you enjoyed this book. Would you please do me a favor?

Like all authors, I rely on online reviews to encourage future sales. Your opinion is invaluable. Would you take a few moments now to share your assessment of my book on Amazon or any other book review website you prefer? Your opinion will help the book marketplace become more transparent and useful to all.

Thank you very much!

ACKNOWLEDGMENTS

To write a book is a strange experience. Most of the time, it is a rather lonely business. You sit at your desk and think: What do I want to convey? What is my point of view? What do I have that will contribute to the product tribe? And it requires some discipline to keep writing week after week after week.

But then, on the other hand, it's also a team sport: it takes a family to watch your back, friends to cheer you on, my editor to help me put my thoughts into book form, well-appreciated colleagues who discussed all my ideas over a glass of red wine, and many, many, wonderful people who made the book even better with their feedback throughout, and especially at the end of the process.

I want to say a big THANK YOU to all of you. Even at the risk of forgetting one or two, here are all the people without whom the book would not exist:

Thanks to Andree and Frida for being the wind under my wings every day.

Simon and Vera: You helped me make this big dream come true!

My parents, Monika & Hans Schwenk, and the rest of the family for their support for so many years.

Peter Economy for being the best possible editor and my partner in crime. Will miss our Tuesday calls.

Arne Kittler—I love you, man!

Thanks to Marty Cagan and Martin Eriksson for being my heroes, for believing in me, for your advice, and for writing the forewords.

Thanks to all those who had an open ear during the entire writing process, gave feedback on superearly versions of the manuscript, and, therefore, helped a lot: Christina Wodtke, Shaun Russell, Sophia Höfling, Gabrielle Bufrem, Eva Maria-Lindig, Heike Funk, Daniel Dimitrov, Tony Llewellyn, Lena Haydt, Alicja Marcyniuk, and Kristina Walcker-Mayer.

Another thank you goes out to the people who read the full manuscript and provided insightful and helpful feedback: Kate Leto, Emily Tate, Barry O'Reilly, Tobias Freudenreich, Mirja Bester, Inken Petersen, Björn Waide, Wolf Brüning, Rainer Gibbert, Alexander Hipp, Adir Zonta, Ole Bahlmann, João Pedro Craveiro, Alexander Schardt, Luis Cascante, Nick Brett, Miguel Carruego, Daniel Bailo, Nacho Bassino, Robiert Luque, Aaron Stuart, Alide von Bornhaupt, Thomas Leitermann, Mareike Leitermann, and Konradin Breyer.

Thanks to every person writing, publishing, and sharing their take on product management, and to the thought leaders of our tribe! Most of my ideas are based on your work, so I'm standing on the shoulders of giants! To name just a few of the people I get regularly inspired by: Jeff Patton, Teresa Torres, Marc Abraham, John Cutler, Steve Portigal, Jeff Gothelf, Denise Jacobs, Matt LeMay, Tricia Wang, Indi Young, Laura Klein, Barry O'Reilly, and C. Todd Lombardo.

Thanks to my Mind the Product family: Analisa Plehn, James Mayes, Janna Bastow, Chris Massey, Martin Eriksson, and the rest of the gang. You are the main reason why I have met so many smart people over the years, including all of you. <3

Thanks to my female leadership role models Barbara Ising, Heike Funk, Julia Brewing, and Birgit Hedden-Liegman. You definitely had an impact on my career.

Thanks to Diana and Philipp Knodel for being my office buddies and for cheering me up when I needed it the most!

Thanks to all my clients and coachees: Working with you has refined the way I teach others.

Thanks to all the developers, designers, and product folks I have ever worked with—I learned something from each one of you!

ABOUT THE AUTHOR

Petra Wille is an independent product leadership coach who's been helping product teams boost their skillset and up their game since 2013. Alongside her freelance work, Petra co-organizes and curates Mind the Product Engage Hamburg, Germany.

Made in United States
Orlando, FL
31 July 2022